Balliol
Studies

Balliol
Studies

Edited by

JOHN PREST

LEOPARD'S HEAD PRESS

Published in 1982 by
Leopard's Head Press Limited
69 Aldwych, London WC2B 4DY

© 1982 Balliol College, Oxford

ISBN 0 904920 07 0

*Printed in Great Britain at the
University Press, Cambridge*

Contents

List of Illustrations

Acknowledgements

The College wishes to thank the Reverend the Master of Campion Hall for permission to reproduce the sketch of Benjamin Jowett taken from Gerard Manley Hopkins' notebook B II fo. 90, and reproduced in Article 6, plate 1.

The copyright of Article 3, plate 1 rests in the Bodleian Library (Vet. A 3 f 1393), and that of Article 8, plate 1 in the Museum of the History of Science.

Preface

The decision to publish a volume of essays commemorating the seven hundredth anniversary of the presentation of the College's first Statutes in 1282 was taken on 30 May 1979. Richard Hunt agreed to act as editor, and it would have been the happiest thing had he lived to see these *Balliol Studies* through the press.

Little attempt has been made to 'drum up' contributions, and none to link them to any central theme. Several articles which were already written and awaiting publication were held back, by the kindness of their authors, in order that they might appear upon this occasion. Others, whose completion still seemed at that time far off, were hurried forward to the same end. Taken together, the eight articles thus present a fair sample of the many inquiries now being undertaken into the history of the College by the curious in every decade.

JOHN PREST

1   JEREMY CATTO

The first century of
Balliol men, 1260 – 1360

This is an enlarged version of the article which appeared in the
Balliol College Record for 1980.

THE FIRST CENTURY OF BALLIOL MEN, 1260-1360

It is tempting to suppose that the spirit of an institution is merely subjective, or at most the ephemeral quality given by a particular generation or a single dominating individual. No doubt that is sometimes the case; but the character of a corporate body is often surprisingly tough, and can impose itself on its individual constituents more than they would like to admit. It is legitimate to ask, in particular, whether Balliol with its palpable, if indefinable spirit was wholly the creation of Jowett or his immediate predecessors, or whether perhaps it can be traced much further back, to the College's remote origins when the first group of "poor scholars" of Northumberland, maintained by the pittance of the Balliol family, began their studies in Oxford. Their names, almost without exception, are forgotten: even the date of that unexpectedly fruitful event can only be determined within the broad limits of 1255 and 1266. Does any particle of a powerful tradition descend from these primal genes, cross-fertilised as they have been many times over by the recruitment of determined, strong-minded men? Did the walls of Mareys Hall, St. Margaret's Hall or perhaps Sparrow Hall in the Broad, now occupied by the Master's Lodgings, already resound to Aristotle's logic hurled back and forth? Did its doors open to let out a phalanx of first-class men, ready to rule the *res publica* as it ought to be ruled, and whether it liked it or not? And was Gordouli chanted there behind the ivy, or the rue, creeping up the Broad Street front, as Wyclif, an early Master, fancifully evoked it? The present contribution is not an attempt to write, or rewrite, the early history of Balliol; it will merely attempt to set out, in the light of these perhaps fanciful speculations, what evidence we have on the sorts and conditions of Balliol men, corporately and where possible individually, during that first century, and to present some impressions of the College's original character and the forces which formed it.

It is bound, therefore, to be brief. Unfortunately, all that the College has preserved from its first century are the records of its carefully assembled property. Unlike the other medieval colleges, no bursarial rolls or *compoti* survive to show what the Fellows spent their money

3

on: perhaps because they had so little, if we are to believe the College's
historians, though there is ground to think that Balliol's original
poverty has been one of its oldest myths. However, some information
about the scholars can be garnered even from the deeds: they appear
in a few of them as witnesses, and in one, dated 1321, all sixteen of
the original foundation are named. As one of its first procurators or
'external masters' — leading University figures designated by the
Founder to look after the infant College — was Friar Richard of
Durham, and he happened to write a chronicle, some of his occasional
references to scholars at Oxford very likely have Balliol in mind. From
an early date the College acquired books: its earliest benefaction was
no real property but a text of Boethius' *De Musica*, bequeathed by
1276 before even the first College Statutes.[1] A number of manuscripts
have been preserved which appear to contain the lectures of a few
early Fellows. Finally, the biographical collections of the late Dr.
Emden, himself a notable contributor to Balliol history, has made
possible a skeleton prosopography of the early College, which brings
into focus the regional connections of the members, those most
elemental and enduring of loyalties even among the new educated
careerists.

   The first Oxford colleges, on the whole, came into existence for the
Highland Zone of Britain — havens for the least secure portion of the
university population, the northerners, the south-westerners, and — in
unendowed halls — Welshmen and Irishmen. In these communities
there was little distinction, except seniority, between undergraduates
— scholars — and masters: the few members of a college were all
"Fellows". The northern scholars came up together, stuck together,
and sometimes stayed together, forming hard regional freemasonries
in the officialdom of the fourteenth century. A Merton connection,
partly northern, occupied much of the king's service. Balliol men, at
this period, grasped far less successfully at the levers of power: but,
like Exeter men from the south-west, Queensmen from the north-west,
and Oriel men as it turned out from Nottinghamshire and Lincolnshire,
Balliol began as a distinctly regional college. The original impetus had
come from, and was sporadically revived by, the Bishops of Durham.
One bishop laid the endowment of a house of poor scholars as a
penance on his neighbour, John Balliol, the lord of Bywell and Barnard
Castle; another persuaded his widow, Lady Devorguilla, to perpetuate

the endowment; a third, many years later in 1340, re-endowed the College at the expense of two other neighbours. For the Durham establishment Balliol was one of several expedients — University College was a second, and the monastic Durham College a third — in the task of turning rude northerners into competent officials and parish priests It was jealous of the available places: even the Warden of Merton received a sharp rebuke from the Prior of Durham for an inadequate northern intake.[2]

Only in the formal sense, then, was John Balliol, the Bishop's recalcitrant neighbour, founder of the College: a reluctant ancestor, we may be sure. Seen in another perspective, he was merely the first, if the greatest, of the lay subjects of the See of Durham to find himself serving the educational ambitions of that church. Perhaps, therefore, we should recognise as the real founder the bishop who imposed the "poor scholars" on his generosity, Walter Kirkham. He was a well known civil servant and intimate of Henry III, like Walter de Merton, though his services to education, if ultimately at least equal, were in the immediate context far less lavishly performed than his colleague's, and not at his own expense. Though a court bishop with Exchequer experience behind him — a Treasury connection has often benefited Balliol — he did his best for clerical education in his diocese, and was remembered by the Balliol Franciscan, Richard of Durham (if his hand can be seen in this passage of the Lanercost Chronicle) as "a man of authority, respected and feared by bullies".[3] Neither he nor his successors, however, found their way on to the College's *rotulus benefactorum*. Though the influence of the Bishops of Durham is evident on several occasions in the first Balliol century, for some reason they remained in the background.

In the event, as a regional society the new college may well have disappointed them. The patronymics of the early Fellows do not suggest that many of them originated in the diocese: the first Principal or Warden (as the Head of House was styled until 1340), Walter de Foderyngeye, was probably one of the Huntingdonshire connections of Lady Devorguilla, heiress of the Scottish Earls of Huntingdon.[4] In spite of her endowments of Balliol in the 1280's largely from Northumberland's wealth, only three Fellows in the first half-century, Thomas of Heworth (c. 1300), Thomas of Humbleton (1310), and perhaps William de Merkeland of Chester-le-Street (before 1311), seem to have

come from beyond the Tees.[5] The endowment of the College and its
Statutes of 1282, it is true, were effected by two prominent northern
masters, the Franciscan theologian Hugh of Hartlepool and the Principal of Neville's Hall, Mr. William Meynill, perhaps one of the Mey-
nills of Bywell who witnessed some of Devorguilla's charters.[6] In
practice, however, they seem to have ordered the College more for the
convenience of the University than for the Foundress's compatriots;
and if the church of Durham was far richer and more venerable, the
University was on the spot, and its masters, on questions of endowment, notably single-minded. The Statutes issued in her name, without
any very obvious justification in the text, were interpreted as providing
funds exclusively for scholars in the Faculty of Arts; once they began
to study theology, they had to resign.[7] As Merton, or the religious
orders, catered for theologians, an endowment of the Arts faculty
suited the University authorities well. In this way Balliol acquired a
role in the University's *cursus honorum*, under the guidance of its
external masters. These procurators, though originally northerners,
seem after 1300 to have been simply prominent masters, one of whom
was often a Franciscan friar and the other sometimes the Chancellor
himself.

Thus a quite different pressure was brought to bear on the young
College; regional affiliations had to be weighed against the needs of
Oxford scholars in general. In this process, the role of friar Richard
of Durham, the personal agent of Lady Devorguilla and a figure as
much at home with the masters of Oxford as among the rude gentry
of the northern counties, was probably crucial. From 1284 he had
acted on her behalf in assembling for the College its earliest Oxford
property, the houses on the front quadrangle site; after 1290 he seems
also to have acquired its earliest London property in St. Lawrence
Jewry.[8] As the author of a now-lost chronicle, he may be claimed as
the first Balliol historian, and it is gratifying to note that the excerpts
apparently preserved in the chronicle of Lanercost Priory stand out,
in a bleak period of historiography, for their liveliness, their large
horizons, and their entertaining gossip — a good start to a long tradition. Perhaps Richard of Durham preserves the first vignette of life at
Balliol, which he dates to 1281:

> Certain scholars residing at Oxford retired to sleep one
> night after supper. One of them, less careful about his com-

fort than the rest, though as merry and lively as any, went to his usual bed in some upper chamber. About midnight, his companions, alarmed to hear him shouting, striking out and gnashing his teeth, went and roused their fellow lodgers who, hastening to his bedside, found the man speechless, acting as if on the point of death; and even more amazing, his whole body presented such a horrible appearance that he looked more like a black Ethiopian than a Christian. And so, as all of them thought his peril was urgent, one of more fervent faith exclaimed, 'let one of us begin the gospel of St. John, and I hope it will relieve our patient'; whereupon the others, moved by faith, began to recite the gospel in parts, not knowing the whole of it; and lo! the evil spirit went out of him. And in the hearing of them all, the great stone stair that led to the door of the chamber shook to the ground, and after the spirit's exit such a stench was left behind that they all thought they would be suffocated. But the sick man, restored to life by the sound of the holy words, soon afterwards reverted from his blackened appearance to his natural looks.[9]

The distant roots of Balliol's fabled African partiality can perhaps be traced to this early College miracle.

Lady Devorguilla died in 1290, and her son John, whose interest in the College seems to have been minimal, embarked on his short career as King of Scotland. This brief hubris of the House of Balliol ended in the deposition, imprisonment, and eventual exile of King John at the hands of Edward I, and the confiscation of the Balliol lands in England. For the College the nemesis of the Founder's kin ought to have been disastrous. That, far from collapse, the next generation was a period of new patrons and new endowments was probably due to a little gentle nursing by the University. Within fifteen years Balliol had probably doubled her wealth with three major endowments from benefactors quite unconnected with Founder or College: money for the College Chapel from Ela, Countess of Warwick, in 1293; the advowson of the church of St. Lawrence Jewry in London from Mr. Hugh of Vienne in 1296; and, above all, the valuable Burnell's Inn on the site of Christ Church's Blue Boar building from Mr. William Burnell in 1304.[10] These windfalls are explicable when it is remembered

that all three patrons were notable benefactors of the University, as
the founders of loanchests for poor scholars: a grateful Chancellor
must have gone out of his way to tack on something for Balliol too.[11]
So, while Balliol prospered, the threads binding her to her earliest
patrons must have been correspondingly weakened.

As, after 1290, money flowed in from all quarters, so, it seems, did
scholars. The moving spirit at the time, and perhaps the real creator
of College tradition, was the first Principal, Mr. Walter de Foderyngeye. Originally perhaps a Huntingdonshire pensioner of the Foundress, Foderyngeye's career after ceasing to be Principal about 1295
was in the Chapter of Lincoln; and there is a recognizable group of
Fellows from Lincolnshire and Huntingdonshire at this period, which
managed to perpetuate itself until about 1360: Walter and perhaps
Henry de Foderyngeye, Hugh of Warknethby, Geoffrey of Horkestow,
a Leverton, a Lusby, a Pipewell, and a Radford.[12] Walter de Foderyngeye's interest in Balliol extended to his last days in 1315, when he
left a house in Merton Street to the College. A more surprising group
are the three Cornishmen, John of St. Germans (1295), Hugh of St.
Ives (1306-7), and Stephen of Cornwall (Principal in 1307).[13] South-
westerners, like northerners, tended to stick together; a decade later
their aspirations would be catered for by the fledgling Exeter College.
The solidarity of these regional coteries and their propensity to perpetuate themselves in particular halls and colleges was a source of
endless friction. Perhaps it was avoided at Balliol by the comparative
brevity of the Fellows' tenure. A large number of Balliol men reappear
as Fellows of Merton shortly afterwards; others carried the torch further afield: Henry de Warknethby to Univ., William of Leverton to
Oriel, Richard of Radford to Queen's, Simon of Holbeche to Peter-
house, Stephen of Cornwall to Paris. It is possible that some of them
entered religious orders for the sake of further theological study: a
John of St. Germans was a monk of Worcester by 1299, studying
theology at Oxford; a Hugh of St. Ives professed as a monk of Canterbury in 1316, returning later to the Oxford schools; and the Franciscan
theologian Thomas of Pontefract appears just as Thomas of Pontefract, Fellow of Balliol, passes from view.

The most striking characteristic of these early Balliol men is their
commitment to the academic life, in a period when university study
and teaching was usually a phase in a career crowned elsewhere. Men

like Richard of Radford and William of Leverton seem to have spent their whole lives teaching in Oxford, though not of course in Balliol. They were the core of the University's corporate identity and traditions. The early fourteenth century was a period of great intellectual distinction at Merton, but there is reason to think that Balliol has been uncharacteristically modest about the contribution of her earliest sons to the scientific and philosophical achievement of the age. The first of many surviving works from Balliol pens — and incidentally the College's first contribution to *literae humaniores* and the study of ancient philosophy — comes from William Bonkes, a Fellow associated with Foderyngeye in two deeds of 1292 and slightly later. They are a collection of lectures on Priscian and on several works of Aristotle, the textbooks of the Faculty of Arts, preserved in Gonville and Caius MS.344: one of the earlier monuments of Oxford's Aristotelian learning. The philospohy of Bonkes is a virgin field, waiting to be tilled by one of his successors in the tradition of Balliol Aristotelianism. A second series of lectures can be identified with the unexpected help of a deed of Balliol's property in School Street, now beneath Exeter gardens: it is a deed of conveyance, datable to c. 1304, transferring the property from an undergraduate scholar, Peter Bradley, to his colleague Mr. William of Gotham. As an internal transaction between nominal feoffees, it is witnessed by a further group of Fellows: Mr. Thomas of Pontefract, Mr. Adam of 'Burle' (not Kurle, as transcribed by Salter in his edition of Balliol deeds), *dominus* (i.e. bachelor) Stephen of Cornwall, *dominus* Richard of Campsall, *dominus* Geoffrey of Tendryng *et aliis*.[14] Two of the witnesses, Burley and Campsall, and Peter Bradley are found again as the authors of questions on Aristotle in another Gonville and Caius manuscript, No. 668, a notebook in a hand of the beginning of the fourteenth century: and since the volume is an integral collection of *questiones dati* by particular masters it seems likely to be of Balliol provenance, and the other lectures represented in it to be Balliol lectures too. One of them is dated 1301, but Bradley's must have been several years later, as he was only an undergraduate in 1304.[15] Once again here is evidence of the prominent part taken by Balliol in the teaching of the Faculty of Arts, and it is easy to see why the University cherished the College in these years.

The second Caius manuscript also provides evidence of the presence

in Balliol of a far more distinguished man, the philosopher Walter
Burley. He is there found associated with Mr. Adam Burley lecturing
on Aristotle's *De Anima*; Adam expounded the first two books and
Walter the third. That the two were related is likely, as a quarter of a
century later they were still found together in the pursuit of papal
provisions.[16] Unlike Adam, however, he went on from Balliol to
Merton, and thence to Paris: and as one of the most original, and by
far the most influential, of medieval interpreters of Aristotle, Burley
seems to have been the first Balliol man to influence thought outside
England. The Caius manuscript throws light on the earliest, Balliol,
phase of his thought: three of his four sets of lectures exist only in
this manuscript, though one, *De potenciis anime*, must have been
published by the stationers and so circulated more widely. Burley,
indeed, was the first really considerable scholar and philosopher among
the new collegiate Oxford men whose intellectual distinction was
beginning to rival that of the friars. In his own eyes he was probably
a conservative thinker, who owed more to the rationalistic, highly
intellectual traditions of Albert the Great, Thomas Aquinas and the
Dominican school than to the metaphysical brilliance of his Franciscan
contemporary Duns Scotus; and much of his mature work was devoted
to refuting a new fashion of thought, the logical scepticism of William
of Ockham. These intellectual affiliations are already discernible in *De
potenciis anime*, and it would probably not be far from the truth to
see his sober and scholarly Aristotelianism as characteristic of Balliol
about 1300, in contrast to the fireworks of Franciscan metaphysics.
It formed the mainstay of his work throughout his life, his final contribution being the production of commentaries on the *Ethics* and
Politics which would be the standard expositions for a century. Balliol
as well as Merton can perhaps claim a share of the credit for this early
contribution to the moral and political philosophy which in a later
age would be peculiarly its own.[17]

That Burley's residence at Balliol can be detected only because of
the chance of survival of a deed and a notebook suggests that the
College's medieval roll of honour must have been underestimated;
the suspicion is confirmed by a deed of 1321 whose witnesses, evidently the whole College, include Thomas Bradwardine, and by the
decision of the external master promulgated in 1325, revealing that
Richard Fitzralph had been a Fellow.[18] Thus incidentally the two

other leading secular intellects of early fourteenth-century Oxford
are revealed as Balliol men. Bradwardine, like Burley, went on to
Merton and to fame as both a physical theorist and a theologian. A
highly original thinker in both fields, he was also a close adviser of
Edward III, and as such an example, not merely of the scholar who
graduates from learning to public service, but of the intellectual who
actively pursues his studies outside the university, in the 'real' world.
Bradwardine's major theological work, *De causa Dei* (1344) was
written in the intervals of his political duties; its doom-laden sense of
human impotence in the face of the predestined course of events may
have been sharpened by the experience. Although very much a Mer-
tonian by then, he exemplifies the variety of distinction achieved by
Balliol men in other places.

Richard Fitzralph, unlike Burley and Bradwardine, did not proceed
to Merton. An Irishman from Dundalk, he exemplified the College's
unusually open doors. Though in theological controversy inclined to
the *via media* — as Etienne Gilson said, he belonged to "la race aimable
de ceux qui pensent qu'on exagère les différences" — his later career
as a stern critic of the friars was provocative enough, and like a good
Balliol radical his propensity to defy authority grew with age. As the
posthumous Marcuse of the Lollards, he could still raise hackles thirty-
five years after his death.[19]

The document which incidentally notes Richard Fitzralph's Balliol
past is a rejection by the external masters of the Fellows' request to
be allowed to study in other faculties than Arts, despite the custom
of the College and the intention, albeit only implicitly expressed, of
the Foundress. Such a change would have made Balliol, like the new
colleges of the early fourteenth century, something more of a lifelong
body of men instead of a brief association of Masters of Arts. In the
light of their stated wishes, it is safe to assume that the form of the
new endowment of Sir Philip Somerville in 1340, by which six new
Fellowships in Arts were established and the election of six existing
Fellows to study in higher faculties permitted, was effectively laid
down by the Principal and Fellows themselves. This radical new departure was made by means of a curious transaction, and the document
in the College muniments which ought to furnish the legal record of
that transaction is itself not above criticism.[20] First of all, a complete
new constitution of the College, including the new post of Master,

appears to be enacted by a benefactor without previous Balliol connections, as the condition of the grant of an advowson, two ploughlands
and twenty acres at Longbenton in Northumberland. It would be
reasonable to expect new Statutes to be made by one of the authorities
with jurisdiction over the Principal and Fellows: the Crown; the
Bishop of Lincoln as diocesan; the Chancellor of the University; or
the two external masters who had acted effectively in 1325. To find
them made as a condition of even a substantial benefaction is surprising; the proceeding, indeed, is arguably irregular, and possibly, insofar
as it modified existing Statutes, invalid in law.

Secondly, the Somerville Statutes are recorded in the College muniments in a charter which clearly is not what it purports to be. Ostensibly a confirmation by *Edwardus dei gratia Scotorum Rex* of the
grant of Sir Philip Somerville which it quotes *in extenso* (thus forming
the record of his Statutes), it incorporates the formal assent to the
grant of the Bishop and Prior of Durham, the Chancellor of Oxford
and the Principal and Fellows of Balliol, but then tails away unfinished
with neither a date nor a locating clause. It is indeed sealed, but the
seal is that of Sir Philip Somerville himself. The college historians are
united in seeing here a final act of munificence on the part of the
head of the Balliol family, the exiled pretender to the throne of
Scotland, Edward Balliol; but this cannot be the case. With neither
date, place nor appropriate seal, the confirmation fails even the most
elementary diplomatic test.

What actually happened? Indubitably the Statutes, insofar as they
applied to the internal structure of Balliol, were effective. It has never
been necessary, fortunately for the College, to produce in their defence
the dubious document on which they rested. Nor were they a pious
fraud perpetrated by the Fellows to outflank their irksome confine-
ment to the Arts faculty and foisted on a complaisant benefactor.
Sir Philip Somerville's grant, with the declarations of Bishop, Prior,
University and College (but without the confirmation of Edward
Balliol) was entered in the Register of the Bishop of Durham and is also
included in a Durham cartulary of about 1400.[21] There is, therefore,
a Durham connection. Sir Philip Somerville, though his principal seat
was in Staffordshire, was a substantial Northumbrian landowner; the
Bishop of Durham, as the paramount spiritual and temporal power in
the north, was a natural patron. A more or less contemporaneous

grant to Balliol of the advowson of Abbotsley in Huntingdonshire, by Sir William Felton, provides a parallel instance: for Felton, primarily a Northumbrian landowner, was another neighbour of the Bishop. The inference is confirmed by some other provisions of the Somerville Statutes: scholars from the region would have a preference in elections to the new arts fellowships; and above all, the whole College would be subject to a Master who would himself need confirmation by the Warden of Durham College, and to the virtually visitatorial powers of subsequent Bishops of Durham. These provisions are an echo of Bishop Kirkham's care for the education of the "poor scholars" of Northumberland; they can only have been inspired by his current successor. Since this was the great bibliophile bishop, Richard of Bury, the patron and friend of Bradwardine, Burley and Fitzralph and one of the wiliest figures in the politics of his time, both the method and the purpose can be understood.

The Somerville Statutes, then, represent a compromise between two interests, that of the Fellows who needed college endowment to proceed to higher faculties, and that of the Durham establishment who sought rather more basic educational opportunities for their compatriots. Balliol was to modify its 'open doors' policy and once more accept a regional bias. As for Edward Balliol's purported confirmation, it must have been drafted at Balliol in the hope of inducing the last representative of the Founder's kin to append his seal: the seal of Sir Philip Somerville may have been obtained first, in order to verify the grant which the Pretender was requested to confirm. As the Founder's residuary legatee, his confirmation would counter any claim of incompatibility between the new Statutes and the old. If so, however, the effort was a failure, and the draft returned to Balliol unconfirmed. The College has been fortunate in escaping any exploitation of the legal loophole this failure potentially opened.

It was perhaps inevitable that the College and not the Bishop, subtle as he was, should have reaped greater advantage from the implied bargain. The Fellows seem in practice to have contributed no more, in the generation after 1340, to education beyond the Tees than they had in the previous half-century. Only four Fellows of this period had evident connections with the north-east: two, Hugh of Corbridge, the first Master, and Thomas Farnelow, were Fellows already in 1340; Hugh Felton was probably related to the benefactor, Sir William; and only William Pegworth may have been preferred by reason of his origin in the diocese of Durham.[22] On the other hand, the previous open-doors policy seems to have given way to a powerful Yorkshire connection: in the 1350's the names of Masters from prominent Yorkshire families stand out in the College records: John Waltham, Hugh of Wakefield, William of Wilton, John Hugate, John Wyclif.[23] Of all the regional freemasonries of the fourteenth century, that of York was perhaps the strongest and most self-perpetuating: from the time of Archbishop Giffard in the thirteenth century to that of Archbishop Scrope in the fifteenth, interrelated groups of Yorkshire clerks dominated the Privy Seal and Chancery. How and when this remarkable influx into Balliol began is now difficult to establish. It is likely, however, that the arrival of John Waltham, a nephew of the powerful Archbishop of York, John Thoresby, some time before 1349, had something to do with it; and the Archbishop may have played a part in the preferment of John Wyclif. The latter is the first to have reversed the usual order and proceeded from Merton (in 1356) to be Master of Balliol (1360), a progression so singular that it suggests he may have been a Fellow of Balliol before 1356.[24] At Balliol, at any rate, he was among his own countrymen, and his future promotion as Warden of Simon Islip's Canterbury Hall probably owed something to Islip's close associate, Thoresby. By adopting its new Statutes, then, Balliol had gained coherence as a community, but it had lost its singular universality.

Wyclif's brief reign as Master marks a natural turning-point in the history of Balliol. The scholars and teachers of the Faculty of Arts gave way to the theologians, builders, and bibliophiles of the fifteenth century: men of the world, generous in their gifts of property and books to the College. Wyclif himself was evidently ambitious to play a great public role, and his radicalism owed much to disappointment. But like many of his predecessors he was beyond doubt a committed and painstaking, perhaps an inspired lecturer, and — like some his successors — as a result his philosophical thought was heard with attention as far away as Prague. The grim radical image projected by his works is relieved, on a closer reading, by many touches of humanity and humour. Balliol men at least can cherish, in spite of its aggressive Yorkshire expression, the unequivocal belief in the power of ideas and the unashamed learning which he inherited and handed down.

NOTES

1. Balliol College MS. 317; see R.A.B. Mynors *Catalogue of the Manuscripts of Balliol College* (Oxford 1963), pp. 334-5.
2. *Oxford Formularies* ed. H.E. Salter, W.A. Pantin, and H.G. Richardson (Oxford Historical Society 1942), I p. 227.
3. *Chronicon de Lanercost* ed. J. Stevenson (Edinburgh 1839), p. 69.
4. A.B. Emden *Biographical Register of the University of Oxford to A.D. 1500* (Oxford 1957-9), II p. 703.
5. *Ibid.*, II pp. 929, 982-3; Emden 'The last pre-Reformation *Rotulus Benefactorum* and list of obits of Balliol College', *Balliol College Record, Supplement* (1967), p. 8.
6. Emden *Biographical Register*, II pp. 920, 1271-2.
7. Statutes of 1282, in *The Oxford Deeds of Balliol College* ed. H.E. Salter (Oxford Historical Society 1913), pp. 277-9; interpreted in this sense in 1325, cf. *ibid.* pp. 285-6.
8. Emden *Biographical Register*, III p. 1712, s.n. Slikeburne; identified as the chronicler by A.G. Little *Franciscan Papers, Lists and Documents* (Manchester 1943), pp. 42-54; and named as feoffee of the London tenement in Balliol College Archive E. 7. 14.
9. *Chronicon de Lanercost* transl. Sir H. Maxwell, *Scottish Historical Review* VI (1908-9), p. 282.
10. Balliol College Archive B.22. 16-25; Emden *Rotulus Benefactorum*, p. 6; *The Rolls and Register of Bishop Oliver Sutton* ed. R.M.T. Hill, IV (Lincoln Record Society 1958), pp. 83-5, 95, 97, 132; Salter *Balliol Deeds*, pp. 91-137.
11. *Statuta Antiqua Universitatis Oxoniensis* ed. Strickland Gibson (Oxford 1931), pp. 101-6, 120.
12. Emden *Biographical Register*, II pp. 703, 963, 1136, 1171; III pp. 1484, 1541-2, 1992.
13. *Ibid.*, I p. 491; III pp. 1626, 1627.
14. Salter *Balliol Deeds*, p. 141; the date can be approximated by the academic progress of Richard Campsall, for which see Emden *Biographical Register*, I pp. 344-5.
15. E.A. Synan 'Master Peter Bradlay on the "Categories"', *Mediaeval Studies* XXIX (1967), pp. 273-327; 'A Question by Peter Bradlay on the "Prior Analytics"', *ibid*, XXX (1968), pp. 1-21.
16. *Idem* 'Four Questions by Adam Burley on the "Liber Sex Principiorum"', *ibid.* XXXII (1970), pp. 60-90.
17. On Burley see C. Martin 'Walter Burley' in *Oxford Studies presented to Daniel Callus* (Oxford Historical Society 1964), pp. 194-230.
18. E.B. Fryde and J.R.L. Highfield 'An Oxfordshire Deed of Balliol College', *Oxoniensia* XX (1955), pp. 40-5; Salter *Balliol Deeds*, pp. 285-6.
19. On Fitzralph see now Katherine Walsh *A Fourteenth Century Scholar and Primate: Richard Fitzralph* (Oxford 1981).
20. Balliol College Archive D.7.5; Salter *Balliol Deeds*, pp. 286-99.

21. *Registrum Palatinum Dunelmense* ed. T.D. Hardy (Rolls Series 1873-8), pp. 381-97.
22. Emden *Biographical Register*, I p. 484; II pp. 668, 676; III p. 1452.
23. *Ibid.*, II p. 979; III pp. 1955, 1973-4, 2055, 2103-6.
24. J.A. Robson *Wyclif and the Oxford Schools* (Cambridge 1961), pp. 10-14.

2 ANTHONY KENNY

Reform and Reaction in Elizabethan Balliol, 1559–1588

Plate 1. Rebellion the effect of monasteries.

REFORM AND REACTION IN ELIZABETHAN BALLIOL, 1559–1588

In the latter part of the reign of Queen Elizabeth I the English Roman Catholics were a divided community. In 1594 there died in Rome Cardinal William Allen, the founder of the seminary at Douai from which missionary priests were sent annually to England. After his death no English Catholic, at home or abroad, enjoyed a similar universal respect. No one succeeded to his Cardinal's hat, and the Catholics in England remained without a bishop. In the absence of an obvious head drawn from the secular clergy, the English Jesuits assumed the leadership of the English Catholic mission. In England itself the Jesuits were no more than a handful, but they were much better organized than their secular brethren, and they had great influence in Rome. The Jesuit Rector of the English College there, Father Robert Persons, was not only the leader of the Jesuit party among the English; he was often taken by the highest authorities in the Papal Curia as the spokesman for all the English Catholics. A section of the secular clergy in England bitterly resented the predominance of the Jesuits and the influence of Persons, and they challenged both in a barrage of polemical pamphlets and a series of appeals to Rome. These appellant clergy had no single leader with authority comparable to Persons'; but during the last years of Elizabeth their most forthright spokesman was Dr. Christopher Bagshaw, long a prisoner with some thirty other priests in Wisbech Castle.[1]

This was not the first time that Persons and Bagshaw had taken opposite sides in a dispute. Some twenty years earlier they had both been Fellows of Balliol, and it was at Balliol that they acquired a lifelong dislike and distrust of each other. The substance of the Appellant controversies between the Catholics at the turn of the century is not our concern; but the disputes throw an oblique light upon the history of Balliol: for the pamphlets exchanged in these quarrels, by raking up old scores, provide our most vivid source of information about daily life in the College in the early Elizabethan period. The narrative which follows draws largely on these texts, checked where possible against contemporary material in the College archives and the records of the

University.[2] By tracing the history of these two Fellows we can tell the story of reform and reaction in Elizabethan Balliol.

At the beginning of the Queen's reign Balliol was an insignificant college in a half-deserted university. The foundation was able to support half a dozen Fellows, while Merton could provide for fifteen and New College for seventy. In Queen Mary's days the Protestant scholars of Oxford had been purged: now it was the turn of the Catholics to depart or be deprived. In spring 1559 an Act of Supremacy established the Queen as supreme governor in matters ecclesiastical and an Act of Uniformity replaced the Mass with the services of the Book of Common Prayer. All were to attend the new services each Sunday under pain of one shilling fine, and Visitors were sent to Oxford to exact an oath to the Queen's supremacy and to remove superstitious utensils from college chapels. Many Catholics left their colleges rather than take the oath: in New College two years later there were twenty-four Fellows still in residence who refused to subscribe to the settlement. By 1561 every Marian Head of house but one had been driven out; during the decade twenty-nine Fellows were expelled from New College, and nine from Merton; other colleges suffered losses in proportion to their numbers. Balliol's two neighbours Trinity and St John's, both founded in Mary's reign, were notorious for popery well into the 1570's. Only Christ Church and Magdalen were comparatively painlessly converted to the new establishment: the latter in particular, under its new President, Lawrence Humfrey, became the centre of Oxford Calvinism.[3]

In tiny Balliol no Fellow was deprived in 1559; but the Master, William Wright, resigned on 15 July 1559 and the Visitor, Thomas Watson, was removed from his see of Lincoln and committed to prison. Three Fellows had resigned shortly before. The Visitors imposed a new Master, Francis Babington of All Souls', a protegé of Robert Dudley, later Earl of Leicester. To fill gaps in the fellowship two young students, not yet B.A.'s, were elected probationer Fellows: John Atkinson and Adam Squire. Master Babington did not hold office long: he was advanced to be Rector of Lincoln in 1560, and shortly became Vice-Chancellor though he was rejected as Dean by the Students of Christ Church. He was succeeded as Master of Balliol by Anthony Garnet, the chaplain of the Earl of of Northumberland.[4]

During the decade 1560–70 there were never more than six Fellows in the College: they rotated between themselves the College Offices, taking turns to be Senior and Junior Bursar, Senior and Junior Dean, and Notary or Keeper of the Register. In most years there were also two probationer Fellows, usually recent bachelors, completing a trial year before being elected *socii perpetui*. In addition the records of charges and commons in the Bursars' books show that there were often other senior members in residence, doctors and masters not on the foundation, often ex-Fellows who had remained or returned after the termination of their fellowship.

There is no clear record of the number of junior members at this period. Each Fellow had a scholar to wait on him, and the Master had two; there were two Bell exhibitioners and the names of undergraduate commoners are to be found in the Bursars' books. The Balliol matriculation lists do not begin until 1572, and are in any case probably incomplete: they commence with a list of residents showing eight scholars, nine matriculated servitors, and twenty-nine other undergraduates.[5] In 1560–65 the number was probably less: it fluctuated with the popularity of individual tutors. We do not know what kind of teaching, if any, was provided by the Fellows at the beginning of the reign: the register is full of grants of long leave of absence, and Master Garnet seems to have devoted much of his attention to the College estates in the North Country.[6]

It was in 1564 that Robert Persons came to Oxford. Born in Somerset in 1546, he had been educated by the vicar of his parish of Nether Stowey; he was sent to St. Mary Hall and studied logic there for two years before migrating to Balliol.[7] In the year of his arrival in Oxford the Earl of Leicester became Chancellor of the University. Leicester took a great and growing part in Oxford affairs, taking the appointment of Vice-Chancellors into his own hands, and frequently intervening in the business of Convocation. He strove to stiffen the Protestantism of the University, though his patronage was extended, wittingly or unwittingly, to Catholic sympathizers as well as to Calvinists. In the year after his appointment a visitation of Balliol endeavoured to bring the College into line with the new reforms.[8]

Elections to fellowships were normally held four days after St. Catherine's Day. On 29 November 1565 the Master and Fellows were about to proceed to an election when a letter from Bishop Bullingham of Lincoln forbade them to do so. There were five Fellows: Richard

Shagnes, the senior Bursar, the sole Marian survivor; Squire and
Atkinson, now senior Dean and Notary respectively; and the Chaplain
George Godsalf and Robert Hammond, who had both become full
Fellows in the previous year. The Master was Robert Hooper who
had succeeded Garnet in 1563. The governing body was not of one
mind about the correct response to the Bishop's letter. Atkinson, and
the two junior Fellows Hammond and Godsalf, refused to vote as
instructed by the Master and were declared contumacious. It was decided to proceed with the election, on the grounds that the Statutes
should be obeyed rather than the Visitor, and that in any case the
Master and Fellows had the right to choose the Visitor, and Bishop
Bullingham had never been elected. Accordingly the two probationer
Fellows, John Tunckis and Thomas Coventry, were promoted to full
fellowships.

On 14 November Dr. Humfrey of Magdalen and two others came
to the College as commissaries of the Bishop of Lincoln. They were
admitted only under protest. When they exhibited an agreement between the College and Bullingham's predecessor John Longland, estab-
lishing the Bishop of Lincoln as Visitor *ex officio*, their jurisdiction
was reluctantly accepted. The election of Coventry and Tunckis was
not quashed, however: Tunckis remained a Fellow for some years,
and Coventry resigned his fellowship voluntarily in 1566 to embark
on a legal career of great distinction. But the contumacious Godsalf,
now Junior Bursar, once more found himself in trouble, and on
1 February he was deprived of his fellowship for carrying arms within
the College and for disobeying the Vicegerent. One of the charges laid
against him was perjury: this almost certainly meant that his adherence
to the oath of supremacy was insincere and that he was a cryptopapist.
Certainly, after his departure from the College he was ordained abroad,
and returned to England as a missioner; he was captured, and banished
in 1585 after two years imprisonment in the Tower.[9] His colleague
Hammond refused to be a party to his expulsion and left the College
meeting in chapel: he was again declared contumacious but retained
his fellowship until 1570.

On the 4 March following (1565/6) the commissaries issued a set of
ordinances governing the religious discipline of the College. The
communion was to be duly ministered and given into the hands of the
communicants in the order set forth in the Book of Common Prayer;

all who were of age should partake three or four times in the year, under pain of a fine of 3s 4d at the Master's discretion. All must resort to the chapel in the time of service and common prayer, and they shall "behave themselves in such godly manner that they hinder not the worde of God to be sedde or songe, nor disturbe others". Perhaps there had been unruly scenes in protest against the new services, as at Merton where some of the Fellows had flung the new psalter into the flames, preferring to sing Popish hymns around the fire. Latin service books not approved by the Queen, and any other superstitious books, are to be handed over to the Master to be destroyed; they are to be replaced by a Bible, a communion book, the psalter and the book of homilies, and all services are to be in the vernacular. There is to be no invocation of the Saints and no praying for the dead. The Master is to take the entire College with him to the University sermons. Those who miss the weekly services are to be fined one shilling, and to be expelled if they offend three times. Those who miss regular morning prayers are to be whipped if they are undergraduates, and otherwise be batteled with one farthing fine. Members of the College are to worship in the College chapel and not in the parish church, and a Minister for the chapel is to be chosen within three months.

A year after this visitation Queen Elizabeth paid her first ceremonial visit to Oxford. She was entertained for a week upon a rich diet of orations in classical tongues and disputations on scholastic topics. It is an indication of the obscurity of Elizabethan Balliol that not one Balliol man is mentioned among the performers in Wood's full account of the elaborate proceedings. One of the most brilliant disputants to distinguish himself in the Queen's presence was a twenty-six year old Fellow of St. John's, Edmund Campion, who seemed poised for a glittering career in the academic and ecclesiastical establishment.[10]

It was in the year of the Queen's visit that Robert Persons migrated to Balliol. His keen intelligence was soon recognized, and after a brief period in the College he was promoted to a scholarship. He was at this time, in externals at least, a Calvinist; but he was subject to a number of Catholic influences. His father was reputed to be sympathetic to Catholicism, and he came to admire Campion who was becoming more and more suspect of Popish leanings. Adam Squire, the only man in Balliol who approached him in intellectual gifts, was ostentatious in his conformity to the established religion: he was elected

Senior Proctor in 1567. But Squire was succeeded as Proctor by
Campion; and it was in Campion's proctorship that Persons took his
B.A. According to a confidential autobiography he wrote years later
as a Jesuit, he tried to persuade the Proctor to exempt him from
taking the required oath acknowledging the Queen's ecclesiastical supremacy. Campion was sympathetic, but the Junior Proctor refused to
be suborned. "Out of juvenile ambition" Persons recalled "I pronounced the oath with my lips while detesting it within my heart".
He proceeded B.A. on 31 May 1568; in the same year he became a
probationary Fellow of the College, and in November 1569 a full
Fellow.[11]

It is difficult to be sure exactly where Persons stood in matters of
religion in his Balliol days. In later years he always wrote as if he was
Catholic at heart and conformed only to further his Oxford career.
His Balliol contemporaries, writing in later controversies, recalled
him as an enthusiastic Calvinist, taking tutorials in divinity from Squire
and reading the works of Calvin with Thomas Hyde, a junior colleague
who was a decided Protestant. As late as 1572 he was said to have
been responsible for selling rare manuscripts from the library in order
to restock it with works of reformed theology.[12]

Quite possibly, in his early days at Balliol, he had not made up his
mind between the old religion and the new ways. Many Oxford dons
of the 1560's may have refused to make a clear-cut choice. The generation to which they belonged had grown used to liturgical changes which
turned out to be short-lived: it was unwise enthusiastically to welcome or stubbornly to oppose the current theological fashions. The
Queen might die, or marry a Catholic prince; on the other hand she
might turn into as fierce a persecutor as her father and sister. So far
no Catholic had been put to death for conscience' sake, and the fines
for recusancy seem to have been irregularly exacted. On the other side,
there had not as yet been any clear Papal ruling promulgated which
forbade Catholics to attend the new services. Those who favoured
the old ways did not yet face an intolerable conflict between religious
loyalty and patriotic allegiance. The divisions between English Catholics and English Protestants were not yet as rigid as they were soon to
become.

At the end of the decade all this changed. In 1568 William Allen,
once a Fellow of Oriel, founded an English Catholic seminary at

Douai: henceforth priests fired with counter-reformation ideals were sent annually to England, frustrating the Government's hope that the old religion would fade gently along with memories of Queen Mary's days. In 1569 there was a Catholic rebellion in the North, led by Master Garnet's patron, the Earl of Northumberland; in 1570 the Pope excommunicated Queen Elizabeth and declared her a usurper: the Bull of excommunication released her subjects from their allegiance. After the Pope's bull the government had a case for regarding every Catholic, and especially every Catholic priest, as a potential traitor. In the event few Catholics plotted to overthrow the Queen, and most of those executed as traitors between 1570 and 1603 were innocent of any overt action against her temporal power; but things might have turned out differently if the Popes had been successful in any of the invasion attempts they sponsored which culminated in the Armada of 1588.[13]

As Catholic resolve stiffened, the government became more determined to stifle popery at home. At Oxford Chancellor Leicester ordered a new visitation of the University, "ever and anon" in Wood's words "summoning those that smelt of Popery or Popishly affected, suspending, imprisoning, or expelling them".[14] A commission was sent to search out heretical books, and scholars suspected of Catholic views were summoned for examination. Exeter College suffered particularly heavily from the visitation: the Rector and several Fellows were expelled. In Balliol suspicion fell most strongly on two Fellows just senior to Persons: Richard Garnet and Robert Benson.

Richard Garnet had been elected Fellow on the same day as Persons became a probationer, 29 November 1568. He was Notary for the next year; but in August 1569 he was granted leave of absence for the following year on the rather odd grounds that poverty, hunger, and debt prevented him from pursuing his studies. (Was a Fellow's stipend, then, inadequate to keep him from starvation?) He does not seem to have taken the leave, because he was elected Dean on 21 October, though he resigned less than a month later. He was summoned to appear before the commission; when he failed to present himself he was threatened with deprivation of his fellowship if he had not answered the charges against him by 6 July 1570. He failed to do so, and was declared a non-Fellow on 8 October. It fell to Persons to record the sentence in the Register since he was Notary for the year:

his name appears last in a list of signatures headed by that of John
Pierse, the new Master who had succeeded on 17 May 1570.[15] Garnet
was an intimate friend of Persons', who felt his departure keenly. He
was put in prison: "the first" Persons later recalled "to give an example of constancy and fortitude to the University". He was able to
escape abroad, apparently with the intention of becoming a priest;
but in Persons' words he was "entramelled in an unexpected marriage"
like another Romeward Balliol fellow in a later age, W.G. Ward.[16] He
disappears from history except for occasional presentation in the
recusancy rolls "with his wife and poor children".[17]

Robert Benson, the Chaplain, likewise fell under suspicion.[18] One
Haddon, a scholar of the College, accused him of perjury — presumably
meaning thereby disaffection to the oath of supremacy. Cross-
examined, Haddon was unable to substantiate the charge, but named
as his source another scholar, Wood. Haddon was whipped in the
chapel in front of all the scholars, and Wood was likewise sentenced
to six strokes of the birch, but as he refused to take his punishment
he was sent down. Benson retained his fellowship for another year.
But it was at this time that Edmund Campion threw up his Oxford
career and went abroad. Within three years he had become a Jesuit at
Rome.

Meanwhile, Persons began to stand out among the Fellows of Balliol.
His later career was to reveal him as a man of many gifts, in particular
of quick intelligence, enviable erudition, and arresting style. By his
death he had written a series of works more substantial than those of
any other Balliol Elizabethan. Throughout his life he could attract
and enchant men younger than himself on very brief acquaintance. It
is therefore entirely credible when we are told by his younger brother — then his scholar and servitor in Balliol — that he was much in
demand as a tutor and gathered around him more than thirty pupils,
who must have amounted to about half the entire number of junior
members.[19] We know the names of a dozen of them; at least four of
them later became priests abroad.[20] Whether or not Persons at this
period believed and taught Catholic doctrines — he certainly conformed in public to the established discipline — it is not surprising
that with hindsight people remembered him as propagating popery in
Balliol.

The tuition of pupils at this time was often a matter of private arrangement between the tutor and the pupil or his parents; but in 1571 Persons was given an official teaching post in the College. In May John Pierse went to be Dean of Christ Church, the first step in a career of preferment which would take him to the archbishopric of York. He was succeeded as Master by Adam Squire, who had continued to live in College as a senior commoner after retiring from his fellowship in 1567. On his appointment it was agreed that henceforth each Master of the College should be obliged, for as long as he held the mastership, to hold the living of Fillingham in Lincolnshire, and out of the revenues of the benefice to pay each year for three College lecturers, one in Greek, one in Logic, and one in Rhetoric. Persons was appointed the first lecturer in Rhetoric at an initial stipend of six pounds per annum; Tunckis, now Senior Fellow, was lecturer in Greek, and Adam Hill, Persons' exact contemporary as Fellow, was lecturer in Logic.[21]

It was some time before the new lecturers could begin their courses. In the first month of the new mastership a pestilential fever dispersed the society and the Fellows were given leave to go where they would. They did not reassemble until 2 February 1571/2. Persons was now, in addition to rhetoric lecturer, Junior Dean and Notary. He did not admire the new Master, and the two were soon at loggerheads. Some of Persons' Somerset friends claimed to have been induced to part with money to Squire in return for worthless investments, and Persons assisted them in litigation in Oxford. "There was great ado about it" reports Persons' brother "in so much that Squire was like to have been put out of his mastership, had he not had very good friends". Persons also took it on himself to rebuke the Master in general terms for "his evil life": our first hint of the reputation Squire was later to acquire as a heartless lecher.[22]

There were those in Oxford at this time who later reported that Persons himself in those days was "not of the best fame concerning incontinency".[23] Certainly he gained a reputation as a dandy and a roisterer:

The fellow was much noted for his singular impudency and disorder in apparel, going in great barrel hose, as was the fashion of hucksters in those times, and drawing also deep in a barrell of ale.[24]

This was shortly after a University statute had forbidden any Head of house, graduate, or scholar, to wear any "cut hosen or hoses lined with any other stuff to make them swell or puff out".[25] Persons himself, summing up his Balliol days after twenty years as a Jesuit, lamented privately "I was no use to my pupils either in word or example, being totally at that time dedicated to vanity".[26]

It was in this first year of Squire's mastership that Christopher Bagshaw came to Balliol. He was the son of a Lichfield innkeeper who had been sheriff of the town in 1564. He may have been a pupil of Persons; certainly he came under his jurisdiction as Dean. He completed his undergraduate course with remarkable speed, and took his B.A. in 1572.[27] George Abbot, who was later Bagshaw's colleague as a Fellow of the College before going on to become Archbishop of Canterbury, recalls

> Bagshaw, being a smart young man, and one who thought his penny good silver, after that he had his grace to be batchelor of arts, was with some despight swinged by Persons, being dean of the colledge: *Hoc manet alta mente repostum*: And Bagshaw afterwards coming to be fellow, was most hot in prosecution against Persons.[28]

Bagshaw became a probationary Fellow in 1573, one of an unusually large batch of six; Persons claims to have had a large hand in his election. But Bagshaw joined the faction headed by Squire of those who resented what they regarded as arrogance and censoriousness on the part of Persons, and who were determined to drive him out of the College. Abbot relates how the quarrel came to a head:

> Dr Squire and Bagshaw being desirous of some occasion to trim him, this fell out: In the year 1572 Parsons had been bourser and being joyn'd in office with one Stanclif, a very simple fellow, he took the advantage of the weakness of his colleague, and falsified the reckonings much to the damage of the colledg, as also deeply polling the commoners names, whereof there was store in the colledg; and withall, not sparing his own scholars: By all which means it was thought that he had purloin'd one hundred marks. His office expiring at St. Luke's tide, there were some that between that and February 1573 scanned over the books,

being moved thereto by the secret complaints of some of
the commoners their scholars.

Bagshaw left his own account of the proceedings, which is similar to
that of Abbot. Both men were writing thirty years after the events,
and had an interest in blackening Persons' name. Is there any contemporary evidence to support the charge that Persons was a corrupt
Bursar of Balliol?

Under the Statutes the Bursars had charge of the food supplies and
the administration of the College buildings and estates; with the Master they had exclusive access to the Treasury and to its chests. They
were obliged to render accounts twice in the year, on St. Luke's day
(18 October) and within three days of the 16 July, at an audit meeting of the Master and Fellows. In 1571 they were given charge of all
commoners' battels, discharging the College for them and reserving
to themselves the profits of bread, drink, baking etc.. New Bursars
were appointed annually after the Luketide accounting. Persons was
appointed Senior Bursar in October 1572, with James Stancliff as
junior colleague, a Fellow of two years standing.[29]

The new Bursars took over at a difficult time. A minute of a College
meeting on 20 October records the decision that since the College
has been reduced to poverty and squalor by the depradations, negli-
gence and death of previous Masters, Fellows, Bursars and commoners,
in order to redeem its name and fortune the Master and Fellows are
to be charged rent for their rooms for the current year. The minute is
signed by the Master and the five current Fellows, Tunckis, Wilson,
Persons, Hyde and Stancliff.[30] Clearly, the College was in a mood for
economising, and scrutinising accounts, and when the Bursars presented their interim accounts on 7 July 1573 they were submitted to a
stringent audit. Squire and the other three Fellows recorded in the
Register that on examining the accounts they found negligent omis-
sions, imprudent business dealings, superfluous expenditure and altogether unparalleled extravagance. There was the sum of £11 of excess
expenditure for which no justifying cause appeared, and so the governing body refused to discharge the Bursars of that sum. Despite this
rebuke, Persons and Stancliff continued in office: by the end of the
financial year the accounts were in balance and £7 10s was handed
over to the next Bursar. Having resigned as Bursar in due course,

Persons became Dean for a second time towards the end of 1573.

Persons' final accounts are preserved in the College archives among the Bursars' *computi*. It is, of course, impossible to tell from them, now that the vouchers have all disappeared, whether there is any substance in the charge of falsification. But a number of things suggest that the allegation was not altogether void of foundation. If Bagshaw is to be believed, Stancliff joined in accusing his brother Bursar of forgery. Persons, when rebutting the smears on his Balliol record in the pamphlets of Bagshaw and his fellow Appellants in the early 1600's, does not defend his record as Bursar, other than by implying that all the charges made against him at Balliol were the result of anti-Catholic prejudice. One of the Fellows whom in 1601 he called as witness to his good behaviour, John Wilson, was in fact one of the four signatories of the censure on the Bursars. But the most important piece of evidence against Persons' bursarship comes from a friendly source. When the forgery charge became current in 1601 Henry Garnet, the Jesuit superior, did his best to give the story the lie. He tracked down a Catholic in a debtor's prison who had been one of Persons' successors as Bursar. This man, he reports in a letter to Persons in Rome, had been pressed by the English Catholic malcontents to make propaganda against him. One of the allegations was that Persons as Bursar had entered into the College account book, against a certain piece of work, a sum greater than that found in his own private accounts. The "good fellow", however, refused to cooperate with the detractors, and was now "standing firm." None the less, the best that Garnet could report to Persons of him was this:

> To the second count he answers that anyone who knows the customs of Oxford can well imagine that Bursars receive a percentage on every pound, and it is the custom for them to receive a gratuity from tradesmen.[31]

It all sounds as if the wisest course for Persons in 1601 would have been to admit to irregularities in his conduct as Bursar, but to point out that they had occurred when he was a heretic or schismatic not yet converted to Catholicism, and not yet a member of the Society of Jesus. But he suffered from a life-long inability ever to admit publicly that he had been in the wrong.

The accusation that as Bursar he disfurnished the library of ancient

works to make room for heretical tomes seems to be less solidly founded. During his year of office there is no record of the purchase of
any book for the College; only an entry of 3d for the carriage of books
to London which could, no doubt, refer to the disposal of surplus
Catholic works. There is a record of a purchase of a chain to attach
to the library a new book given by the Master: but the library benefactors' book shows that Squire's gift was not a Calvinist tract but the
collected works of the fourth century apologist Lactantius. Indeed a
superficial search of the earliest library catalogues and accession books
suggests that very few Calvinist books found their way into the library
before the 1580's.[32]

Persons's *computi* cannot settle the charges made against him: but
they do throw light on many details of Elizabethan College life: the
recurring feasts and gaudies, the provision of special wine for the rare
celebrations of the Lord's Supper, the progress and equipment of the
new garden. The entries do not make easy reading. Persons' crumpled
and energetic hand, now familiar to researchers of state papers in
many a European archive, presents puzzles even in the well-tempered
orthography of latin epistles. In the *computi* Persons wrote, like other
Fellows of the period, an extraordinary macaronic Bursary jargon:

Item pro clavibus pro the new cubbard in the buttery

Item pro the yrons pro the whilbarrowe et pro factione eiusdem.

An interesting item in the petty expenses is the purchase of two pairs
of gloves to be given by the Master to Lord Montague. Lord Montague was the only lay peer to vote against the Act of Uniformity in
1559, and he never forfeited the favour of the Queen in spite of his
unconcealed Catholicism. This suggests that even the conformist
Squire found it worthwhile to court the most important Papist in the
country just in case the death or marriage of the Queen brought a
sudden alteration in religion.

The episode which led to Persons' expulsion from the College occurred at Christmas, 1573. Writing anonymously years later, Persons
interpreted the episode as an attempt by Bagshaw to steal away one
of his pupils. He narrated it thus.[33]

F. Persons being gone to London at Christmas time, M.
Bagshaw allured unto him a very proper youth called M.
James Hawley of whom F.P. being tutor, had special care

both for his good parts, and for his friends who lyved in
London, and with whom F.P. remayned at this tyme. The
manner of drawing him was (as we understand) by carrying
the said youth forth by night being of very tender age, to
certayne commedies which F. Persons had forbidden at his
departure, for feare of inconvenience that might ensue in
such thing, and having committed this fault he persuaded
the youth that F.P. would not pardon it, and so when he
came home M. Bagshaw kept this youth shut up in his owne
chamber, and would not suffer him to go to F.P. when he
sent for him, nor yet when he came for him himselfe, under
pretence of fere that he would punish him over rigorously.

The quarrel between Persons and Bagshaw led to the calling of a
special College meeting. We have several accounts of this occasion,[34]
but they do not agree why the meeting was called. Persons says that
it was he who "called a public chapter of all the fellows laying open
the iniury done to him" claiming that the Statutes called for the expulsion of Bagshaw for refusing the Dean access to one of his own
pupils. Bagshaw says that Persons' account is "not onely voyd of substance, but of all probability or colour of truth", and says that twenty-
nine or thirty junior members of the College came before the Master
and Fellows to complain of Persons' overcharging. Abbot, too, distinctly implies that it was allegations of corruption as Bursar which
led to Persons' being "put to the push in the colledge chapel."

All sources agree that Persons received no satisfaction for his complaints against Bagshaw: instead, the Master and Fellows pressed a
number of charges against him. There were now ten Fellows, six of
whom had been elected at the same time as Bagshaw; of the ten at
most two were sympathetic to Persons, John Wilson, the only Fellow
senior to him, and George Turner, one of the six juniors. The Master,
according to Persons, alleged "that he perverted a great part of the
youthes of the house and that it was not meet that a man of his back-
wardness of religion should have so many schollers and pupils." It
was also alleged that Persons was disqualified to be a Fellow since he
was a bastard, and it was required by the Statutes that every Fellow
should be born in lawful wedlock. This charge, however, could not
be proved, and was indeed almost certainly false.[35] The Fellows therefore did not deprive Persons of his fellowship, but urged him to resign

it voluntarily, offering him three months grace to prepare his departure. They threatened, he tells us, that if he would not do this, "they would violently ioyne together to have him out with all his schollers, whatsoever became of it, and that they would that very night cast out by force and fury both his and all his schollers stuff without the college, and he should seek his remedy as he might."

Persons entertained, but quickly abandoned, the idea of an appeal to the Visitor. The new Bishop of Lincoln, Thomas Cooper, was a former Dean of Christ Church who had shown himself a firmly Protestant Vice-Chancellor: he was unlikely to be sympathetic to a man reputed a crypto-Papist. So Persons agreed to resign his fellowship; but he obtained consent to a compromise.

> Before the assembly broke up, he entreated that his giving over might be conceal'd, by reason that it would be disgraceful unto him with all men, but especially with his scholars and their friends, and for these causes humbly prayed, That he might keep his scholars, chamber &c, and be reputed as a fellow in the house, the matter being concealed from all the boys and the younger sort in the house.

This rather Jesuitical proposal was accepted; Persons tell us that the other Fellows took an oath of secrecy. Thus "the matter was ended, and all made great frends, as to outward show appeared."

The outcome of the meeting was recorded in the College register under the date of 13 February 1573/4. First comes Persons' resignation (see plate), which may be translated as follows:

> I Robert Persons Fellow of Balliol College resign all my right, title and claim that I have or may have to my fellowship in the same College: I do this of my own free will and under compulsion on the thirteenth day of the month of February in the year of our Lord 1573.

This follows the customary form for renunciation of a fellowship, save that instead of saying that he resigns *sponte et non coactus* (of my own free will and *not* under compulsion) he wrote *sponte et coactus*. The oxymoron was perhaps not an unnatural Freudian slip for a man who was writing under compulsion that he was resigning of his own free will.[36] Below the resignation there follows in the Notary's hand:

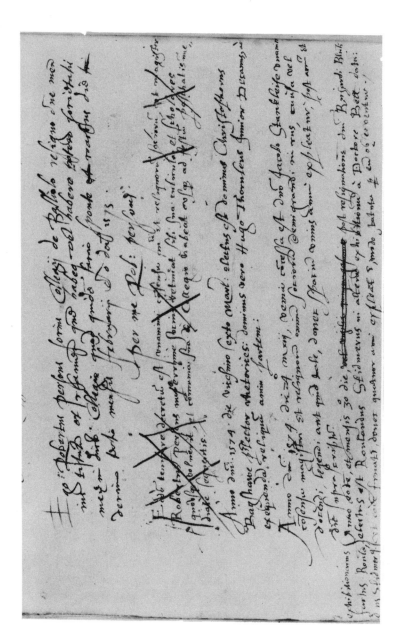

Plate 2. Persons' resignation in the College Register, 13 February 1573/4.

At the same time it was decided by the unanimous agreement of the Master and the remaining Fellows that Master Robert Persons lately Fellow shall retain his rooms and his scholars for as long as he will, and that he shall have his commons from the College until Easter day next.

The secret of Persons' resignation was not well kept. Perhaps Master Squire never intended to keep it. Archbishop Abbott reports:

When Parsons was expell'd, he was one of the deans of the colledg, and so by his place was to keep corrections in the hall on the Saturdays. The next time therefore of correction, which was on the day of Parsons his expulsion, or soon after, Dr. Squire causeth Parsons to go into the hall as dean, and to call the book and roll &c, and then cometh Dr. Squire himself in, and as if it had been in kindness to countenance him (but in truth more profoundly to deride him) he calleth him at every word, Mr. Dean, and desireth him often to have a strict care to the good government of the youth; and not only for a fit, but all the time of his year that he was to continue in office. Some of the commoners knew all this pageant, and laught the more sweetly.

The Bursar's book, which records which Fellows took their commons week by week, notes Persons as continuing to eat at common table for several weeks after 14 February, and as continuing to draw his stipend until Easter 1574.[37] Indeed, during Lent, while the Master was absent in London, he attempted a counter-attack upon the hostile faction. He alleged that they had eaten flesh secretly in their rooms, and had encouraged some of his own scholars to do so; moreover that one of his pupils, Simms, who had refused to eat with them, had had some cheeses or puddings stolen from his own chest at the instigation of the anti-Catholic Fellows. He reported the matter to Simms' father and tried with his aid to prosecute the pudding thieves before the Vice-Chancellor's court. He had some hope that the thieves might be imprisoned, for the Vice-Chancellor, Dr. Martin Culpeper, now Warden of New College, had long lived in Balliol as a senior commoner and had always been friendly disposed towards him. But the Protestant Fellows notified Squire in London, who informed his patron, the Earl of Leicester, of the threatened proceedings. The Chancellor wrote a sharp letter to the Vice-Chancellor telling him to proceed no further, "saying that he understood of such an attempt as meaning of one evil affected in religion towards others that were good protestants, for a trifle of eating a little flesh". Persons incurred great infamy, Bagshaw tells us, for bringing men of good reputation in danger of their lives for a juvenile prank, and the expression "Persons' puddings" became a common byword.[38]

This story was well aired in the prolix Catholic controversies of the 1600's: it naturally caused great merriment to Protestant pamphleteers. Thus Matthew Sutcliffe in his *Full and Round Answer to N.D. alias Robert Persons the Noddie his foolish and rude warneworde*, amid a number of gibes at Persons' humble birth, says this:

> It may be thought that taking of puddings was a great matter, considering especially, that the wealth of the tripewife his mother consisted in tripes, puddings, and sources; but see Gods hand against this prosecution of takings of puddings: he is now so swollen like a blacke pudding, that the memory of Parsons puddings will not lightly be forgotten. A man shall hardly find a fitter fellow to play Ballio the baud, then Persons being a baudy, burley, pudding-growne fellow, and very like the baud in Plautus . . . . . with his bumbasted and barell-like bellie, and eyes greenish like grass.[39]

The Chancellor's stay of proceedings was taken by Persons' enemies as the signal of final victory. They no longer felt obliged to keep his resignation secret. He complains:

> Against their oathes they published that F. Persons was not fellow of Balliol Colledge, and further in their fury they ran to the next Church of S. Magdalyn and rang the bells backward as if fire had begun in towne, and being asked of the people what it meant, they answered, that a great Papist was fyred out of Balliol Colledge that day.

Even for Persons, this was too much. In Abbot's words "understanding all his knell which was rung out for him, for very shame he got him away to London."[43]

In later life Persons wrote as if it had been long publicly known that he intended to travel overseas. But if he had at the time a firm intention to become a Catholic abroad, he concealed it even from close friends. In London he sought shelter with an old schoolfellow, James Clark of the Middle Temple. "Mr. Parsons" said Clark "it is now some years since we were schoolboys together, and I have often heard that you are since become a great Papist. I would be glad to be satisfied to the contrary." Persons assured him that this was a calumny bruited abroad by his enemies, and especially Dr. Squire: he was no Papist, and did not intend to be; he intended to travel to Padua to study medicine.[41]

He left England in June, and in Louvain his irresolution ended: he was reconciled to the Catholic Church by the Jesuit William Good, and made the spiritual exercises of St. Ignatius. After some months in the study of civil law at Bologna he entered the Society of Jesus in Rome in July. After ordination in 1578 he became a penitentiary at St. Peter's. He probably did not expect to see England again: the Jesuits had as yet no English mission, and Campion, who had been a Jesuit since 1573, was at present a schoolmaster in Prague.[42]

The departure of Persons did not bring peace to Balliol, nor did it put an end to suspicions of popery. On 7 May 1575 the Master and four other Fellows signed a decree expelling from their fellowships John Wilson, George Turner and Christopher Bagshaw. It is interesting to see Bagshaw's name in company with those of the two Fellows whom Persons recorded as having been Catholicly inclined at the time of his own expulsion. Had Bagshaw undergone a conversion in the meantime? We cannot say, because the sentence of expulsion was quashed by the Visitor's commissaries on 3 June and the Register entry cancelled so thoroughly that the reasons for the attempted expulsion are quite illegible.[43]

There is some evidence that some of Persons' pupils were dispersed. One of his favourite pupils, Alexander Briant, is found matriculating at Hart Hall in 1574.[44] His brother George remained at Balliol, but when he supplicated for his B.A. on 3 July 1575 grace was granted only on condition that he purged himself of the suspicion of papistry in the presence of the Vice-Chancellor.[45] Others of his former pupils followed him across the sea and became seminary priests. Among the six probationer Fellows elected in 1576 two were future seminarists:

William Staverton, who was ordained in Rome, and Thomas Pilcher who was to be executed at Chideock in Dorset in 1587.[46]

Adam Squire, the Master of the house, remained resolutely Protestant. He took his D.D. in 1576 and chose for the topics of his disputation the following items of contemporary controversy:

Does purgatory exist? No.
Should prayer be made for the dead? No.
Does the Holy Spirit desert the elect when they sin? No.[47]

He had been Vicar of Cumnor since 1568, and in 1577 he became a Canon of St. Paul's; as Master he was also Rector of Fillingham in accordance with the decree of 1572. In 1576 he was one of a small committee appointed to revise the University Statutes. In the pursuit of his own career he was ambitious and unscrupulous: he was constantly involved in litigation,[48] but he was careful to retain the favour of the Chancellor, the Earl of Liecester. He finally left the College in 1580, after frequent absences in London in previous years. He married the daughter of Bishop Aylmer of London, and was provided for by being made Archdeacon of Middlesex. He cuts rather a poor figure in Strype's life of the bishop:

> The man was somewhat fantastical, as appears in that he would needs preach his own wedding sermon; which he did from that text, It is not good for Adam to be alone . . . He proved an unkind husband and a dissolute man.[49]

During the last years of Squire's mastership Bagshaw was the most senior and influential Fellow. He was Senior Dean in 1576, and again in 1578; in 1577 he was Senior Bursar, holding office in company with James Hawley, Persons' theatre-going pupil, as his younger colleague. Like Squire, Bagshaw was a pluralist: he was Principal of Gloucester Hall from 1579–81, and held the prebend of Gaia Minor in Lichfield Cathedral from 1578–81. During Squire's absences Bagshaw acted as Vicegerent. In August 1579 he summoned the Bursar, Matthew Pindar, to answer charges in the chapel. The nature of the charges is not clear, but Pindar failed to appear, having been thrice admonished, and so Bagshaw declared him contumacious and deprived him of his fellowship, appointing Pilcher as Bursar in his place. Many entries in the Register at this period show that the Fellows distrusted each other totally in financial matters: repeated injunctions attempt to make the Bursars more accountable, and it was found necessary to decree that the Treasury, to which the Master and two Fellows held the three keys, should be opened only in the presence of the entire governing body.

By now a number of Persons' former pupils had returned to England and were ministering clandestinely as Catholic priests. Alexander Briant had gone to Douai in 1576 and was now back in England, where he reconciled Persons' father to the Roman church in 1579. Thomas Ford, who had been a pupil of Persons before becoming a Fellow of Trinity in 1567, had now been a missioner in England for three years. The first of the seminary priests to be executed for treason was Cuthbert Maine, who suffered at Launceston in 1577: he had been in former times Chaplain of St. John's College. In 1579 a second seminary overseas was founded, in the house of the old English Hospice in Rome. Persons helped in its establishment, and it was entrusted to the Society of Jesus. Dr. Allen now persuaded the Jesuit authorities to send Jesuit missionaries to England to work alongside the secular priests from the seminaries. The first to be sent were Edmund Campion and Robert Persons.[50]

Persons, though the younger man, was made superior; the two set off from Rome, along with thirteen secular priests, in April 1580. The two Jesuits landed separately in June. They had been given instructions not to meddle in political affairs; but the spiritual nature of their mission was compromised from the outset by an inept simultaneous Papal military venture in Ireland. They travelled round England comforting Catholics, reconciling the lapsed and administering the sacraments. Persons set up a clandestine printing press from which Catholic tracts were distributed. When the University of Oxford assembled for the degree disputations of June 1581 each M.A. found on his bench in St. Mary's a copy of Campion's *Ten Reasons*.

One of the first acts of the Jesuits on arrival in England had been to assemble a meeting of the senior missionaries already in England, including Persons' former colleague at Trinity, George Blackwell. They communicated to these priests two recent Papal decisions: first, that attendance at Anglican churches was strictly forbidden, and secondly that the Papal excommunication of the Queen did not oblige Catholics for the present (*rebus sic stantibus*) to rise against her. The first provision placed the Catholic laity in a more difficult position than ever;

the second did nothing to relieve the government's suspicions of treason, because of the conditional nature of the dispensation from the
obligation to rebel.

Persons' letters of this year give an arresting and moving description
of the missionaries' lives: of their secret progress from manor house
to manor house, of the risks taken by their hosts and of their own
hairsbreadth escapes from the pursuivants who roamed the country-
side in search of them.[51] In July 1581 Campion was betrayed and
arrested; with him was taken Thomas Ford. Alexander Briant had
already been captured: he was now in the Tower, and was several
times racked in order to reveal the whereabouts of Persons and his
printing press.

> Because he would not confess where he had seen father
> Parsons, how he was maintained, where he had said mass,
> and whose confessions he had heard, they caused needles
> to be thrust under his nails; whereat Mr. Brian was not
> moved at all, but with a constant mind and pleasant coun-
> tenance, said the psalm *Miserere*, desiring God to forgive
> his tormenters.[52]

In the letter in which Persons reported to the Rector of the English
College in Rome about the cruelties used on Briant, he also complained
of the brutality of Bishop Aylmer. Having listed the Bishop's cruelties,
he went on:

> But vengeance of a sort seems to have pursued him immed-
> iately; for he had married his own daughter whom he espe-
> cially loved, to a certain preaching minister (for they usually
> all marry for the most part within their own tribe of minis-
> ters), and to enhance his daughter's position had made him
> Archdeacon of London. This man, while on a visitation of
> his district, was caught by the magistrates with another
> man's wife. This having been brought to the notice of the
> father-in-law, the son-in-law in order to induce him to take
> a more lenient view of the matter, was willing to add to his
> offence. So he forged, in his wife's name, a letter full of
> passion, to a certain knight, and pretending that he had inter-
> cepted it, produced it to his father-in-law as an excuse for

his lapse. The latter was extremely distressed, but when he found out afterwards that the whole affair had been invented by his son-in-law, he flew into a passion and is said to have given the Archdeacon a tremendous thrashing, not with the pastoral staff, but with a butcher's cudgel. It is with prelates of this sort forsooth that we are fighting.[53]

The delinquent Archdeacon was, of course, none other than the former Master of Balliol. The quarrel between father-in-law and son-in-law was no mere Papist canard: the Bishop's correspondence with the Lord Treasurer about Squire's misbehaviour can be read in Strype's biography.[54]

Persons' letter was written in August. In the same month his secret press was discovered and dismantled at Stonor Park; he himself took an opportunity to slip abroad. Campion, Briant, Ford and a dozen others were tried in November. Campion and Briant, with Ralph Sherwin, a graduate of Exeter College and the English College in Rome, were hanged, disembowelled, and quartered at Tyburn on 1 December 1581.[55] The three of them — and Persons *in absentia* — were found guilty of a totally fictitious plot to compass the Queen's deposition and death. By the spring of next year the Attorney General, Sir John Popham (Balliol 1551–4) had found a more convenient method of bringing recusant priests within the treason statute. Imprisoned priests were asked their opinion of the pope's deposing power, and invited to say what they would do in the event of an invasion on account of religion. This "bloody question", often put to victims on the rack, brought many a priest to the scaffold in the coming years. One of the first to be put to the question was Thomas Ford: he answered, to the inquiry about a papal invasion, that "it would be time enough to determine what was to be done, when the case should happen". He was executed at Tyburn in May 1582 with John Shert of Brasenose and another priest.[56]

The 'Jesuit invasion' and the executions made a stir in Oxford. Dr. Humfrey of Magdalen, now Regius Professor of Divinity, preached a sermon against Campion and Persons and the Jesuits as the Pharisees of the age; he published a painstaking rebuttal of Campion's *Ten Reasons*.[57] But many of the younger members of the University were moved to imitate the Catholic martys, and crossed overseas to the

seminaries. One of the most senior to do so was Christopher Bagshaw.
A few weeks after the execution of Campion and Briant he ceased to
take his commons in Balliol; by 17 July 1582 he had presented himself at Dr. Allen's seminary, now in Rheims. He was ordained at Laon
in the following May, and sent on to Rome as the head of a contingent
of seminarists in August.[58] Dr. Allen described him as being "pre-
eminent in age and in the scope of his learning", but Allen's Vice-
Rector wrote privately to the Roman college that they would find
him "irascible, difficult, and troublesome".

The departure of Bagshaw and his comrades worried the English
authorities. Balliol had acquired the reputation of being, in the words
of a recent historian, "an enclave of reaction".[59] An anonymous
memorialist informed the Privy Council in summer 1583

> That Balliol Colledg hathe not been free from the suspicion
> of papistrie this longe time it appeareth by the men that
> have been of the sayme house, namelye, Brian and Parsons.
> With Parsons and since his departure from the colledge hath
> Turner, Bagshaw, Staverton and one Pilcher been fellowes:
> all which were grevously suspect of religion. And certaune
> it is that this Pilcher is gone this year from thence to Rhemes,
> looking dailye for Bagshaw as he did report . . . Staverton
> is in like manner departed the colledge, and it is thought that
> both Bagshaw and he be gone over the sea. It is said that
> Turner also either is gone or shall goe beyond the seas
> with a physician, to whom the Q. Majestie has geven leave
> to passe and to take one with him. It is thought some of
> these have lefte their resygnation of their fellowship with
> theyr schollers whom they have trayned up, as Bagshaw to
> Elis his scholler, and Staverton to his scoller Blunt, which
> two yf they be fellows, the College will remain in its de-
> served name of suspicion of papistrie. This may be foreseen
> in causing the Master . . . to place those which be knowne
> to be zealous and godly. The election is at Saynt Katherine's
> day or after presentlye.[60]

A letter was indeed sent by the Privy Council to the College, and
Blount was passed over when he stood for election. He was, however,
nephew to Lady Paulet, the widow of the founder of Trinity; by her

influence he was elected to a fellowship there next Trinity Sunday. But he did not stay long, and three Protestant Fellows of Balliol notified the government that he had taken a bunch of Trinity scholars overseas to Rheims. Blount became a Jesuit, and eventually became a successor of Henry Garnet as provincial of the English mission.

Persons meanwhile, in exile in France and Flanders, was active in many ways in promoting the Catholic cause. He wrote a number of controversial and devotional books; one, the *Christian Directory*, was so successful that it became a best-seller in England in a pirated Protestant edition. He was tireless in devising plans for invading England and replacing Elizabeth with a Catholic sovereign, and in trying to persuade officials in Rome and in Spain to see that these plans were put into effect. In 1584 we find him writing to Mary Queen of Scots in captivity, offering her advice on how to escape, and recommending the name of a possible husband. Some of his letters, including this one, were intercepted by government decipherers, and he was soon known as an archtraitor. He was named as such, with Dr. Allen, in a royal proclamation in 1589. The fiasco of the Armada put an end to the possibility, but not to his hopes, of installing a Catholic sovereign on the throne.

Bagshaw, like Persons, was later to become involved in political manoeuvre. His career as a priest in Rome was stormy. He resented being treated on equal terms with undergraduate seminarists many years his junior, and he raised such tumults in the English College that the Cardinal Protector was forced to make a Visitation. He was not exactly expelled, but forced to depart in the same ambiguous manner as Persons had left Balliol.[61] Persons, then in Paris, wrote to the Rector of the College that he was delighted that Bagshaw had been "mortified".[62] Bagshaw went to Padua, where he acquired a Doctorate with astonishing speed; unless it was obtained by outright purchase, it must have been on the basis of his Oxford reputation. He reached Rheims in April 1585 and was sent on to England. Only two months before there had been passed an Act against Jesuits and secular priests (27 Eliz. c.2) making it treason for an English subject ordained beyond the sea to set foot in England. Henceforth any priest returning to England did so at the peril of his life. Bagshaw was captured very soon after arrival: by September he was in prison in the Tower of London. After a visit to Lichfield on parole he was sent to join a company of priests imprisoned in Wisbech Castle. There he remained for thirteen years.[63]

It was at Wisbech that there occurred the first public quarrel between pro-Jesuit and anti-Jesuit factions among the Catholic clergy. A majority of the priests adopted a semi-monastic regime under the Jesuit William Weston; Bagshaw was one of two leaders of the minority who objected to the new discipline as hypocritical and divisive. The points at issue were at first comparatively trivial items magnified by the strain of prolonged imprisonment. But Catholics outside the prison were drawn into the dispute, and more important matters became involved.[64]

A number of the English Catholics complained that Persons' treasonable activities abroad led to more rigorous persecution of the innocent in England. They also complained that their attempts to secure a bishop to lead the English secular clergy were frustrated by the Jesuits in order to preserve their supremacy over the English mission. The discontent grew to a climax when in 1597 Persons became Rector of the English College in Rome and purged it of anti-Jesuit elements, and when he secured the appointment in 1598 of his old associate, George Blackwell, as archpriest over the clergy in lieu of a bishop.[65]

Blackwell was regarded by influential members of the secular clergy as a Jesuit catspaw. "All Catholics must hereafter depend upon Blackwell" wrote Bagshaw "and he upon Garnet and Garnet upon Persons, and Persons upon the Devil, who is the author of all rebellions, treasons, murders, disobedience, and all such designments as this wicked Jesuit hath hitherto designed against her majesty, her safety, her crown and her life."[66] Bagshaw and his party organised a number of appeals to Rome against Blackwell's authority. In their quarrel against the Jesuits they enlisted the support of the English authorities, who were quick to exploit the dissensions among the Catholics. Bishop Bancroft of London arranged for Bagshaw's release and eventual banishment, and facilitated the printing of anti-Jesuit books by Catholic priests. In the last year of the reign thirteen of the appellant party signed a protestation of allegiance to the Queen, affirming their loyalty to the Pope but rejecting the Papal deposing power and offering to shed their blood for the Queen should there be a Roman invasion.[67]

In the battle of books between the Appellants and the Jesuits the old quarrels in Balliol were raked up and set before the public. The Appellant John Mush, blaming all the discords on the Jesuits, mentions Persons as a man who

> was driven out of Oxford University with universal applause and ringing of bells, not for the sake of religion as he vainly boasts but because he always delighted in sedition, faction and the writing of slanderous pamphlets.[68]

This passage provoked Persons, in his *Briefe Apologie* in favour of the Archpriest, to give the detailed account of his expulsion from which I have quoted above. Persons' book drew a reply from a former Fellow of St. John's Dr. Humphrey Ely, entitled *Certaine Briefe notes upon a Briefe Apologie*, to which Bagshaw contributed an appendix giving his own account of the events in Balliol in 1574. The pamphlets became more and more vituperative. One Appellant, Watson, went so far as to blame the present quarrels on Persons' vindictive nature: he was seeking revenge on Bagshaw for turning him out of Balliol. Part of a page-long rhetorical question in his *Decacordon of Ten Quodlibeticall Questions* reads thus:

> who that had seen & knowne him in Oxford and his dealings there, how seditious, wanton and factious this lewd bastarde's conversation was: how for his libelling & other misdeameanours he was thrust out of Balyoll college (and not for religion as he vainely vaunts) doctor Bagshaw being then fellow of the same college, and his stiff adversarie in the matter objected against him, which I verily thinke is cause of a great hatred in all the Iesuits against the said doctor now, as an accident proper to that society to be revengefull to death: how he became so infamous there being then master of arts, that they hissed him out with whouts and hoo-bubs, and rang him thence with bells.

Protestant controversialists naturally enjoyed the spectacle of the Papists tearing each other to pieces in print. Thomas Bell's *The Anatomie of Popish Tyrannie* contains an anthology of Appellant denunciations of Persons.[69] It was indeed the writings of the Appellant controversy that fixed Persons forever in the English consciousness as the archetype of the crafty, scheming, treacherous Jesuit.

The controversy was long, involved, and bitter. "Why can you not put up with each other, you who are prepared to put up with so very much?", said the exasperated Pope Clement VIII to the quarelling English Catholics.[70] Historians are divided about the significance of the Archpriest controversy. Some see the Appellants as the forward-looking party to the dispute, willing to reach agreement with the English government, and give loyalty to a heretical sovereign in exchange for toleration: ecumenists, almost, before their time. Others regard the Appellants as being, on the contrary, an anachronism: conservatives hankering after the established hierarchies of the middle ages and unappreciative of the streamlined counter-reformation missionary methods of the Jesuits.[71] But whatever the principles at stake, no one who reads the pamphlets and memoranda of the two factions can fail to see that personalities were no less important than principles in the minds of the combatants. And of all the conflicts of personality, none was more influential than the one which had begun so many years earlier at Balliol.

The appellant clergy eventually won a bishop from Rome: but that was not until 1623, by which time both Persons and Bagshaw had gone. Persons died in 1610 after thirteen years as Rector of the English College in Rome. Astonishingly, he still awaits a biographer. Successive archivists of the English Province of the Society of Jesus have published much of the documentation on which a life must be based, but none has yet come forward to tell the full story of this most interesting of Balliol Elizabethans.[72]

Bagshaw makes only one further appearance after Persons' death. In 1612 he held a teaching post at the Sorbonne. The English ambassador's chaplain, Daniel Featley, published under the title *Transubstantiation Exploded* an account of a disputation which he held with Bagshaw in Paris. His report, as might be expected, gives the victory handsomely to himself. After recording a telling point he made about the Greek text of the Gospel account of the last supper, he ends his narrative:

> At these words he arose from his chair and brake off the disputation. D. Bagshaw as it seemeth sitting upon thornes would not stay to hear out M. Featley's full answer.

And with that the disputatious Bagshaw disappears from history.

NOTES

1. See P. Hughes *Rome and the Counter-Reformation in England* (1942), and J. Bossy *The English Catholic Community 1570–1850* (1975).
2. Especially C. Bagshaw *A sparing discouerie of our English Iesuits, and of Fa. Parsons proceedings vnder pretence of promoting the Catholike faith in England* (1601), R. Persons *A brief apologie, or defence of the Catholike ecclesiastical hierarchie, & subordination in England* . . . , (St. Omer 1601), and Bagshaw's appendix to H. Ely *Certaine briefe notes upon a briefe apologie set out under the name of the priestes united to the archpriest* (Paris 1603).
3. See P. Williams 'Elizabethan Oxford' forthcoming in the *History of the University of Oxford*.
4. Balliol College Register 1514–1682 (henceforth BCR), pp. 82–88. The Bursar's book of the period records on 17 June 1559 the purchase of the Book of Common Prayer, the Bible, the Psalter and the Homilies. In 1559 and 1563 there are entries recording the destruction of altars. The Bursars' book itself is lost, but notes taken from it by Clark are in the Bodleian, MS.Top. Oxon.e.124/10. I am indebted for this reference to Dr. J.H. Jones.
5. The list is given in A. Clark, *Register of the University of Oxford, 1571–1622*, II (Oxford 1885) p. 30.
6. According to MS.Top.Oxon.e.124/10, f.101 there was in 1558/9 a praelector in natural philosophy; but we hear no more of him in the next decade. Garnet was in residence, according to the list of commons, only 28 weeks in 1560 and only 2½ weeks in 1561.
7. Persons' own notes for his autobiography are published in Volume 2 of the *Publications of the Catholic Record Society* (henceforth *CRS*). See p. 13.
8. The proceedings leading up to the Visitation are recorded in BCR; the injunctions are to be found on p. 108.
9. See G. Anstruther *The Seminary Priests: A dictionary of the secular clergy of England and Wales 1558–1850*, volume 1, 1558–1603, (Ware 1969), s.v. Godsalve. Godsalf's brother also became a priest; he too described himself as a Balliol graduate.
10. A. Wood *The History and Antiquities of the University of Oxford* (Oxford 1792). The most up-to-date account of the Visitation is in Williams *op. cit*; the most vivid is in Evelyn Waugh's *Edmund Campion* (1953).
11. *CRS* 2, pp. 13ff. The dates of the promotions are in BCR.
12. Bagshaw, in Ely, appendix p. 32.
13. The most judicious account of this interweaving of religion and politics is still A.O. Meyer *England and the Catholic Church under Queen Elizabeth* trans. J.R. McKee (1967).
14. Wood *op. cit*, p. 167.
15. BCR, p. 120.
16. *CRS* 2, p. 15.
17. Garnet's younger brother Henry became superior of the Jesuits in England and was executed as privy to the Gunpowder Plot. See P.G. Caraman *Henry*

Garnet, 1555–1606 and the Gunpowder Plot (1964). Richard's son Thomas was executed as a priest in 1608.

18. BCR, p. 119. Persons is described in Wood's *Athenae Oxonienses* ed. P. Bliss, 5 vols (1813–20) II p. 62, and in H. Foulis *The History of Romish Treasons and Usurpations* (1671) as Chaplain-Fellow of Balliol. But I can find no trace of this in his autobiographical writings or in the College registers; it is unlikely that he ever took Anglican orders. The error may have arisen through a confusion between "Robertus Bensonus" and "Robertus Personius" in the records.

19. CRS 2, p. 30.

20. The names we know, in addition to Persons' own brothers in Balliol, are Seaner, Southcott, Hill, Sidney, Culpeper, Hawley, Simms, Briant, Ford, Yeomens and Fennell; the biographies of the last four are in Anstruther's dictionary of secular clergy.

21. BCR, p. 128. The fees for Commoners were fixed in 1572 as 10s for the son of a peer, 6s 8d for the son of a knight, 5s for the son of an esquire, and 2s 6d for a plebeian.

22. CRS 2, p. 30: Persons *Briefe Apologie* pp. 193ff. The worthless investments are described, bafflingly, as "dicing flies". Persons is said to have written a "libell . . . against D. Squire, wherein he touched a certain Ladie".

23. Archbishop Abbot, quoted in Wood *Athenae Oxonienses*, II p. 64.

24. M. Sutcliffe *A full and round answer to N.D. alias Robert Parsons the Noddie his foolish and rude warne-worde* (1604), p. 222.

25. Wood *History*, p. 153. Williams *op. cit.* gives many instances of Leicester's obsessive concern with the apparel of Oxford men.

26. CRS 2, p. 15.

27. See Anstruther, s.v. Bagshawe.

28. This and the following quotation are taken from Abbot's letter of 1601 printed from Foulis in Bliss' edition of Wood's *Athenae*, II p. 64.

29. See G.R. Duncan 'An introduction to the Accounts of Balliol College' forthcoming as an appendix in the *History of the University of Oxford*.

30. See the Bursars' *computus* under the date 20 October 1572.

31. CRS 39, p. 315.

32. The library holdings of the 1570's can only be estimated by checking the publication dates of the works listed in the seventeenth century catalogue. C. Dent in 'The Protestants in Elizabethan Oxford' (Oxford D. Phil. thesis 1980) has a lengthy survey of Calvinist holdings in Oxford libraries; he does not mention Balliol.

33. *Briefe apologie*, p. 198. In his private memoir (*CRS* 2, p. 17) Persons identifies Hyde, as well as Bagshaw, as a leader of the hostile faction.

34. Besides Persons' two accounts, there is one in Abbot's letter cited in n.28 and another in Bagshaw's *Sparing Discoverie*, pp. 42–3, as well as in the appendix to Ely, p. 33.

35. A great deal of ink flowed on this topic in the early 1600's. The historian may not be totally convinced by testimonials to the virtue of Persons' mother drawn up by Jesuits who met her only in advanced age (*CRS* 2, p. 666), but

the story that he was the son of the parson who educated him is proved to be chronologically impossible by a letter of Persons' brother John to the Dean of Totnes in 1602 (*CRS* 2, pp. 40ff). John Persons was a respectable Anglican clergyman who would have been only too glad to place a pair of sheets between his own conception and that of the traitorous Jesuit. Probably the only basis of the bastardy story was Persons' surname.

36. Some time before Abbot examined the record in 1601 a correction was made: "*et*" was blotted out and "*non*" set over. Henry Savage, Master of Balliol in 1668, puzzled over the entry when writing his history of the College *Balliofergus*. "This *non*" he says "was written with the same hand as the *et* under it was written with, so therefore writing his resignation with a running hand, he mistook: upon a review whereof, he blotted out the (*et*) and wrote (*non*) over it immediately; and that he should of purpose write such a contradiction as sponte et coactus cannot be incident to a wise man and a scholar." But Abbot says that the "*non*" was in a later hand, and recalled seeing the "*et*" when he first came to the College uncorrected. At the present time the cancellation of the "*et*" is still perceptible, but the "*non*" is invisible, so that we cannot tell whether Abbot or Savage was in the right.

37. In 1574 February 14 was Sexagesima Sunday; Ash Wednesday was on 24 February and Easter on April 11.

38. The pudding story is told in the *Briefe Apologie*, p. 201, and in the appendix to Ely, p. 34.

39. *Full and Round Answer*, p. 227.

40. It was presumably at this time that the Notary's entry was struck out of the Register record of the proceedings of 1574. Savage noted in 1668 "It was a publick Act of the College. He therefore was a lewd person that crossed it, which yet remains legible enough and not revoked . . ." Savage's notes are in Balliol MS.429; I am indebted for this reference to Mr. V. Quinn.

41. See the letter of Clark printed in T.G. Law *The Archpriest Controversy* (Westminster 1896), I p. 241.

42. *CRS* 39, p. xi.

43. BCR, p. 166.

44. Both Robert and Thomas Persons and a Privy Council informant, all quoted elsewhere in these notes, say that Briant was Persons' pupil at Balliol; and his name figures in the list of scholars in the Bursar's book excerpted in MS. Top.Oxon.e.124/9. Hence the matriculation at Hart Hall cannot have been the beginning of his University career. Such migration and late matriculation is quite common during this period, see L. Stone in *The University in Society* I (1975), a reference for which I am indebted to Dr. J.H. Jones.

45. Clark, II p. 105.

46. See Anstruther, under their names. The martyrdom of Pilcher is narrated in the Catholic equivalent of Foxe's *Book of Martyrs*: Bishop R. Challoner's *Memoirs of Missionary Priests from the year 1577 to 1684*, 2 vols, (Manchester 1803), p. 104.

47. Clark, I p. 194.
48. Squire's litigation can be traced in the Bursars' *computi* and in a number of university records (e.g. Clark, II p. 105). The most interesting *computus* entry records that in 1580 the College paid commissioners to go to London to examine Squire in company with Dr. Julio, the Queen's physician who cut a scandalous figure in Leicester's circle. Dr. J.H. Jones drew my attention to this entry.
49. J. Strype *Historical collections of the life and acts of Bishop Aylmer* (Oxford 1821), p. 123.
50. The fullest recent account of the mission of Campion and Persons is E.E. Reynolds *Campion and Persons* (1980). For Persons' part in the founding of the English College in Rome, see A. Kenny 'From Hospice to College' in *The Venerabile* XXI, pp. 218–273.
51. Persons' letters of this period have been published and translated by L. Hicks S.J. in *CRS* 39.
52. Challoner, p. 36, quoting a contemporary source.
53. *CRS* 39, p. 89.
54. Martin Marprelate related that Aylmer "went to buffets with his son-in-law for a bloody nose." The jest was relished by puritans as well as by papists.
55. Campion, Briant and Sherwin were among forty martyrs canonized by Pope Paul VI. Saint Alexander is, so far as I know, the only Balliol man to have been officially declared a saint.
56. Challoner, pp. 43–4.
57. L. Humphrey *Iesuitismi Pars Prima et Secunda* (1582).
58. T.F. Knox *The First and Second Diaries of the English College, Douay* (1878) gives the arrival of Bagshaw under the date: see further references in Anstruther s.v. Bagshawe.
59. C. Dent *op. cit.*, p. 666.
60. Printed from the original in the P.R.O. in Knox, p. 363. Knox prints there also the letter from the Fellows of Balliol cited in the next paragraph.
61. Persons in *CRS* 4, p. 116. The Visitation is printed in an appendix to Meyer.
62. *CRS* 39, p. 215.
63. The fullest account of Bagshaw's later years is in P. Renold 'The Wisbech Stirs' in *CRS*, 51.
64. The story of the Wisbech stirs is told from an anti-Jesuit point of view by T.G. Law's edition (1889) of Bagshaw's *True relation of the faction begun at Wisbich* (1601), and from a pro-Jesuit point of view in Renold, and in Father Caraman's *William Weston* (1955).
65. The fullest account of the circumstances in which Persons became Rector of the English College is A. Kenny. 'The Inglorious Revolution 1594–1597' in *The Venerabile* XVI, pp. 240ff.
66. Bagshaw *A sparing discouerie . . .*, p. 80.
67. The dealings between the Appellants and the Protestants are fully documented in Law *Archpriest Controversy*.

68. J. Mush *Declaratio motuum ac turbationum quae ex controversiis inter Iesuitas* . . . (1601).
69. He helpfully provides an Index, where under Persons there are these entries: Persons is an arrant traytor; Persons is a bastard; Persons is a monster of mankind; Persons is a gypsey; Persons setteth the Englich crowne on sale; Persons spendeth four or six crownes weekly on postage.
70. In the Brief *Cum Nobilissimum* quoted in Hughes, p. 303.
71. For the former view, see Meyer; for the latter, Bossy.
72. Father J.H. Pollen published materials towards Persons' biography in *CRS* 2 and 4; Father L. Hicks edited his letters and memorials up to 1588 in *CRS* 39. The introduction to the latter volume is the fullest account in print of Persons' early life. While this article was in press, I was pleased to learn that Father Francis Edwards S.J., has prepared for publication a full-length biography.
Final note. The woodcut on p. 18 is taken from F. Carleton *A Thankfull Remembrance* (1627).

ACKNOWLEDGEMENTS

I am indebted to a number of scholars who made comments on an earlier draft of this article and drew my attention to references, in particular to Dr. J.H. Jones, Mr. J.M. Prest, and Fr. J. McConica. I am grateful for having been allowed to read in MS Penry Williams' study of Elizabethan Oxford and Gregor Duncan's study of the Balliol accounts. I found the Rev. Christopher Dent's D. Phil. thesis on Elizabethan Protestants most helpful. Finally, I am very grateful for the assistance so generously given by Dr. P. Bulloch, Mr. V. Quinn and Mr. A. Tagliello in the Balliol library.

3 CHRISTOPHER HILL

Dr. Tobias Crisp, 1600–1643

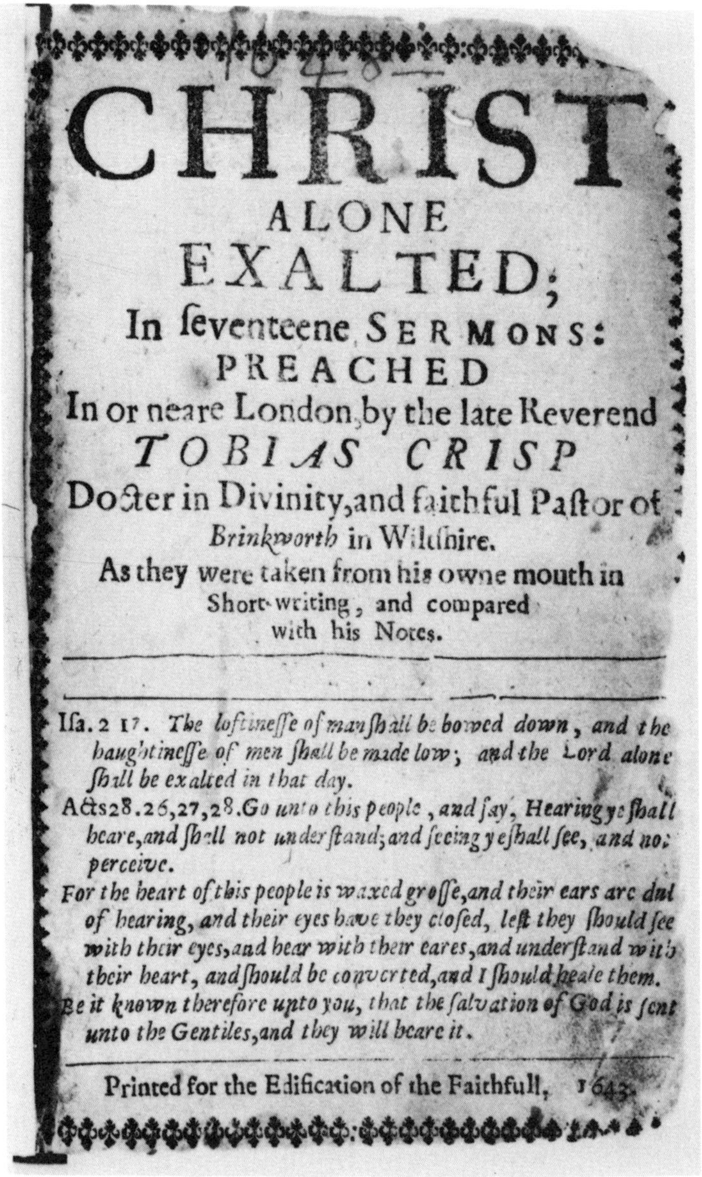

CHRIST

ALONE
EXALTED;

In feventeene SERMONS:
PREACHED

In or neare London, by the late Reverend
TOBIAS CRISP

Docter in Divinity, and faithful Paſtor of
Brinkworth in Wiltſhire.

As they were taken from his owne mouth in
Short-writing, and compared
with his Notes.

Iſa. 2 17. *The loftineſſe of man ſhall be bowed down, and the
haughtineſſe of men ſhall be made low; and the Lord alone
ſhall be exalted in that day.*

Acts 28. 26,27,28. *Go unto this people, and ſay, Hearing ye ſhall
heare, and ſhall not underſtand; and ſeeing ye ſhall ſee, and no:
perceive.*

*For the heart of this people is waxed groſſe, and their ears are dul
of hearing, and their eyes have they cloſed, leſt they ſhould ſee
with their eyes, and hear with their eares, and underſtand with
their heart, and ſhould be converted, and I ſhould heale them.
Be it known therefore unto you, that the ſalvation of God is ſent
unto the Gentiles, and they will beare it.*

Printed for the Edification of the Faithfull, 1643.

Plate 1. *Christ alone exalted*, title page.

DR. TOBIAS CRISP, 1600–1643

I

Balliol has had a number of radical theologians, from Wyclif who was condemned as a heretic in 1381–2 to Jowett who was charged with heresy before the Vice-Chancellor's court in 1863. But radical Balliol theologians are hard to find in the seventeenth century, when they proliferated everywhere else in England. Apart from Crisp, I know only of John Cooper (matriculated 1640) who succeeded the arch-anti-Trinitarian heretic John Bidle as master at Crypt School, Gloucester, in 1647. Cooper has himself a small place in histories of Socinianism.[1] Tobias Crisp is not renowned in the annals of the College. He gets only two disparaging sentences in the College History.[2] Yet in his time, and for many years after his death, he was a well-known, not to say notorious figure.

The seventeenth century was not the most glamorous period in Balliol's history. During the civil war, when Oxford was the royalist headquarters, Balliol "seems to have been treated little better than a tavern". No doubt in consequence, under Charles II Balliol men "by perpetual bubbing made themselves perfect sots".[3] In 1653 the College was so insignificant that a man who drew up a list of Oxford colleges forgot to mention Balliol.[4] But in the following year a former chaplain of New College, who had made a compact to reappear after his death in order to establish the immortality of the soul, was able to find his way to Balliol and there redeemed his pledge.[5]

Tobias Crisp was born in 1600 in Bread St., London, a prosperous area where John Milton was born eight years later. Tobias was the third son of a well-to-do family. His merchant father had been sheriff of London. Tobias's elder brother was Sir Nicholas Crisp of the Salters' Company, who was engaged in the slave trade between West Africa and the West Indies. He too became sheriff of London, was a trained band captain and M.P. in both the Short and the Long Parliaments of 1640. He had imprudently become a customs farmer in that year, that is to say one of the very unpopular government financiers. He was also a monopolist, and for this he was expelled from the House of Commons. He was perforce a royalist during the civil war, equipping a privateering fleet for the King.[6]

Tobias's connections and outlook seem to have been very different from his brother's. He was educated at Eton, which did not then mean quite what it means now. In 1642 he took his B.A. at Christ's College, Cambridge, the year before Milton entered the College as an undergraduate. Crisp incorporated at Balliol to take his M.A. in 1626. His D.D. followed much later. He married the daughter of Rowland Wilson of the Vintners' Company, another prominent London merchant. Wilson commanded a City regiment for Parliament during the civil war, was alderman and sheriff of London and a Trustee for Crown lands when they were sold in 1649. He was a recruiter M.P. for Calne, Wiltshire, and a member of the Commonwealth's Council of State. He became a friend of Bulstrode Whitelocke, who courted his widow after Wilson died in 1650.[7] Tobias Crisp and his wife had 13 children before his death in 1643. From the start Tobias seems to have had Puritan leanings. In 1627 he was deprived of his first living, the rectory of Newington Butts, on a charge of having entered into a simoniacal contract. This may be less reprehensible than it sounds: Crisp had been presented to the rectory only a few months earlier by a group which had leased the presentation from the Bishop of Worcester. They may have incurred the wrath of the hierarchy as a Puritan group trying to present Puritan ministers, like the Feoffees for Impropriations, who flourished between 1625 and 1633 before being suppressed by Archbishop Laud.[8]

In the same year 1627 Crisp was presented to the vicarage of Brinkworth, Wiltshire — the county with which his father-in-law was to be associated. Here Crisp became famous for his lavish hospitality: "a hundred persons, yea and many more, have been received and entertained at his house at one and the same time, and ample provision made for man and horse". His substantial fortune enabled him to refuse "preferment or advancement", and Crisp stayed at Brinkworth until in 1642 persecution by royalist soldiers drove him back to London, where he died a year later.[9] His preaching appears however to have left memories behind him in Wiltshire.[10]

In the year before his death Crisp preached in London. Among others Laurence Clarkson the future Ranter heard him hold forth against all existing churches - Anglican, Presbyterian, Independent, Baptist (the last three of which had appeared publicly only since

DR. TOBIAS CRISP

1640). "Be in society or no, though walked all alone, yet if he believed that Christ Jesus died for him, God beheld no iniquity in him". The prose style is Clarkson's but the sentiments are unmistakably Crisp's. Clarkson read all his books as they came out and tried to become one of those in whom God saw no sin — or so he tells us.[11] Clarkson was to carry Crisp's antinomian doctrines well beyond anything Crisp advocated.

Crisp's sermons were published posthumously in 1643 and later: it is unlikely that they could have been published before 1640. "Taken in short writing and compared with his notes", their genuineness is attested by his son.[12] But we must recall that they were delivered at a time of rigid ecclesiastical censorship and control, so he had to be careful what he said.

II

Crisp is primarily concerned with the problem of reconciling predestination and free will, God's omnipotence and human freedom — not a new problem. His starting point seems to have been dissatisfaction with traditional Calvinist predestination which — he thought — led many to despair because they could not believe in their election. His initial reaction in the sixteen-twenties was towards Arminianism, then becoming fashionable at court and soon to win control of the Church of England through the Laudians. But Crisp had been brought up to have a strong gut-hatred of popery, and as the Thirty Years War progressed the danger of Roman Catholic domination on the continent (and then in England) alarmed him as it did many other English protestants. Laudian Arminianism revived sacramental emphases which Crisp disliked and which he — again like many others — saw as a reversion to popery.

He expresses himself cautiously, but he makes pretty clear his anxiety about both the foreign and the domestic situation. "Look upon the present time, now you may see what sadness fills the hearts and faces of men, yea even of God's own people . . . They look every hour when they shall be cut off by the sword". There is no certainty "that our lives and estates shall be spared".[13] "How many among you, yea and of the uppermost form (bishops) have warped of later times and have turned their faces to return back to the fleshpots of Egypt".[14] Thomas Goodwin expressed similar anxieties in 1639 — more openly because he was writing in exile. He foresaw the subjugation of protes-

tantism in its last refuge in Europe, England, because of the conni-
vance with popery of men like the Laudian bishops. "It were happy
for other states professing the Calvin[ist] religion if they could wash
their hands of the blood of the churches not only not assisted but betrayed by them".[15] Because we know that nothing came of such fears,
we perhaps underestimate their strength in forging the near-unanimity
with which in 1640–1 the Long Parliament set about destroying the
power of the Laudian clergy, and of royal ministers in whom they had
no confidence. Events in Germany in the sixteen-twenties had created
a real and lasting fear of popery, and a suspicion that members of
Charles I's government were its accomplices.[16]

Crisp's aversion from justification by works spills over into anxiety
about the covenant theology which, thanks to preachers like William
Perkins, John Preston and Richard Sibbes, had become almost orthodox among Anglican protestants until the Laudian challenge of the
sixteen-twenties. The covenant theology attempted to smuggle works
back into Calvinism by arguing that God contracted to save those
who kept his covenant. Their good works would not earn the elect
salvation, but would testify to their state of grace. It was an under-
standable attempt by harassed clergymen to preserve their flocks from
the despair to which Calvinism was apt to lead. Perkins argued that a
sincere and strong desire for grace is presumptive evidence that grace
is at work in the soul: God accepts the will for the deed. Crisp thought
that sincerity and good intentions were not enough,[17] and that the
covenant theology led to presumption. Those who looked for assurance of salvation in the good works that they performed came to rely
on their own merits rather than on Christ.

Crisp's own solution was to go back to pristine Calvinism before
Theodore Béza and the covenant theologians had watered it down.[18]
In Crisp's view the elect are ordained to salvation from all eternity;
they cannot fall from grace. This, as we shall see, seemed to his critics
to run the risk of antinomianism, of encouraging those who believed
that their election was secure to indulge in all manner of licentious
practices. Crisp's answer was that *no* person is capable of works pleasing to God; all — elect and reprobate alike — are sinful and filthy. We
are saved only because "the Lord hath laid on him [Christ] the iniquity
of us all" (Isaiah 53. 6). This was the text for sermons III to XVII of
the 1643 volume. (The association of this passage with the Messiah

was commonly accepted by seventeenth century theologians.)

Crisp's onslaught on the covenant theology arose from his dislike of its legalism, its implied bargaining with God: "you give me salvation, and I will give you faith, and works too". "Even true faith", Crisp wrote, "is no condition of the covenant".[19] "The new covenant is without any conditions whatsoever on man's part". Man "is first justified before he believes, then he believes that he is justified".[20] Crisp was anxious to emphasize that the elect were saved before they were born. Christ himself "is not so completely righteous but we are as righteous as he was; . . . Christ became . . . as completely sinful as we". Crisp insists with almost monotonous repetition that "as soon as ever [a believer] hath committed this sin, . . . the Lamb of God . . . hath already taken away this very sin".[21] To restrict justification until after a man believes in Christ is to bring to life again the covenant of works, to trouble the consciences of those who are convinced that they are under the hatred of God.[22]

The source of all this is Crisp's determination to relieve believers of "horror in their consciences", of the superstition of scarecrow sins which Milton deplored. Stand "fast in the liberty wherein Christ hath made you free, and do not again entangle yourselves with such yokes of bondage that neither you nor your fathers were able to bear".[23] He was against preaching the terrors of the law, the wrath of God, damnation and hell-fire. The object of such sermons, if preached at all, should be not to terrify but to reassure believers that they are secure from damnation.[24] Crisp strongly disapproved of preachers who "fetch blood at the hearts of children with their causeless cautions, and then rejoice to see them in their spiritual afflictions, which methinks is an inhuman cruelty. . . . Children must not want their food for fear of dogs".[25] In 1643, the year when Crisp's sermons were first published, the future Leveller William Walwyn was also concerned lest "many of you may, through sense of sin and of wrath due for sin, walk in a very disconsolate condition: fears and terrors may abound in you". Such fears were the product of "the grossest antichristian error that ever was". Like Crisp, Walwyn attacked the doctrine that God accepts "our wills for our performance".[26]

Crisp was worried about those who "are apt to think their peace depends on this subduing of sin" which they find impossible. "Fetch peace where it is to be had", was his advice. "Let subduing alone for peace".[27] "Sadness in any believer whatsoever . . . in respect of his jealousy of his present and future estate", shows that he is "out of the way of Christ". "I believe many poor souls have been held under hatches the longer because some have withheld Christ from them, or themselves have not dared to think Christ belongs to them". "Christ doth not look for your pains; he came to save those that could not tell which way to turn themselves". Believers "must not fear their own sins". "The Father forces open the spirit of the man, and pours in his Son, in spite of the receiver".[28] "This grace of the Lord's laying of iniquities upon Christ is applicable to persons even . . . before they have mended their ways", Crisp insisted again and again, though he recognized that it is a view which "will find great opposition in the world", because it gives "way to looseness".[29]

Crisp's continuing concern was to escape from the formal self-righteousness of those who believed that their election was demonstrated by their good works. "Even the most blameless walking according to God's law, not only before but also after conversion, is truly counted but loss and dung".[30] "Righteousness is that which puts a man away from Christ".[31] Good works should be performed only because they are profitable to others, not with any idea that they confer merit on the doer. Loving mankind anyway "is no evidence of our being in Christ. For publicans and harlots love one another".[32] "When we labour by our fasting and prayer and seeking the Lord . . . to take away his displeasure, . . . do you serve God or no? Do you not serve yourselves?" "Is there not much self mixed in your performances?"[33] Men must be taken off "from performing duties to corrupt ends", from "idolizing their own righteousness".[34]

Since the elect are saved from the womb, Crisp logically concludes that neither prayers, tears, fasting, mournings, reluctancy and fighting against our corruptions have "the least prevalency with the Lord". "They move God not a jot. . . . God is moved only from himself".[35] God hears only Christ's prayers.[36] It was a doctrine later adopted by the Muggletonians. I have argued elsewhere that they derived it from Clarkson, who joined the sect in the late fifties; and Clarkson almost certainly derived it from Crisp.[37]

For all Crisp's hostility to the covenant theolgians, he could be as unpleasantly legalistic as any of them. "The Lord's justice", he wrote, must "be satisfied to the full"; "reparation must be had".[38] This recalls Milton's doctrine of Christ's sacrifice on the cross: "Die he or justice must".³⁹ But Crisp dwells quite unnecessarily on the pleasure which Christ's sufferings give God. "It is Christ's personal bearing of iniquity upon the cross once for all that gives unto the Lord the full pleasure and content to his own heart's desire". Nor does this pleasure and content derive from the salvation of mankind. "Christ's main aim is at the giving his Father content"; that "poor sinners are saved . . . is a subordinate thing".⁴⁰ Crisp's use of the word "purchase" to describe Christ's sacrifice caused uneasiness to his nineteenth century editor.⁴¹

III

I think we should assume that Crisp did not believe that all men were saved. But his rhetoric in insisting that God applies "the laying of iniquities upon Christ" to the ungodly, to the worst of sinners, long before they repent, exposed him to accusations of preaching universal grace. However ungodly a sinner may be, "what hinders but that thou mayst have as good a portion in him as thy heart can wish?"⁴² It is rash to speak of those who are still unconverted as damned: their names may be in the Book of Life though they do not yet know it.⁴³ "There is no man under heaven . . . , if he do but come to Christ, . . . shall be rejected of him". "There is no better way to know your portion in Christ than upon the general tender of the gospel to conclude absolutely he is yours; and so without any more ado to take him as tendered to you, on his word; and this taking of him, upon a general tender, is the greatest security in the world that Christ is yours".⁴⁴ Crisp is anxious here to assure the worst sinner that there is still hope: he may have a better chance of salvation than the formally righteous. But his way of expressing it laid him open in the seventeenth century to the charge of preaching universal redemption; even his nineteenth century editor annotates such passages uneasily.

To contemplate the possibility that divine grace might be offered to all does not seem terribly shocking in our liberal age; but to the orthodox in the seventeenth century it seemed horrific. Private property, social inequality, and the state which protected both, were all accepted as the consequence of the wickedness of the mass of fallen mankind, of the fact that God's grace was limited to the few whom he had chosen. Reject the comfortable doctrine of original sin, and the floodgates might be opened — to ideas of human equality such as the Quakers were to preach, to democratic theories such as the Leveller Walwyn advocated, to the communism of the Diggers.⁴⁵

Above all, it seemed to Crisp's contemporaries that licentious and immoral conclusions might be drawn from this theology. The orthodox had always known that the heresy "they can commit no sin offensive to God" appealed especially to "some of the meaner ignorant sort of people".[46] But with the breakdown of ecclesiastical control and of censorship in the revolutionary sixteen-forties such creatures were able to express themselves freely. As a horrified Balliol poet put it:-

No teaching now contents us the old way
The layman is inspired every day,
Can we pray and preach *ex tempore*; the priest
With all his learning is despis'd and hiss'd
Out of the church. . . .

The world is a great Bedlam, where men talk
Distractedly, and on their heads do walk,
Treading antipodes to all the sages
And sober-minded of the former ages.[47]

In the forties and fifties the world was temporarily turned upside down: ideas previously unthinkable were freely expressed. Coppe and Clarkson, whom their contemporaries called Ranters, preached against monogamy and in favour of free love. ("Polygamy's no sin/In a free state", Washbourne growled.)[48] And Clarkson at least had listened to Crisp.

Crisp died too early to see the full and scandalous development of popular antinomianism in England, but he certainly contributed to it, however innocent his intentions may have been. It is easy to pick out sentences in his sermons which might reasonably alarm the orthodox. "To be called a libertine is the most glorious title under heaven; take it for one that is truly free by Christ."[49] Sin, Crisp declared, is finished. To the question "Is thy conscience Christ?" he replied in the affirmative.[50] "Suppose a believer commit adultery and murder?" Crisp asked himself. And he replied that before he even confesses his sin "he may be as certain of the pardon of it as after confession". "I know the enemies of the gospel will make an evil construction of it", Crisp admitted.[51] He had earlier recognized that some believed "this kind of doctrine opens a gap to all manner of licentiousness and presumption". His answer was "only such as are rejected and given up of God" would so abuse the doctrine.[52] "Nothing doth more establish a restraint from sin", he asserted. "The children must not want their bread because dogs abuse it".[53] Like Milton, Crisp was so concerned with the freedom of the elect that he virtually ignored the existence of the unregenerate.

It was to the elect that Crisp addressed himself when he declared "If you be freemen of Christ, you may esteem all the curses of the law as no more concerning you than the laws of England concern Spain or the laws of Turkey an Englishman". "I am far from imagining any believer is freed from acts of sin," Crisp expostulated; "he is freed only from the charge of sin. . . . God doth never punish any believer, after he is a believer, for sin". "You are in as true a state of salvation, you that are believers, as they that are now already in heaven".[54]

Crisp regarded it as "a gross, notorious and groundless slander that I should affirm that an elect person should live and die a whoremonger and an adulterer . . . and be saved." But it was hardly enough in the sixteen-forties merely to assert that the elect "person is changed in conversation."[55] "Good works or inherent righteousness are necessary attendants on free grace."[56] No-one can "out-sin the death of Christ."[57]

Crisp counter-attacked. "People are afraid to speak out of things that are Christ's, for fear of giving liberty." Milton might have echoed the phrase. "And in the mean while other things shall be set up above Christ", Crisp continued with growing irony; "the divine rhetoric of repentance and humiliation, the prevalency of tears to wash away sin, and our conscionable walking, will commend us to God at the last day. Here must be a magnifying of man's righteousness; and when these come to be examined they are but rhetorical expressions."[58] By Crisp's theology "the freeman of Christ is let loose to enjoy the free spirit."[59]

If Crisp had survived to see what some who thought themselves Christ's freemen did with the free spirit, he might have realized the inadequacy of his perfunctory assurances that it could not be used to undermine traditional morality.

IV

Crisp's views were not unprecedented. In the security of a West Riding valley Roger Brearley, curate first of Grindleton, then of Kildwick, taught not dissimilar doctrines from 1615 to 1631. His hearers seem to have been even more heretical than he was. Among accusations made against the Grindleton congregation in 1617 were the doctrine that to "ask [God's] pardon for failing in matter or manner is a sin; the Christian assured can never commit a gross sin," and so "must never think of salvation".[60]

The collapse of censorship in the early forties, which allowed Crisp's sermons to be printed, also led to the printing of writings by other antinomian theologians. John Eaton died in 1641. His *The Discovery of the most dangerous dead Faith* was published in that year, "set forth . . . (as they say) by Dr. Crisp".[61] Eaton's *The Honey-comb of Free Justification by Christ alone* was also published posthumously in 1642, edited by Robert Lancaster, who was to edit Crisp's sermons. Eaton declared there was "no sin in the sight of God". He too was concerned to escape from the revival of justification by works which he saw in the covenant theology, and in particular from "the popish rotten pillar that God accepts the will for the deed".[62] In the same year as Crisp's *Christ Alone Exalted* and Walwyn's *The Power of Love* appeared, Henry Denne published *The Doctrine and Conversation of John Baptist*. In this he too attacked Perkins's doctrine of the will for the deed: "all that desire to be rich are not rich", he observed sardonically. Eaton's, Denne's and Crisp's books were all condemned by the Westminster Assembly of Divines in August 1643.[63] The Assembly had "an eminent Christian . . . secured in gaol for promoting the publishing of Dr. Crisp his works",[64] though the Prolocutor of the Assembly, Dr. Twisse, was said to have remarked that the opposition to Crisp's sermons arose from the fact that "so many were converted by his preaching and (said he) so few by ours".[65]

By 1644 the House of Commons was becoming worried about antinomianism. A succession of sermons preached to the House on the occasion of its monthly fast kept the subject before the attention of M.Ps. In January the Scottish Presbyterian Samuel Rutherford denounced antinomianism: he named Crisp in the margin when he printed the sermon.[66] Rutherford's Scottish colleague Robert Baillie took up the cry a month later, followed by Herbert Palmer in August.[67] In October Edmund Calamy attacked those who preached against days of national humiliation on the ground that "God is never displeased with his people", and that "the very being of their sins is abolished out of God's sight".[68] He did not name Crisp, but the allusion seems fairly clear. "National sins", Crisp had preached, "bring about national judgments, yet all the sins of the times cannot do a member of Christ a jot of hurt (even though you have had some hand in them)".[69]

In 1643 John Sedgwick published *Antinomianism Anatomized*. Baillie followed up his sermon by *A Disswasive from the Errours of the Time* (1645). Three fat volumes of Thomas Edward's *Gangraena* appeared in 1646. In one of them he reported an apparently antinomian lady who told a minister that "to kill a man, to commit adultery, or steal a man's goods" were no sins.[70] Thomas Bedford's *An Examination of the chief points of Antinomianism* (1647) devoted two chapters to Crisp.[71] Samuel Rutherford too returned to the fray in *A Survey of the Spirituall Antichrist* (1648), naming Crisp among others on his title-page; and there were many others.[72] In 1644 Stephen Geree, elder brother of the better-known John Geree, had directed *The Doctrine of the Antinomians . . . Confuted* specifically against Crisp, "so magnified of many".[73] Antinomianism, Geree observed, was "most plausible and pleasing to flesh and blood": and he referred to Crisp in this connection.[74] He pays tribute to the popular appeal of Crisp's theology in the new circumstances of the 'forties. Crisp's "strains of rhetoric . . . do marvellously allure and ensnare the minds of many simple and unsettled souls". His doctrine "will most abundantly please the carnal palates of the worst men in the world, even atheists, drunkards, rioters and rankest rebels that can be". Geree associated Crisp with Brearley and Eaton, and accused him of preaching universal grace and election: for him Christ belongs "to all sinners without exception of any particulars".[75]

Others were contributing to what Geree called these "sweet poisons".[76] Clarkson later wrote that Giles Randall ("a great antinomian", Edwards called him)[77] and Paul Hobson taught "such a doctrine as Dr. Crisp, only higher and clearer".[78] Edwards quoted Hobson as saying "I am persuaded when I used all these duties" — prayer, penitence — "I had not one jot of God in me" — a phrase of Crisp's which his critics had made notorious.[79] John Saltmarsh, William Dell, early Quakers and many others popularized the heresy. William Erbery praised Crisp.[80] But the full libertine consequnces of antinomiansim remained to be drawn by the Ranters.[81]

Robert Towne, from the Grindleton area, wrote an answer to John Sedgwick in 1644. In this he declared "If you believe sin, death and

the curse to be abolished, they are abolished. . . . They that believe
on Christ are no sinners."[82] Abiezer Coppe in 1649 repeated Crisp's
and Towne's announcement that sin was finished. God's service,
Coppe said, is "perfect freedom and pure libertinism", a word that
Crisp had used. But Coppe concluded from this that "I can . . . love
my neighbour's wife as myself, without sin". He claimed that God
was "that mighty Leveller."[83] Laurence Clarkson, "Captain of the
Rant", had written a Leveller tract in 1647. He genuinely held, or said
he held, the views which Crisp's critics had most feared. He systema-
tized the ideas which Edwards's antinomian lady had so shamelessly
put forward. "There is no such act as drunkenness, adultery and theft
in God", Clarkson wrote. "Sin hath its conception only in the imagination. . . . What act soever is done by thee in light and love, is light
and lovely, though it be that act called adultery. . . . No matter what
Scripture, saints or churches say, if that within thee do not condemn
thee, thou shalt not be condemned".[84] He went even further to claim
that "None can be free from sin till in purity it be acted as no sin".[85]
In sexual matters at least Clarkson practised what he preached.
Another Ranter, Jacob Bauthumley, proclaimed that God is "glori-
fied in sin"; many others alarmingly suggested that sin had been
invented by the ruling classes to keep the lower orders in place.[86]

V

In 1655 Richard Baxter introduced a tract against antinomianism
by Thomas Hotchkis, "minister at Stanton-by-Highworth, Wiltshire",
who "liveth not far from the place where Dr. Crisp did exercise his
ministry". After naming Eaton, Towne, Randall, Simpson and
Saltmarsh, Baxter concluded "but the man that most credited and
strengthened their party was Dr. Crisp". In consequence antinomianism was stronger in Wiltshire than elsewhere.[87] Hotchkis had
written (but not published) an *Examen* of Crisp's Third Volume
(1648).[88] Henry Pinnell, who wrote a preface to the 1648 volume,
knew Crisp personally. "Upon mine own experience and more than
twelve years' knowledge" he vindicated the author "from all vicious
licentiousness of life, and scandalous aspersions cast upon him".[89]
Pinnell's antinomianism was more plebeian than Dr. Crisp's. "All the
learning I had at Oxford", he observed, "I laid out and improved in
opposing the truth". He was no "whit the fitter to be a minister
because of the repute and notion of scholarship". "I got more from

simple country people, husbandmen, weavers, etc., about Brinkworth, Southwick and those parts in Wiltshire, than ever I did or got here by books and preachers".[90] Brinkworth was the living held by Crisp from 1627 to 1642.

Pinnell, formerly chaplain in Colonel John Pickering's regiment, became a separatist preacher at Brinkworth after leaving the Army.[91] This he did in two stages. In December 1646, disillusioned with Parliament's policy, he resigned, but he rejoined in the summer of 1647 after the rank-and-file revolt led by the Leveller-influenced Agitators. But by the end of the year, when the generals had routed the Agitators, "the Army, which was once so beautiful and lovely in mine eye, is now become most black and ugly, God having made me ashamed of my fleshly confidence therein." After expostulating with Cromwell, who listened politely and thanked him for his plain dealing, Pinnell finally abandoned the Army.[92] In the fifties he published alchemical treatises and made an important translation of works by Croll and Paracelsus.[93]

The "cheese" area of north-western Wiltshire, which embraces Brinkworth, Highworth and Southwick, was an area of poorly-paid part-time cloth-workers, which in the early seventeenth century saw weavers' riots and religious heresy. It was strongly Parliamentarian at the beginning of the civil war; from it Clubmen favourable to Parliament later came.[94] There were antinomians there in the fifties, though it is not clear — in spite of Baxter — how far Crisp's teaching had influenced them. Richard Coppin preached "frequently in those parts", collecting "sundry disciples" from "the profane sort of people . . . who do hold that there is no resurrection, no day of judgment, no salvation, no damnation, no heaven nor no hell but what it is in this life". ("I do less wonder", Hotchkis commented, "that the antinomian preachers are accounted by the ignorant and profane multitude truly comfortable preachers".)[95]

Thomas Webbe, of an old Wiltshire clothing family, was rector of Langley Burhill. He was alleged to be "one of Lilburne's faction" (i.e. a Leveller), was friendly with Joseph Salmon and praised Abiezer Coppe. Webbe was alleged to claim to "live above ordinances, and that it was lawful for him to lie with any woman". His epigram, "there's no heaven but women, nor no hell save marriage" suggests a certain light-heartedness; "the Lord grant we may know the worth of hell,

that we may for ever scorn heaven" is worthy of Blake.[96] William
Eyre, minister of a gathered congregation in Salisbury, another son
of an old Wiltshire family, published in 1654 a defence of antinomianism, *Justification without Conditions*, which Hotchkis, Baxter and
others attacked.[97] In 1656 there was an antinomian group in Lacock,
one of whose members echoed Coppin to say "there was neither heaven
nor hell except in a man's conscience"; another thought "whatever
sin he did commit, God was the author of them all and acted them in
him".[98] Langley Burhill and Lacock are both in the "cheese" area of
the county.

<h1 style="text-align:center">VI</h1>

The most interesting seventeenth century antinomian, another
undergraduate of Christ's College, was John Milton. Milton was in
London during the last year of Crisp's life, when he was attracting a
good deal of attention. Milton may or may not have heard him preach:
it is very unlikely that he did not read the sermons when they were published. In 1645 Milton defended "the maids of Aldgate" who claimed
to be incapable of sin because they were "godded with God". Milton
believed, like Crisp, that "the entire Mosaic Law is abolished". "We
are released from the decalogue". "Everyone born of God cannot sin".
"The practice of the saints interprets the commandments". "The
greatest burden in the world is superstition . . . of imaginary and scarecrow sins", which "enslave the dignity of man". Apart from the last
clause, all the above sentences might have been written by Crisp. Milton
was careful, like Crisp, to stress that such ideas gave no authority for
licence; but he too was denounced by his contemporaries as a libertine.
Like Crisp, he was so concerned with the liberty of the elect that he
hardly bothered about the consequences which the unregenerate
might draw from his writings. The same is true of his doctrine of
divorce, where he gave very great liberty to the husband to put away
his wife in cases of incompatibility of temperament, oblivious apparently of the possibilities of abuse. And *The Doctrine and Discipline
of Divorce* created scandal because it — like Crisp's sermons — was
published in the vernacular. Most of Milton's antinomian ideas were
too dangerous to be published even veiled in the decent obscurity of
a learned language.[99]

Crisp anticipates both Gerrard Winstanley the Digger and Milton in
his interesting belief that "Christ is to be considered collectively: that

is, he is not only Christ as he is one person of himself; but he is Christ as he himself in that one person is united to the persons of all the elect in the world. We and they make up but one collective body". To the union of the Father and the Son, and of the two natures in Christ, we must add the mystical union which makes "Christ the Mediator . . . one with all the members of Christ jointly".[100] The Godhead is too remote for man to approach, but when Christ's humanity is united to it, it becomes more accessible.[101] Winstanley associated a version of this doctrine with belief in the advent of a communist society, brought about by Christ rising in all men and women.[102] The evidence for the idea in Milton is less clear-cut: it is stronger in *Paradise Lost* than in Milton's theological treatise, the *De Doctrina Christiana*. I had set out the evidence for Milton holding some such doctrine before the possibility that he might have derived it from Crisp occurred to me.[103] Some scholars have expressed scepticism of Empson's theory that at the end of time Milton's God will abdicate his power to this collective Christ, to all the saints.[104] The clear exposition of the "collective body of Christ" in Crisp — a more respectable source than Winstanley, and one which Milton is more likely to have read — perhaps reinforces the case for accepting some such doctrine in Milton.

VII

In 1690, when the press was again freer, Crisp's sermons were reprinted by his son. They caused a great scandal. Crisp's main critics now were Presbyterians, anxious to disavow antinomianism lest it bring discredit on the reputation of dissent. Daniel Williams's *Gospel-Truth Stated and Vindicated: Wherein some of Dr. Crisp's Opinions Are Considered and the Opposite Truths Are Plainly Stated and Confirmed* (1692)[105] led to fierce controversies with Congregationalists. The furore ultimately broke up the recently-formed union between Congregationalists and Presbyterians. Isaac Chauncy, one of the first to withdraw from the union, declared that "according to the opinion of our modern divines", Luther "was an antinomian himself, and Calvin but a little better".[106] Richard Baxter now thought Crisp's views antichristian, and that opposition to them was a cause which "will endure no indifferency or neutrality".[107] An anonymous tract published in 1693, *Crispianism Unmask'd*, reverts to the social threat implied in Crisp's doctrine, with a dark reference to "Mr. Saltmarsh

and such like men . . . in those days". If only the learned read Crisp,
no harm will be done. "But when I saw that the book was bought up,
and read, and (which is more) applauded by the common readers, I
thought it was time" to protest. Crisp's doctrine "cuts the sinews of
all the duties and exercises of Christianity". Why should we bother to
be good if nothing we do is acceptable to God?[108] "By means of
Crisp's book", we are told by the pious biographer of Bishop Bull,
"the poison of antinomianism soon spread, not only in the country
but infected London too".[109]

Congregationalists rallied to the defence of freedom of expression.
Crisp's son Samuel wrote on behalf of his father in 1691 and 1693,
pointing out that the Presbyterian attitude recalled the Westminster
Assembly's attempt to suppress Crisp's sermons in 1643.[110] These
sermons were again reprinted in 1791: perhaps a significant date if
we recall that they were first published in the revolutionary sixteen-
forties, and reprinted after the revolution of 1688. There was a further republication in 1832: the editor was still nervously aware that
controversial conclusions could be drawn from Crisp's doctrine.

VIII

A final question, to which I have no clear answer, is Was Tobias
Crisp as simply innocent as he appears? When it was suggested to him
that libertine conclusions could be drawn from his doctrine he pro-
tested with outraged incredulity; and so far I have assumed that he
erred on the side of naivety rather than of duplicity. Yet this raises
worrying questions too. Crisp was no unsophisticated provincial; he
was the son, brother and son-in-law of highly-powered London business men, all of them deeply involved in City and national politics.
The circumstances in which Tobias was deprived of his first living
suggest either that he committed the sin of simony or that he was
deceiving the ecclesiastical authorities in the interests of what he
thought a good case — neither the act of a political innocent.

Crisp was certainly aware of the accusation that his doctrine opened
a door to all licentiousness. But his answer was alarmingly inadequate
for so clever a man. He said in effect, the elect could by definition
not indulge in licentious practices (as we may be pretty sure that he
himself did not). He gave no indication at all of how we know who
the elect are, how we differentiate between elect and unregenerate,
how we distinguish those who wrongly believe themselves to be elect.

He must have known that this was one of the crucial questions of seventeenth century protestant theology. The covenant theologians answered it by saying that the visible elect could be known by their good works: they were not saved by their works but their works demonstrated that they were saved. Crisp utterly rejected works as evidence of salvation at the same time that he widely extended the freedom of the elect. Like Milton, Crisp appears to regard the unregenerate as totally unimportant; he says nothing about them at all. Curious for a man with fifteen years pastoral experience in Wiltshire.

The question then arises, Who are the unregenerate? How many people are we talking about? If you believed with the covenant theologian Thomas Shepard that they were 99.9% of the population, or even with Dean Donne that they were two out of every three,[111] could you just ignore them? Did Crisp believe that all men and women would be saved, as some Ranters did? Did he believe that salvation was offered to all who threw themselves on Christ, as Milton perhaps did, and as many were to suggest in the sixteen-forties? Did he believe in hell? Many came to regard hell as an inner state rather than a geographical location.[112] Crisp once wrote rather testily of those who were not satisfied with his doctrine: "for aught I know they may have their deserved portion in the lowest part of hell".[113] It is an ambiguous remark, committing him to nothing: could the ambiguity be deliberate?

I think it unlikely that Crisp was as unorthodox as Milton became: but the evidence does not exclude the possibility that he was moving in that direction. Men had to be very careful how they expressed themselves on such questions. The possibility of universal salvation was not raised in print in England till 1648, by Winstanley and Coppin: though almost certainly it had been discussed verbally much earlier. Most of Crisp's sermons were presumably delivered under the Laudian régime, when it would have been foolhardy in the extreme to commit oneself on paper to unorthodox opinions.[114]

So the question must remain open. We just do not know what Crisp's attitude to Ranters and suchlike would have been if he had lived to see them. All we can say is that some of them looked back to him with respect. Crisp's ideas excited the lower orders in the sixteen-forties and again in the sixteen-nineties; they still caused discomfort to the orthodox two hundred years after his death. It would be a pity to allow such a Balliol man to be forgotten. We all try to provoke: but which of us can hope to enjoy so long a posthumous life?

NOTES

1. *Calamy Revised* ed. A.G. Matthews (Oxford 1934), p. 133; E.M. Wilbur *A History of Unitarianism in Transylvania, England and America* (Harvard University Press 1952), pp. 196–7.
2. H.W.C. Davis *A History of Balliol College* (revised by R.H.C. Davis and Richard Hunt, Oxford 1963), pp. 104–5.
3. C.E. Mallet *A History of the University of Oxford* (1924–7), II pp. 365, 422.
4. Edward Waterhouse *An humble Apologie for Learning and Learned Men* (1653), pp. 68–9.
5. Keith Thomas *Religion and the Decline of Magic* (1971), p. 593.
6. D. Brunton and D.H. Pennington *Members of the Long Parliament* (1954), pp. 54–57; M.F. Keeler *The Long Parliament* (Philadelphia 1954), p. 147.
7. Brunton and Pennington *op. cit.*, p. 59; D. Underdown *Pride's Purge: Politics in the Puritan Revolution* (Oxford 1971), p. 234; B. Worden, *The Rump Parliament, 1648–1653* (Cambridge 1974), p. 224.
8. D. Lysons *The Environs of London*, I (1792) p. 394; my *Economic Problems of the Church from Archbishop Whitgift to the Long Parliament* (Panther ed.), p. 64 and chapter XI *passim*. It is possible indeed that Crisp may have been presented to Newington Butts by the Feoffees.
9. *Dictionary of National Biography*. The reference to Crisp's refusal of advancement may be intended as retrospective rebuttal of the charge of simony.
10. See pp. 66–7 below.
11. L. Clarkson *The Lost Sheep Found* (1660), p. 9.
12. T. Crisp *Christ Alone Exalted: in Seventeene Sermons* (1643), title-page. Subsequently referred to as *Seventeene Sermons*.
13. *Seventeene Sermons*, pp. 386–7.
14. *Crisp's Christ Alone Exalted, . . . Being the Complete Works of Tobias Crisp, . . . containing Fifty-Two Sermons* ed. J. Gill (1832), pp. 406–7. Hereafter referred to as *Fifty-Two Sermons*. The word in brackets occurs in the printed version, though presumably Crisp was not so specific in his manuscript. Cf. Milton's addition of an anti-episcopal headnote to *Lycidas* when he reprinted it in 1645.
15. T. Goodwin *An Exposition of the Revelation* in *Works* (Edinburgh 1861–3), III p. 174.
16. For one example among many of such anxieties in a layman in the sixteen-twenties, see R. Cust and G. Lake 'Sir Richard Grosvenor and the Rhetoric of Magistracy', *Bulletin of the Institute of Historical Research* LIV (1981), pp. 42–53.
17. *Seventeene Sermons*, p. 443.
18. R.T. Kendall *Calvin and English Calvinism to 1649* (Oxford 1979), chapter 13.
19. *Seventeene Sermons*, p. 60; cf. pp. 43, 58; cf. *Fifty-Two Sermons*, pp. 174–7.
20. *Fifty-Two Sermons*, pp. 86, 91.

21. *Seventeene Sermons*, pp. 89, 146–7.
22. Crisp *Christ Alone Exalted*, III (1648), pp. 273–8. Hereafter cited as Vol. III.
23. *Seventeene Sermons*, pp. 87, 156.
24. Vol III, pp. 129–30, 136; *Fifty-Two Sermons*, p. 22.
25. *Fifty-Two Sermons*, p. 411.
26. W. Walwyn *The Power of Love* (1643), pp. 19–22, reprinted in *Tracts on Liberty in the Puritan Revolution* ed. W. Haller, Columbia University Press (1933), II.
27. *Fifty-Two Sermons*, p. 14.
28. *Ibid.*, pp. 55, 106, 137, 190; II, p. 137.
29. *Seventeene Sermons*, pp. 409, 412.
30. *Ibid.*, p. 6.
31. *Fifty-Two Sermons*, p. 104.
32. *Seventeene Sermons*, pp. 16–17, 28, 452–3.
33. *Ibid.*, pp. 391, 446. This was a point later to be made very forcibly by the Ranter Abiezer Coppe *A Fiery Flying Roll* (1649), pp. 5–9 and *passim*.
34. *Fifty-Two Sermons*, p. 143.
35. *Seventeene Sermons*, p. 182; cf. pp. 283–4.
36. Vol. III, p. 185.
37. See *The World of the Muggletonians* ed. C. Hill and B. Reay, forthcoming.
38. *Seventeene Sermons*, pp. 319–26, 329.
39. *Paradise Lost*, Book III, line 210; Book XII, lines 401–4.
40. *Seventeene Sermons*, pp. 324, 332. Bunyan was equally barbaric:- God "will burn sinners in the flames of hell ... with delight ... for the easing of his mind and the satisfaction of his justice", *Works* ed. G. Offer (1860), II p. 111.
41. *Fifty-Two Sermons*, p. 191.
42. *Seventeene Sermons*, pp. 409, 412, 425–6. cf. Vol. III, pp. 174–9.
43. Vol. III, pp. 179–81.
44. *Fifty-Two Sermons*, pp. 114, 213; cf. pp. 202–3.
45. For Walwyn see p. 59 above.
46. Richard Sibbes *Works* (Edinburgh 1862–4), II p. 316.
47. Thomas Washbourne *Poems* ed. A.B. Grosart (1868), pp. 182–4.
48. *Ibid.*, p. 227.
49. *Fifty-Two Sermons*, p. 122.
50. *Seventeene Sermons*, pp. 156–9, 87.
51. *Fifty-Two Sermons*, pp. 224–6; cf. p. 131; even "a scandalous falling into sin" does not bring a believer under the curse.
52. *Seventeene Sermons*, p. 164; cf. Vol. III, pp. 105, 110.
53. Vol. III, pp. 113, 119–32, 167–8.
54. *Fifty-Two Sermons*, pp. 10, 43, 132; cf. pp. 15–18.
55. Vol. III, p. 326.
56. *Fifty-Two Sermons*, p. 328.
57. Vol. III, p. 362.
58. *Ibid.*, p. 359.
59. *Fifty-Two Sermons*, p. 133.

60. See my *The World Turned Upside Down* (Penguin ed.), pp. 81–5.
61. Stephen Geree *The Doctrine of the Antinomians . . . Confuted* (1644), p. 41. Geree referred to Eaton as Crisp's "master" - *ibid.*, p. 5. But there is no evidence that they ever met, and Crisp's ideas must have been settled long before Eaton's writings were published. Eaton, twenty-five years Crisp's senior, was a Kentishman, who had been vicar of Wickham Market, Suffolk, from 1635 to his death.
62. *The Discovery* . . . , pp. 62–3.
63. Kendall *op. cit.*, pp. 185–8. Like Crisp, Denne was against preachers who "terrify them with hell-fire". He realized that he might "to many seem guilty of that crime which was laid against the apostle, to turn the world upside down" (H. Denne *Grace, Mercy and Peace*, 1645, reprinted in *Records of the Churches of Christ gathered at Fenstanton, Warboys and Hexham, 1644–1720* ed. E.B. Underhill, Hanserd Knollys Soc. 1854, pp. 398, 422).
64. S[amuel] C[risp] *Christ Alone Exalted in Dr. Crisp's Sermons* (1693), p. 7.
65. Tobias Crisp *Christ Made Sin* ed. S. Crisp (1691), p. 4.
66. Samuel Rutherford *A Sermon Preached to the Honourable House of Commons* (1644) pp. 32–7.
67. Robert Baylie *Satan the Leader in chief to all who resist the Reparation of Sion* (1644), pp. 25–6; H. Palmer *The Glasse of Gods Providence towards his Faithfull Ones* (1644), pp. 54–5.
68. Edmund Calamy *Englands Antidote against the Plague of Civil Warre* (1645), pp. 18–19.
69. Vol. III, pp. 28–9.
70. Thomas Edwards *Gangraena* (1646), II p. 6; cf. II p. 146, III p. 107.
71. *Op. cit.*, pp. 50–64. Bedford also attacked Henry Denne, pp. 25–33, 60–70.
72. Rutherford attacked Eaton, Towne, Saltmarsh and Dell as well as Crisp.
73. *Op. cit.*, Sig. B 3.
74. *Ibid.*, Sig A 2.
75. *Ibid.*, pp. 1–2, 5, 26, 41, 46–8, 127, 133–4.
76. *Ibid.*, Sig. A.2.
77. Edwards *op. cit.*, I p. 97.
78. Clarkson *op. cit.*, p. 9.
79. Edwards *op cit.*, I. p. 90. See p. 60 above.
80. *The Testimony of William Erbery* (1658), p. 68. For Erbery see *The World Turned Upside Down*, pp. 192–7.
81. For Ranters see A.L. Morton *The World of the Ranters* (1970), and Frank McGregor 'Ranterism and the Development of Early Quakerism', *Journal of Religious History* Sydney 1978, pp. 349–63.
82. R. Towne *The Assertion of Grace* (n.d. ?1644), p. 23. See also Rutherford 'A Modest Survey of the Secrets of Antinomianism', printed with *A Survey of the Spirituall Antichrist*, pp. 25, 71.
83. Coppe *op. cit.*, I pp. 1–5, 11; cf. p. 62 above.
84. Clarkson *A Single Eye* (1650), pp. 8–12, 16.
85. Clarkson *The Lost Sheep Found*, p. 25.

86. For Bauthumley see *The World Turned Upside Down*, pp. 219–20; for sin generally see *ibid.*, chapter 8 *passim*.

87. Thomas Hotchkis *An Exercitation Concerning the Nature and Forgivenesse of Sin* (1655), Sig. B 2, B 3v.

88. *Ibid.*, p. 152.

89. Crisp Vol. III, Sig. A 8v.

90. H. Pinnell *A Word of Prophecy concerning The Parliament, Generall and the Army* (1648), p. 49.

91. C. Webster *The Great Instauration: Science, Medicine and Reform, 1626–1660* (1975), p. 184.

92. Pinnell *op. cit.*, pp. 2–4, 7–10, 17, 74.

93. Webster *op. cit.*, p. 280. Crisp's successor as rector of Brinkworth was the Presbyterian John Harding, an even more active translator of Paracelsus, *ibid.*, p. 281. Harding was expelled after the restoration.

94. D. Underdown. 'The Chalk and the Cheese: Contrasts among the English Clubmen', *Past and Present* 85 (1979), esp. pp. 30, 39–40; *The World Turned Upside Down*, pp. 46–7, 77, 109; cf. Buchanan Sharp *In Contempt of All Authority: Rural Artisans and Riot in the West of England, 1586–1660* (California University Press 1980), *passim*, and *V.C.H. Wilts*, III p. 102.

95. Hotchkis *op. cit.*, pp. 239, 291–2. For Coppin, see p. 68 below, and *The World Turned Upside Down*, esp. pp. 220–3.

96. *The World Turned Upside Down*, pp. 226–7. Former Levellers in Wiltshire were alleged to have become Ranters, *ibid.*, p. 239. For Salmon, see *ibid.* esp. pp. 217–19.

97. Hotchkis, *op. cit.*, pp. 172–6. Eyre's book gave rise to an exceptionally tedious and long-winded controversy, in which Baxter mentioned Crisp as an antinomian of learning and judgment, *Richard Baxters Admonition to Mr. William Eyre of Salisbury* (1654), Sig. A 3. John Graile (of Tidworth, Wilts.), another participant, associated Eyre with Crisp's doctrines, *A Modest Vindication of the Doctrine of Conditions in the Covenant of Grace* (1655), p. 25; cf. pp. 49, 57. I have not been able to trace any relationship between the reverend William Eyre and Colonel William Eyre the Leveller, also of Wiltshire. If there was any connection it was a distant one.

98. *The World Turned Upside Down*, p. 228.

99. See my *Milton and the English Revolution* (1977), pp. 303, 313–16.

100. Vol. III, pp. 346–7.

101. *Fifty-Two Sermons*, p. 27.

102. See my 'The Religion of Gerrard Winstanley', *Past and Present Supplement No. 5* (1978), esp. pp. 34–7.

103. *Milton and the English Revolution*, pp. 303–5.

104. W. Empson *Milton's God* (1961), pp. 130–46.

105. The Deist John Toland's first appearance in print arose from the Crisp controversy. Toland, still a very young man, rather unexpectedly "greatly liked" Daniel Williams's book, and made an abstract of it which Le Clerc published

in his *Bibliothèque Universelle* Tome XXIII, p. 505. See *Biographia Britannica*, VI (1763) p. 3965.

106. Isaac Chauncy *Neonomianism unmasked: or the ancient Gospel Pleaded* (1692), p. 2.

107. Quoted in W.M. Lamont *Richard Baxter and the Millennium* (1979), p. 267; cf. *Reliquiae Baxterianae* ed. M. Sylvester (1696), p. 43.

108. *Op. cit.*, pp. 3, 50, 54, 61. Crisp is (with Milton) one of the very few seventeenth-century Englishmen to have an -ism attached to his name. See *Milton and the English Revolution*, p. 226n.

109. Robert Nelson *The Life of Dr. George Bull, Late Lord Bishop of St. David's* (1713), p. 260.

110. Tobias Crisp *Christ made Sin* (1691), Preface; S.C. *Christ Alone Exalted in Dr. Crisp's Sermons* (1693), pp. 7–14.

111. *God's Plot: The Paradoxes of Puritan Piety. Being the Autobiography and Journal of Thomas Shepard* ed. M. McGiffert (Massachusetts University Press 1972), p. 9; J. Donne *Sermons* ed. G.R. Potter and E.M. Simpson (Berkeley and Los Angeles 1953–62), VIII, p. 370.

112. *The World Turned Upside Down*, chapter 8 *passim*; *Milton and the English Revolution*, chapter 21, *passim*.

113. Volume III, p. 362.

114. J.R. Jacob in *Radical Protestantism and the Early Enlightenment in England: Stubbe to Toland* (forthcoming) very skilfully demonstrates how after 1660 the radical Henry Stubbe resorted to subterfuge and Aesopian language in order to get his unorthodox views past the censor. I am very grateful to Professor Jacob for allowing me to read his book in advance of publication.

4 GWEN BEACHCROFT

Balliol College accounts in the eighteenth century

BALLIOL COLLEGE ACCOUNTS IN THE EIGHTEENTH CENTURY

In the eighteenth century financial responsibility at Balliol College was vested in the Master and Fellows, *collegialiter congregati* in the College meeting. Every year, on 21 October in Luketide, this body elected from among its members the administrative officers and Prae-lectors for the next twelvemonth.[1] Among these were two Bursars, a Senior and a Junior, whose duties were to collect the moneys due to the College, pay its bills and to record their findings in the tall narrow ledgers still carefully preserved at Balliol. These were short-term officers, appointed to hold office for one year only and hardly ever reelected for an immediate second term, although a Junior Bursar might be elected Senior Bursar the next year and the Senior of one year was often appointed to the Junior post in the ensuing twelve-month. Fellows who showed skill in finance tended to be elected as Bursars several times during their College careers. Outstanding among these was Joseph Sanford, who was Senior Bursar eight times between Theophilus Leigh's election as Master in 1726 and his own death in 1774 and who held office as Junior Bursar eleven times in the same period. Only two others, Charles Godwyn and John Davey, came near his record. Such men spent all their adult lives in the College, were familiar with its recurrent financial problems and aware of the possible solutions. We find them taking charge of the finances at critical times and, as Junior Bursars, reinforcing the efforts of less experienced men who occupied the Senior post (see Table 1). For his important and exacting duties each Bursar received 6s. 8d. a year, paid in two equal six-monthly instalments. In spite of the poor pay, however, some Fellows actively sought election as Bursar. Such was Jeremiah Milles, a Fellow of Balliol from 1696 to 1704, who on 16 October 1702 "waited upon the Master to desire his vote for my being Bursar, which he granted" and who seemed to relish the long hours and hard work involved in receiving and paying out College money and in achieving a balance that would satisfy the Master and several senior Fellows who audited them.[2] He was probably not the only man to be so inclined.

Every financial year, beginning and ending round about St. Luke's

Day, 18 October, the Bursars had to produce two distinct sets of Accounts, the BURSARS' *COMPUTI* and their FINAL ACCOUNT, each in its own set of ledgers and serving a particular purpose. The connection between the two sets has not always been recognised, although it is necessary to the sound interpretation of their signifi- cance. Even as great an authority on the constitution of Balliol College as Andrew Clark, who considered the Bursars' *Computi* "the true Quarry for facts illustrative of the social life of the College", confessed that he was baffled by the Final Accounts. Of them he wrote,

> They apparently balance on a traditional system now unin- telligible. Few patent facts for College history seem deriv- able from them. Blindly and unintelligently I have waded through those that came under my notice. The notes I took from them as a rule have been superseded by better infor- mation from other volumes and so have been cancelled.[3]

Coming from one whose knowledge of Balliol institutions was in many respects unrivalled, this is a most startling verdict. The Final Accounts, in fact, dovetail neatly into the *Computi*, summing up the findings there and filling some important gaps in their information, and give a more complete and more accurate picture of the financial position of the College during the eighteenth century than can be discovered from the *Computi* alone.

The Bursars' *Computi* were presented each year in two six-monthly parts running, the one from St. Luke's to Lady Day and the other from Lady Day to the next St. Luke's. The Final Account was a single set of calculations completing the year's business and arriving at a balance, either favourable or otherwise for the year as a whole. It seems to have taken some six months beyond the end of the year concerned to complete and be passed by the auditors. In 1769 a College Order stipulated that if it were not passed by the Lady Day following the end of his term of office the Senior Bursar would be fined.[4]

The interpretation of College Accounts in the eighteenth century is made more difficult by a method of presenting them very different from what it would be today. The credit and debit sides of each Account are shown, not in juxtaposition but consecutively, each ram- bling over many pages in such a way as makes it all too easy to lose the thread, especially as the accountants did not carry forward the mounting totals of income and expenditure continuously from page to page, but contented themselves with recording only the *Summa Paginae* of each page in turn. Throughout the eighteenth century the layout of both sets of Accounts never changes. To the Bursars, often men with no previous experience of accountancy, the rigid moulds into which they had to pour the many facts and figures required of them must have been a welcome aid, as indeed it is to the modern student also. Once the pattern of entries in any one year is recognised, it can be applied to every other year as well. For the purposes of this article I have selected the year 1734–35, some eight years after Theophilus Leigh's election as Master, and a fairly prosperous time in the history of the College. The two half-yearly Bursars' *Computi* are here shown in Table 2 in parallel columns for easy comparison, and these can in turn be compared with the Final Account given in Table 3.

THE BURSARS' COMPUTI

The Bursars' two half-yearly *Computi* concerned themselves chiefly with one part only of the whole Balliol community, that which consisted of Master, Fellows and Scholars/Exhibitioners who were, at least in theory, the spiritual successors of mediaeval Balliol, a small House of a Master and poor scholars living entirely on the charity of their Founders and Benefactors. Eighteenth century Balliol bore little resemblance to its early predecessor, but its central core, the College proper, was still maintained entirely by the endowments of those same Founders and many generations of Benefactors anxious to preserve its traditions of piety and learning. The far larger number of students outside the College proper, the Commoners and Fellow Commoners, Batlers, and Servitors, often significantly described as the *extranei*, had no statutory claim to benefit from the Society's endowments and paid their ways by their battells and sundry other fees not mentioned in the Bursars' *Computi*. These payments appear only in the Final Accounts, where they represent a substantial part of College income.

The Bursars' *Computi* begin by estimating the income due to Balliol under the general heading of *Recipienda*. Foremost among the expected receipts are the rents from the College estates and lands in general. Each half-yearly *Computus* opens with a list of some thirty-five to fifty holdings or tenancies specified by the place-name or surname of tenants past and present but without describing the type of lease involved. Next comes a section headed *Reditus Status et Reditus Frumenti* due from certain named rectories and farms.[5] In both half-years the corn rents exceeded those in cash, especially in that which included harvest time. In the second half year a further small income in capons is also mentioned. Although arrears in rent were a common feature of the Accounts the College seems to have been successful in collecting some three-quarters of the total rents due in most years. As the rents were paid, the Bursars marked the appropriate entries with the word *Sol*, sometimes adding a special sign like a three-barred portcullis, denoting receipt. Those not paid were not excluded, however from the totals of *Recipienda* due from this source. As in mediaeval monastic accounts, *Arreragia* formed part of the total income shown. This certainly gives the totals entered an air of unreality, but it was a signal that the College in no way resigned its claim on the missing payments, some of which in time did in fact materialise, as will appear later in the Final Accounts.

The next items shown under *Recipienda* are described as *Proficua*, and all seem to have been sums of money, mainly connected with College house-keeping, that were received by the College and not transferred to the Butler, Manciple or any other of its employees. First mentioned under this heading are *Panis* and *Potus*, the main items of the basic commons statutably provided by the College to all its members. Both were purchased from tradesmen outside the College on terms which enabled it to make small profits. All the beer bought each quarter was not necessarily consumed and the remnant could be saved from quarter to quarter and from year to year at a saving to the College. Bread left over could not be kept in the same way, but, bought by so much per dozen loaves, was in practice supplied by the baker at fourteen loaves to the dozen, and here again the College was the gainer, albeit by only a small sum. These profits on bread and beer never rose together much above £20 a year and dropped to less than £10 between them when the student population of the College dwindled. The next two items listed under *Proficua* appear as *Decrementa* and *Incrementa*. No clue as to their meaning is afforded by either the College Accounts or by the 1682–1781 College Register. The first of them certainly does not sound like any sort of profit. However, the term 'Decrements' does occur among documents in some other Oxford Colleges, notably at Trinity and Corpus Christi. Those at

Trinity suggest that there Decrements were charges made by the College for such articles of diet as Mustard, Vinegar, and such other additions to those regularly battelled for by Gentlemen Commoners and Commoners of whatever degree, the payment being made directly to the College and not passed on as fees to the Butler or Manciple.[6] At Corpus too the term applies to spices and condiments nor normally provided and at times even to firewood and coal. It is defined by the historian of that College as "Deductions from the money allowances of any member of the foundation on account of articles of consumption not recognised as due to him by statute or custom".[7] It seems probable that Decrements at Balliol too were of this type, their existence a recognition of the inadequacy of the statutory commons in an age of rising prices and more luxurious standards. They were retained by the College and not transferred to any College servant. Increments, on the other hand, were almost certainly the profits made by the College on such regular articles of diet as butter, cheese and meat bought for the meals served in Hall on lines similar to those described above for the basic commons of bread and beer. They were a much smaller sum than the Decrements, and from the circumstance that from the middle years of the century the figures entered as Increments in this part of the Bursars' *Computi* coincide with those of *Increment*, entered among the *Solvenda* in the Final Account it would seem that this last was transferred to the College. Other *Proficua* consisted of *Mulcta*, fines levied upon it is not sure whom, and *Domus*, charges made to visitors dining in the College Hall, or to their hosts.

On the debit side of the Bursars' *Computi* we find the general heading of *Solvenda* or estimated expenditure. All the payments here entered were made for the benefit of the College proper. First we are shown the sums paid to the Master and Fellows. The first of these consist of the commons due to the Master and Fellows. In 1734–5 the commons for a Fellow's full week of residence of thirteen weeks every quarter had been raised from 2s.6d. to 3s.6d. a week, thanks to an increase in the value of Balliol's estate of Long Benton in Northumberland, and in the hope of encouraging residence.[8] There were also the basic stipends (10s.4d. a week), the extra official stipends of the six Praelectorships (which ranged from £2 to £12 a year), and the payment of the College Officers of 6s.8d a year. These remained unchanged. Fortunately for the Fellows they had other sources of in-

come than those appearing in the Accounts. They earned something
in tuition fees by teaching the large numbers of students outside the
inner circle of Scholars and Exhibitioners and charged their pupils
rents for their rooms in College and for firewood. These fees did not,
however, appear on any College Account until the late eighteenth
century, being privately negotiated with their pupils' parents and we
have no details of the sums involved. Master and Fellows were further
entitled to substantial shares of any profit on the Accounts at the
end of the year, and this was fully recognized at the end of the financial year in the Bursars *Computi*. The remaining items of expected
expenditure in the *Computi* speak for themselves. The taxes, rents
and other dues payable by the College, and the wages of its servants
are given in full as are miscellaneous expenses such as alms to the
Marshal of the Beggars, an offering to the neighbouring Church of St.
Mary Magdalene and, heaviest item of all, the sums owed to the many
building workmen — stonemasons, tilers and carpenters among them
— employed to repair and maintain the College buildings and other
house property.

At the close of the second half-yearly *Computus*, the Bursars
summed up the total *Recipienda* and *Solvenda* for the year as a whole
and declared a balance of £1088.9s.10½d minus £650.11s.5¾d =
£437.17s.5¾d. The surplus on the year's Account was unlikely to
have caused surprise. In no year between 1726 and 1785 did the Bursars' *Computi* show a deficit. The income from endowments was more
than enough to cover the cost of maintaining the Master, Fellows and
Scholars/Exhibitioners, especially as it was not expected to cover the
provision of any of their food beyond their 'commons'. Moreover,
the balance was always unrealistically swollen by the inclusion of
arrears of rent in the total of income due. After the middle of the
century another factor came into play which should be noticed, this
being a remarkable increase in the rents due to the College as a result
of a rise in land values owing to enclosure and other improvements in
agricultural methods. The rent income from Balliol estates in 1726–27
was estimated to yield £645 1s. 4d.; in 1734–35 it was £680 13s. 9d.;
in 1768–69 it had risen to £1517 9s.1½d. and in 1774–75 it reached
£1788 9s.1½d.. There was a corresponding profit shown on the whole
year's working in the Bursars' *Computi*. That profit was distributed
as the so-called Fellowship Dividend.

This was a well-known feature of eighteenth century College finance. As defined by Andrew Clark it "represented an artificial excess of expected income over estimated expenditure" which was divided among the Master and Fellows, the Master receiving a double share *ex officio* and the remnant being set aside for *Domus* or general College purposes. Thus, in 1734–35 Dr. Leigh got £60, each Fellow £30 and *Domus* £17 17s. 4¾d. The *Table of Balliol College Accounts 1726–85* at the conclusion of this article shows that *Domus* usually received a larger share than this, but never much more than that given to any one Fellow. There is much to be said in favour of supplementing the basic statutory emoluments of the Fellows of a College out of profits shown on the Accounts and the practice was common and uncritically accepted in contemporary Oxford. Obviously some method of adjusting the remuneration of Fellows to long-range changes in the value of money was essential. However, the failure to make a larger share of each year's profits available to *Domus* must be open to criticism. Balliol was neglecting the opportunity to set aside a regular yearly sum as a reserve large enough to meet unexpectedly heavy expenses in future years. Only the Master and individual Fellows profited from such improvidence, whether from selfishness or from blindness is an open question. Perhaps in an age when no clear distinction was drawn between current and capital expenditure they should have the benefit of the doubt. The *Computi* show that their shares in the Dividend tended to rise year after year with but slight fluctuations. When in the mid-seventies the College was faced by a financial crisis provoked by exceptionally high legal and building costs it had no reserves to draw upon. In 1775 the Master and Fellows had to ask the Visitor for permission temporarily to suppress a Fellowship to meet their financial problems. Yet no warning of this situation had been so much as hinted at in the *Computi*, whose mounting surpluses suggested a continuing prosperity.

THE BURSARS' FINAL ACCOUNTS

If the *Computi* gave an impression of uninterrupted well being, this was not borne out by the Final Accounts. With these we are on very firm ground, and are presented with facts rather than hopes. The Final Accounts distinguished between expected income and expenditure on the one hand and money actually received and actually spent on the other. Moreover, whereas the *Computi* dealt with the finances of only the Master, Fellows, Scholars and Exhibitioners, the Final Accounts included those of the whole Balliol community. The Fellow Commoners, Batlers and Servitors whose fees were often the College's largest source of income and the feeding of whom was its chief expense.

In examining these, as with the *Computi*, we will take those of 1734–35 as typical. The first part of every Final Account consisted of a statement of the estimated income and expenditure for the year. The first *Recipienda* and *Solvenda* shown are those already recorded in the same year's *Computi*. It will be seen that by including the whole Fellowship Dividend in the likely expenditure the two 'sides' of the Account are shown to coincide at £1088 8s. 10½d.. Then follows a new set of figures, the income due to battells and the estimated cost of supplying the bread, drink, butter, cheese, butcher's meat and all the other provisions purchased by the Bursars in Oxford Market as food for the entire College. These sums were based on the voluminous Books of Battells in which the College Butler kept a daily record of all meals taken in the College Hall by the whole student body and even by the Master and Fellows, who could hardly have subsisted on their statutory commons alone. At the end of every quarter the Butler passed on his lists to the Bursars who lost no time in demanding prompt payment on the battells due. Unfortunately for Balliol battells were notoriously difficult to collect. A long series of College orders sought to make evasion more difficult and to punish defaulters, but the problem remained. The total *Recipienda* and *Solvenda* in the Final Account for 1734–35 are shown as £3454 18s. 7½d., a figure which includes income due from both rents and battells and the total expected expenditure on the whole student body. Also included in the *Recipienda* is a sum of £67 17s. 9d. either in cash or in stock in hand remaining in the Storeroom at the end of the year.

The next section of the Final Account is labelled *Recepta and Soluta*. Under these headings the Bursars show that the chief sources of revenue, i.e. rents and battells for 1734–35, fell short of what had been estimated, amounting to only £3087 2s. 0½d. instead of the hoped for £3454 18s. 7½d., while actual expenditure reached £3386.

The final section of the Final Account consists of a straightforward balance sheet, labelled *Comparatio*. The figures speak for themselves. One entry, however, requires explanation. After giving the *Recipienda* the Bursars emphasise the shortfall in *Recepta* by reporting the total of unpaid rents and battells *"non recepta ex altera parte Libri"*. In the same way the corresponding entry on the debit side refers to a sum *"non soluta ex altera parte Libri"*. Both these refer to the back pages of the ledger in which are shown lists of all outstanding arrears in both rents and battells due that year. These lists show that the un-paid rents included in the total *Recipienda* of the Bursars' *Computi* were neither forgotten nor neglected. It is clear the successive Bursars made strenuous efforts to recover them and often did so, for many of the entries are marked 'Sol.' and the Bursars who later collected them both dated and initialled those which they received. In many years some of the purchases made by the College were not yet paid for. These too were listed at the back of the Ledger. In 1734–5 the Bursars were left in debt to the tune of £68. 5s. 10d. for the provisions in their store-rooms and cellars. In some years the items not already paid for were much more numerous, but this did not mean that the College was defaulting in payments to their suppliers. The Final Account concludes by summing up the *Recepta and Soluta* and showing a deficit of £231. 16s. 8½d. at the close of the year.

Editor's Note

Mrs. Beachcroft's article ends here, but she also prepared tables of the Bursar's *Computi* and of the Final Accounts for the years 1755–56 and 1774–75. In the text she would surely have gone on to explore the growing rent-income and turnover of the College in the middle of the eighteenth century, and the financial crisis which overtook Balliol in the early 1770's when the number of students reached a low ebb. She might then have concluded by showing how this system of accoun-ting lasted, with a gradual transfer of detail from the Bursars' *Com-puti* to the Final Accounts, until the middle of the nineteenth century.

NOTES

1. 'The College Register 1682–1781'. Each year's business opens with a list of the officers and Praelectors elected at the College Meeting on 21 October.
2. 'The diary of Jeremiah Milles, 1700–1701', fo. 43, Balliol College library.
3. Andrew Clark 'Notebooks on the Constitution of Balliol College', vol. V., Bodleian Library, MSS. Top. Oxon. e 124/5.
4. 'The College Register 1682–1781', 29 Nov. 1769, clause 11.
5. Under 13 Eliz. cap. vi the tenants of all new college leases had to pay at least one-third of the old rent in corn or malt at a fixed price.
6. I am much indebted to Dame Lucy Sutherland for this reference, 'Bursars' Directory', Trinity College, Oxford, A. 59, as also for her suggestion that I should study *Dissertation on the Accounts of All Souls College, Oxford, by Sir William Blackstone*, presented to the Roxburghe Society by Sir William Anson (1898).
7. Thomas Fowler *The History of Corpus Christi College, with lists of its members*, Oxford Historical Society vol. XXV (1893), p. 354.
8. 'The College Register 1682–1781', 26 July 1732, records the Visitor's approval of the proposal to put the increased quit rent of Long Benton to this use as an encouragement to residence.

TABLE 1

Summary of the accounts of Balliol College during the Mastership of Theophilus Leigh

	BURSARS' COMPUTI					BURSARS' FINAL ACCOUNTS				
DATE	RECIPIENDA Total for the year	SOLVENDA Total for for year	SUMMA TOTALIS Favourable balance	DIVIDEND Individual share	DIVIDEND Domus	RECEPTA	SOLUTA	BALANCE	DATE	BURSARS
1726–27	1085 17 6	646 7 4	439 10 2	30 0 0	29 10 2	4087 8 1¾	4037 2 6	50 5 7¾	1727	Loveday and Rich
1727–28	1088 19 0¼	528 19 9¾	559 19 2½	40 0 0	39 19 2½	3962 13 8	4058 5 1¼	-95 11 5¼	1728	Sanford and Wilson
1728–29	1092 14 8½	561 17 0	530 17 8½	41 0 0	38 17 8½	3880 12 10¼	3844 7 11¾	36 4 10½	1729	Best and Walker
1729–30	1050 11 7¼	598 19 4¾	451 12 2½	33 0 0	22 12 2½	No entry *Comparatio* survives			1730	Jones and Best
1730–31	1036 6 4½	626 4 2½	410 2 2	30 0 0	20 2 2	4293 0 9½	3893 13 4½	399 7 5	1731	Wilson and Thomas
1731–32	1060 16 8	572 6 5	488 10 3	33 0 0	26 10 3	4260 14 5¾	4197 16 6	62 17 11¾	1732	Thomas and Coxe
1732–33	1061 14 9	622 8 3	439 6 6	32 0 0	23 6 6	3804 14 2	3836 3 6	-31 9 4	1733	Coxe and Quick
1733–34	1041 13 9¼	684 9 6½	357 4 2¾	26 0 0	19 4 2¾	3552 13 4	3554 15 9¼	-2 2 5¼	1734	Sanford and Wilson
1734–35	1088 8 10½	650 11 5¾	437 17 4¾	30 0 0	17 17 4¾	3476 3 6¼	3708 0 2¾	-231 16 8½	1735	Wilson and Thomas
1735–36	1086 14 2¾	657 7 10½	429 6 4½ (sic)	36 0 0	33 6 4½	3747 10 4¼	3984 6 9¼	-236 16 5	1736	Thomas and Coxe
1736–37	1150 5 8½	596 1 3½	554 4 5	47 0 0	37 4 5	3956 14 8¼	3807 7 4½	149 7 3¾	1737	Coxe and Land
1737–38	1169 2 6¼	736 15 9¼	432 6 9	37 0 0	25 6 9	4100 9 7½	4096 13 0¼	3 16 7¼	1738	Godwyn and Land
1738–39	1189 4 10¾	620 1 6¼	569 3 4½	44 0 0	41 3 4½	4106 3 8¼	4098 8 6¾	7 15 1½	1739	Land and Fernyhough
1739–40	1159 7 0¾	617 14 9¾	541 12 3	37 0 0	23 12 3	4081 11 10¼	4073 16 4¾	7 15 5½	1740	Fernyhough and Sanford
1740–41	1150 14 4¾	617 13 4½	533 1 0¼	38 0 0	39 1 0¼	3952 1 9	3963 5 5¾	-11 3 8¾	1741	Sanford and Hunsdon
1741–42	1182 19 5½	636 4 3¼	546 15 2¼	37 0 0	28 15 2¼	4932 5 9	4933 11 9	-1 6 0	1742	Godwyn and Land
1742–43	1129 2 3	651 7 6¾	477 14 8¼	31 0 0	43 14 8¼	3994 11 4¾	3985 2 4	9 9 0¾	1743	Land and Hunsdon
1743–44	1126 7 0¼	606 13 11	519 13 1¼	35 0 0	29 13 1¼	3642 3 6¾	3707 17 2¼	-65 13 7½	1744	Fernyhough and Hunsdon
1744–45	1113 10 10¾	601 9 8¼	512 1 2½	36 0 0	44 1 2½	3506 1 11	3626 15 4¼	-120 13 5¼	1745	Hunsdon and Godwyn

TABLE 1 *continued*

1745–46	1099 2 9¾	581 11 4½	517 11 5¼	37 0 0	36 11 5¼	4302 11 7½	4296 7 5	6 4 2½	1746	Drake and Land
1746–47	1151 4 4	515 18 8½	635 5 7½	42 0 0	47 5 7½	3076 17 7¼	3200 14 3	-123 16 7¾	1747	Sanford and Land
1747–48	1157 19 8¼	505 6 3¾	652 13 4½	47 0 0	41 13 4½	3264 11 6¾	3276 19 8	-12 8 1¼	1748	Godwyn and Hunsdon
1748–49	1128 0 10½	550 3 7½	577 17 3	39 0 0	31 17 3	3248 5 3	3266 1 1½	-17 15 10½	1749	Hunsdon and Darch
1749–50	1162 4 11	583 12 1	578 12 10	41 0 0	45 12 10	3748 15 2	3733 5 5	15 9 9	1750	Drake and Sanford
1750–51	1116 13 0¾	620 11 11¼	496 1 1½	35 0 0	41 1 1½	3094 12 0¾	3066 3 1¾	28 8 11	1751	Sanford and Godwyn
1751–52	1146 14 10¾	609 19 0½	536 15 10¼	45 0 0	41 15 10¼	3393 9 5	3371 16 0¼	21 13 4¾	1752	Godwyn and Hunsdon
1752–53	1146 1 4¼	608 4 3½	537 17 0¾	45 0 0	42 17 0¾	3082 9 3¼	3102 17 8¼	-20 8 5	1753	Hunsdon and Wilmot
1753–54	1361 4 9¼	649 11 5	711 13 4¼	55 0 0	51 13 4¼	3359 16 3	3278 16 9¾	80 19 5¼	1754	Darch and Sanford
1754–55	1500 2 7	556 18 0¼	943 4 6¾	72 0 0	79 4 6¾	3155 12 9¾	3076 1 5	79 11 4¾	1755	Vivian and Godwyn
1755–56	1519 14 3½	533 6 2	986 8 1½	76 0 0	74 8 1½	3538 10 6¾	3329 13 11½	208 16 7¼	1756	Wickham and Godwyn
1756–57	1506 5 0¼	606 13 9	899 11 3¼	60 0 0	59 11 3¼	3476 15 5¾	3245 12 5¼	231 3 0½	1757	Sanford and Godwyn
1757–58	1374 15 6¾	531 2 2¼	843 13 4½	56 0 0	59 13 4½	3595 13 3¼	3221 2 2¾	374 11 0½	1758	Godwyn and Coxe
1758–59	1347 4 9½	641 6 10¼	705 17 11¼	50 0 0	55 17 11¼	3658 16 3¾	3591 9 3½	67 7 0¼	1759	Vivian and Coxe
1759–60	1323 12 9	627 10 5¾	696 2 3¼	50 0 0	46 2 3¼	3126 3 7½	2985 6 0	140 17 7½	1760	Coxe and Sanford
1760–61	1386 10 7½	847 19 9¾	538 10 9¾	39 0 0	31 10 9¾	3240 19 4	3110 19 11½	129 19 4½	1761	Davey and Sanford
1761–62	1285 14 3¼	763 10 10½	522 3 4¾	37 0 0	41 3 4¾	3238 15 11½	2949 14 9¾	289 1 1¾	1762	Sanford and Godwyn
1762–63	1358 10 2½	717 8 1	641 2 1½	46 0 0	43 2 1½	3504 3 5¼	3499 19 2½	4 4 3¾ (sic)	1763	Godwyn and Coxe
1763–64	1041 10 7¼	452 16 1¾	588 14 5½	39 0 0	42 14 5½	2888 12 7½	2838 18 1¼	49 14 6¼	1764	Coxe and Davey
1764–65	1368 18 6¾	698 2 0¼	670 16 6½	48 0 0	46 16 6½	3791 16 7	3826 19 6½	-35 2 11½	1765	Davey and Sanford
1765–66	1429 5 10½	722 16 9¼	706 9 1¼	47 0 0	48 9 1¼	2924 13 8¾	2933 15 2	-9 1 5¼	1766	Sanford and Godwyn
1766–67	1446 11 4½	744 15 7¾	701 15 8¾	50 0 0	51 15 8¾	3003 5 7¼	2992 17 5	10 8 2¼	1767	Godwyn and Coxe

TABLE 1 *continued*

Partner	Year								Year range
Davey and Sanford	1769	80 4 5½	5077 10 9	5157 15 2½	76 10 5¾	82 0 0	978 10 5¾	803 15 3 · 1782 5 8¾	1768–69
Watkins and Sanford	1770	46 5 5¼	4066 13 2½	4112 18 7¾	76 8 7¼	72 0 0	868 8 7¼	940 2 9¾ · 1808 11 4¼	1769–70
Cooke and Sanford	1771	-243 17 0	4103 18 3	3860 1 3	88 17 9¼	81 0 0	979 17 9¼	877 1 5¾ · 1856 19 3	1770–71
White and Sanford	1772	-72 19 5½	4928 16 6½	4855 17 1	84 8 0¼	80 0 0	1044 8 0¼	984 15 9½ · 2029 3 9¾	1771–72
Love and Sanford	1773	-34 16 10	4484 11 10¾	4449 15 0¼	73 7 1½	69 0 0	970 7 1½	1044 18 5¾ · 2015 5 7¾	1772–73
Williams and Davey	1774	-57 1 9¾	4354 18 0½	4297 16 2¾	38 6 3 / 41 19 0¾	37 10 0 / 42 0 0	488 6 3 / 503 19 0¾	464 8 10 / 514 14 1¾ · 952 15 1 / 1018 13 2½	1773–74
Heighway and Davey	1775	-129 8 3¾	5170 16 5¼	5041 8 1½	44 1 5¼ / 38 5 2½	41 10 0 / 37 10 0	542 1 5¼ / 488 5 2½	511 9 1½ / 553 5 11 · 1053 10 6¾ / 1041 11 1½	1774–75
Hutton and Davey	1776	37 16 8½	4443 4 4½	4481 1 1	32 4 6 / 37 12 5	31 6 8 / 34 13 4	439 11 2¾ / 488 5 9	563 13 8 / 595 18 2 · 1003 4 10 / 1084 3 11	1775–76
Wood and Davey	1777	47 1 11¼ (sic)	4656 19 0	4691 18 5¾ (12.2.6 omitted in error)	36 6 11¼ / 24 0 11	37 0 0 / 25 6 8	554 6 11¼ / 378 14 2	466 10 3¾ / 765 16 2 · 1020 17 3 / 1144 10 5	1776–77
Davey and Cooke	1778	137 16 11½	5076 2 2¾	5213 19 2¾	27 2 4¾ / 42 2 2	27 0 0 / 38 0 0	405 2 4¾ / 574 2	719 7 2 / 610 10 11 · 1124 9 6¾ / 1184 13 1	1777–78
Heighway and Cooke	1779	151 3 5½	4806 9 0	4957 12 5½	29 13 6½ / 36 17 6½	29 0 0 / 35 17 6	435 13 6½ / 538 2 6½	655 9 8 / 618 18 2 · 1091 3 2½ / 1157 0 8½	1778–79
Hutton and Davey	1780	-151 0 9¼	5319 13 11¾	5168 13 2½	40 8 1 / 59 8 5¼	40 6 8 / 58 0 0	524 8 1 / 755 8 5¼	596 19 10 / 568 19 8½ · 1121 7 11 / 1324 8 1¾	1779–80
Prosser and Davey	1781	170 16 3	5324 0 7½	5494 16 10½	39 19 6¾ / 38 0 3	39 13 4 / 35 0 0	595 6 2¾ / 528 0 3	718 10 5½ / 641 8 6½ · 1313 16 8¾ / 1169 8 9¼	1780–81
Barter and Heighway	1782	10 4¾	6404 6 4¾	6404 16 9	28 2 1 / 36 8 4¼	27 15 0 / 36 4 0	416 12 1 / 543 4 4¼	680 14 8¾ / 648 7 5¼ · 1097 6 9¾ / 1191 11 9¾	1781–82
Yeatman and Prosser	1783	185 15 10¾	5010 17 4¾	5196 13 3	38 18 2¾ / 52 13 10¾	36 0 0 / 51 0 0	506 18 2¾ / 715 13 10¾	596 5 6¾ / 508 2 9½ · 1103 3 9¾ / 1223 16 8¼	1782–83
Davey and Barter	1784	64 9 6	5563 3 7	5627 13 1	40 13 3¾ / 50 7 6	41 10 0 / 48 0 0	538 13 3¾ / 626 7 6	591 17 5¾ / 593 19 10½ · 1130 10 9¾ / 1220 7 4¼	1783–84
Prosser and Wright	1785	215 12 11¾	5181 7 5¼	5397 0 5¼	44 15 3¾ / 54 2 5	44 14 11 / 54 0 0	536 19 4¼ / 648 2 5	620 17 2¾ / 563 17 7 · 1157 16 6¾ / 1212 0 0	1784–85

TABLE 2

Bursars' Computi 1734-35

First half year, St. Luke's 1734 – Lady Day 1735

Recipienda	£	s	d	
Procuratores Universitatis	0	7	0	sol
Collegium Exoniense	0	6	3	
Phipps	1	0	0	
Almond als Wheatly	0	4	0	sol
Ball als Pain	0	10	0	sol
Ford als Franklyn	0	6	8	sol
Hughs als Buckingham	0	2	6	
London als West	0	5	0	
Burnham als Whitney	0	4	6	
Parochi Stae Ebbae Oxon	0	4	0	sol
Walker als Harward	0	8	0	sol
Finmore als Knapp als Holman	0	6	8	
Dunch	5	0	0	
Hobbs	25	0	0	sol
Wade de Risborough	6	0	0	
Betting als Wheeler	1	6	0	
Sayer	10	3	6	sol
Camera Londini	5	0	0	sol
Dacres als Hayton	5	0	0	sol
Castle als Delahay als John Gregory	0	17	0	sol
Lee als Hankey	1	6	8	sol
Chaplyn als Hankey	3	6	8	sol
Halward de Suckley als Cook	14	4	8	
Thorne in Parochia de Studley Devoñ	9	18	6	
Manerium de Uffton	150	0	0	sol
Colebourn in parochia de Uffton	12	10	0	sol
Huntspil & Cannington in Somerset	3	0	0	
	256	17	7	

Bursars' Computi 1734-35

Second half year, Lady Day 1735 – St. Luke's 1735

Recipienda	£	s	d	
Camera Londini	5	0	0	sol
Ball als Pain	0	10	0	sol
Batting als Wheeler	1	6	0	
Canterbury	1	6	8	
Castle als Delahay als Gregory	0	17	0	sol
Coll. Exon.	0	6	3	
Coll. Merton	0	2	0	
Dacres als Hayton	5	0	0	sol
Dunch	5	0	0	
Finmore als Smith als Holman	0	6	8	sol
Franklyn	0	6	8	sol
Halward de Suckley	14	4	8	
Hobbs	25	0	0	sol
Hughs als Buckingham	0	2	6	
London als West	0	5	0	
Oliver als Chaplyn als Hankey	3	6	8	sol
Otger als Lee als Hankey	1	6	8	sol
Parochia Stae Ebbae	0	4	0	sol
Phipps	1	0	0	
Smith de Woodstock als Johnson als Brown	0	5	1	
Sayer	10	3	6	sol
Taylor als Almond als Wheatley	0	4	0	sol
Tipping als Burnham als Whitney	0	4	6	
Stone de Thorne in Paroch. Studley	9	18	6	
Uffeton pro Manorio	150	0	0	sol
Coleburn	12	10	0	sol
Wade	6	0	0	
Walker als Harward	0	8	0	sol
Huntspill & Cannington	3	0	0	
Beeston	4	12	0	
	262	16	4	

TABLE 2 *continued*

		£	s	d		£	s	d
Pro Caponibus								
Haynes		0	5	0				
Walker al͞s Harward		0	5	0 sol				
Holman		0	5	0				
Camera Londini		0	4	0 sol				
Phipps		0	4	0				
Hicks		0	5	0 sol				
Templar al͞s Crips de Wooton		0	5	0		1	13	0
Abbotsley	Reditus Status	17	9	5½				
	Reditus Frumenti	22	17	7		40	7	0½
Benton M.	Reditus Status	16	2	8				
	Reditus Frumenti	67	17	0		83	19	8
Woodstock	Reditus Status	4	0	0				
	Reditus Frumenti	5	8	10		9	8	10
Nethercote	Reditus Status	1	0	0				
	Reditus Frumenti	1	11	10		2	11	10 sol
Wooton	Reditus Status	0	12	6				
	Reditus Frumenti	0	19	8½		1	12	2½
Oddington	Reditus Status	0	10	0				
	Reditus Frumenti	0	15	11		1	5	11 sol
Moreton	Reditus Status	0	8	0				
	Reditus Frumenti	0	12	11½		1	0	11½
St. Aegid.	Reditus Status	0	8	0				
	Reditus Frumenti	0	11	10		0	19	10
Risholm	Reditus Status	0	4	4				
	Reditus Frumenti	0	14	1½		0	18	5½
						142	4	9

		£	s	d		£	s	d
Woodstock	Reditus Status	4	0	0				
	Reditus Frumenti	5	3	10		9	3	10
Steeple Aston	Reditus Status	2	6	8				
	Reditus Frumenti	3	5	5		5	12	1 sol
Wootton	Reditus Status	0	12	6				
	Reditus Frumenti	0	17	2½		1	9	8½
Risholme	Reditus Status	0	4	4				
	Reditus Frumenti	0	12	1½		0	16	5½
						17	2	1

TABLE 2 *continued*

Proficua (I)

Panis	1 Quartͭ	21 13 06	01 16 01½	
	2 Quartͭ	21 06 00	01 15 06	03 11 07½
Potus	1 Quartͭ	62 16 00	02 13 00	
	2 Quartͭ	49 12 00	02 01 10	04 14 10
Decrementͭ		23 10 10	22 03 00	
Incrementͭ		04 03 00	03 08 00	
1 Quͬ				
Mulcta	01 10 06	2 Quͬ	00 17 00	
Domus	46 19 06		47 07 00	
	76 03 10		73 15 00	
				149 18 0

Admissiones (I)

Soc. Com.	Mͬ Carew Mͬ Buller Mͬ Master Mͬ Rickards	1 0 0
Commensal.	Cox Trap Milles Daniel Prinsep Bennet Carew Wyndowe Jones Sanford	5 0 0
Bat.	Wilkins Gregory Watkins Jones Higgins Wallis	1 10 0
Servient.	Skinner Abbott	0 3 0

Proficua (II)

Panis	Quartͭ 3	41 12 0	3 9 4	
	Quartͭ 4	26 5 0	2 3 9	
Potus	Quartͭ 3	55 12 0	2 6 10	
	Quartͭ 4	48 8 0	2 0 10	
Domus	Quartͭ 3		51 17 0	
	Quartͭ 4		49 7 0	
Decrementͭ	Quartͭ 3		34 1 0	
	Quartͭ 4		32 19 0	
Incrementͭ	Quartͭ 3		3 17 0	
	Quartͭ 4		3 7 0	
Mulct.	Quartͭ 3		0 5 6	
	Quartͭ 4		0 7 7	
				186 1 10

Admissiones (II)

Soc. Com.	Dⁿˢ Edwardus Turner	0 5 0
Commensal.	Dⁿˢ Kedington Dˢ Keene Preston	1 10 0

TABLE 2 *continued*

Praesentationes

	£	s	d
Ad Gradum Baccalaurei in Iure Civili Mr Webber	4	0	0
Ad Gradum Magistri in Artibus Mr Kidby Mr Bound Mr Milles Mr Murray Mr Gilchrist Mr Cooke Mr Millechamp Mr Barter Mr Bidgood	18	0	0
Ad Gradum Baccalaurei in Artibus 1ma Praesent. Ds Sharpe Ds Sargeaunt Ds Stephens Ds Parker Ds Randal Ds Hillman Ds Bridges Ds Walker Ds Lucas	4	10	0
2da Praesent. Ds Norris Ds Hawkins Ds Stephens Ds Sargeaunt Ds Wheeler Ds Agate Ds Allen Ds Bridges Ds Walker Ds Wansborough	5	0	0

Pro Horto

	£	s	d
Mr Kidby Mr Bound Mr Milles Mr Murray Mr Webber Mr Gilchrist Mr Cooke Mr Millechamp Mr Barter Mr Bidgood Mr Carew Mr Buller Mr Master Mr Rickards	14	0	0
Mr Burchinshaw pro Caena 2da	3	0	0

Praesentationes

	£	s	d
Ad Gradum Mri in Artibus Mr Walker	2	0	0
Ad Gradum Baĉ in Arts D. Tarrant D. Yard D. Norrish	1	10	0

Pro Horto

	£	s	d
Dr Edwardus Turner Mr Walker	2	0	0

TABLE 2 continued

Solvenda (Quar̃ 1 & Quar̃ 2)

	Sep̃	Quar̃ 1	Sep̃	Quar̃ 2
Mag. Loci	7	1 11 6	13	2 18 6
Mr Sanford	13	2 5 6	13	2 5 6
Mr Lux	0	0 0 0	0	0 0 0
Mr Wilson	0	0 10 6	0	0 0 0
Mr Thomas	6	1 1 6	1	0 3 6
Mr Coxe	7	1 4 6	8	1 8 0
Mr Godwyn	13	2 5 6	13	2 5 6
Mr Quick	4	0 14 6	3	0 10 6
Mr Land	13	2 5 6	12	2 2 0
Mr Fermyhough	9	1 11 6	13	2 2 0
Mr Dagge	13	2 5 6	13	2 5 6
D^s Walker	13	2 5 6	13	2 5 6
		18 0 6		18 10 0

36 10 6

Stipendia Mag^rii & Soc. (Quar̃ 1 & Quar̃ 2)

	Quar̃ 1		Quar̃ 2
Mag. Loci	10 4	Mr Godwyn	10 4
Mr Sanford	10 4	Mr Quick	10 4
Mr Lux	10 4	Mr Land	10 4
Mr Wilson	10 4	Mr Fermyhough	10 4
Mr Thomas	10 4	Mr Dagge	10 4
Mr Coxe	10 4	D^s Walker	10 4
3 2 0			

6 4 0

Stipendia Officialium (Quar̃ 1 & Quar̃ 2)

Mr Land	0 3 4	Matheseos	6 0 0
Decani Mr Fermyhough	0 3 4	Logicae	1 0 0
Mr Wilson	0 3 4	Poeseos	3 0 0
Bursarii Mr Thomas	0 3 4	Praelect: Ling: Graec:	3 0 0
Notar̃ Mr Coxe	0 3 4	Rhetor.	3 0 0
Bursar.	2 10 0		16 0 0
3 6 8			

19 6 8

Solvenda (Quar̃ 3 & Quar̃ 4)

	Sep̃	Quar̃ 3	Sep̃	Quar̃ 4
Magister Loci	13	2 18 6	7	1 11 6
Mr Sanford	4	0 14 0	9	1 11 6
Mr Lux	0	0 0 0	0	0 0 0
Mr Wilson	0	0 0 0	0	0 0 0
Mr Thomas	9	1 11 0	3	0 10 6
Mr Coxe	10	1 15 0	9	1 11 6
Mr Godwyn	12	2 2 0	12	2 2 0
Mr Quick	5	0 17 0	3	0 10 0
Mr Land	13	2 5 0	13	2 5 6
Mr Fermyhough	13	2 5 0	11	1 18 6
Mr Dagg	13	2 5 0	13	2 5 6
Mr Burchinshaw	13	2 5 0	13	2 5 6
Mr Walker	13	2 5 0	13	2 5 6
		21 6 0		18 18 0

40 4 0

Stipendia M^rii & Soc. (Quar̃ 3 & Quar̃ 4)

	Quar̃ 3		Quar̃ 4
Mag^r Loci	0 10 4	Mr Quick	0 10 4
Mr Sanford	0 10 4	Mr Land	0 10 4
Mr Lux	0 10 4	Mr Fermyhough	0 10 4
Mr Wilson	0 10 4	Mr Dagg	0 10 4
Mr Thomas	0 10 4	Mr Burchinshaw	0 10 4
Mr Coxe	0 10 4	Mr Walker	0 10 4
Mr Godwyn -	0 10 4		
3 12 4			3 2 0

6 14 4

Stipendia Officialium (Quar̃ 3 & Quar̃ 4)

Mr Land	0 3 4	Matheseos	6 0 0
Decani Mr Fermyhough	0 3 4	Logicae	1 0 0
Mr Wilson	0 3 4	Poeseos	3 0 0
Bursarii Mr Thomas	0 3 4	Praelector: Ling: Graec:	3 0 0
Notar̃ Mr Coxe	0 3 4	Rhetor.	3 0 0
Bursar.	2 10 0		
3 6 8			

19 6 8

TABLE 2 *continued*

Commemorationes

	£ s d			£ s d
Mag^r Loci	2 5		Mr Quick	2 5
Mr Sanford	2 5		Mr Land	2 5
Mr Lux	2 5		Mr Fernyhough	2 5
Mr Wilson	2 5		Mr Dagg	2 5
Mr Thomas	2 5		Mr Burchinshaw	2 5
Mr Coxe	2 5		Mr Walker	2 5
Mr Godwyn	2 5			
	16 11			14 6
				1 11 5

Exhibitiones Magistri

		£ s d
A	D^no Blundel	1 0 0
	D^na Peryham	1 0 0
	D^no Snell	5 0 0
		7 0 0

Solutum D^nae Guise   50 0 0

Communae Scholarium

Sep~		Quart 3	Sep~	Quart 4	
0	D^s Mills	0 0 0	0	0 0 0	
13	D^s Sanford	0 16 3	13	0 16 3	
0	D^s Capel	0 0 0	2	0 2 6	Fletcher
12	D^s Parker	0 15 0	12	0 15 0	
13	Farrington	0 16 3	1	0 1 3	
2	Adney	0 2 6	2	0 2 6	
13	Blake	0 16 3	6	0 8 9	
13	Skerrat	0 16 3	7	0 8 9	
13	Mills	0 16 3	8	0 10 0	
13	Brooke	0 16 3	13	0 16 3	
13	Martin	0 16 3	4	0 5 0	
13	Ellicombe	0 16 3	4	0 5 0	
10	Trap	0 12 6	1	0 1 3	
13	Pemberton	0 16 3	2	0 2 6	
		8 16 3		4 11 3	
				13 7 6	

Exhibitiones Magistri

		£ s d
A	D^no Blundel	1 0 0
A	D^na Peryham	1 0 0
A	D^no Snell	5 0 0
		7 0 0

Solut~ D^nae Guise   50 0 0

Communae Scholarium

Sep~		Quart 1	Sep~	Quart 2	
0	D^s Milles	0 0 6	0	0 0 0	
6	D^s Sanford	0 7 6	9	0 11 3	
0	D^s Capell	0 0 0	0	0 0 0	
2	Stephens	0 2 6	0	0 0 0	
0	Adney	0 0 0	3	0 3 9	
0	Blake	0 0 0	7	0 8 9	
0	Skerret	0 0 0	4	0 5 0	
13	Milles	0 16 6	13	0 16 3	
6	Parker	0 7 6	1	0 1 3	
0	Brooke	0 0 0	1	0 1 3	
9	Martin	0 11 3	3	0 3 9	
13	Ellicombe	0 16 3	13	0 16 3	
1	Trap	0 1 3	9	0 11 3	
0	Farrington	0 0 0	2	0 2 6	
			8	0 10 0	Pemberton
		3 2 6		4 11 3	7 13 9

TABLE 2 *continued*

Exhibitiones Scholarium

	Sep̃		Quart̃ 1	Sep̃	Quart̃ 2	
Peryham	2	Stephens	0 3 1	0	0 0 0	
	13	Milles	1 0 0	13	1 0 0	
	1	Trap	0 1 6½	9	0 13 10½	
Senr Soc.	9	Martin	0 6 11¼	3	0 2 3¾	
Bell	0	Brooke	0 0 0	1	0 1 1¾	
Blundel	6	D^{s} Sanford	0 11 6	9	0 17 3	
	0	Skerret	0 0 0	4	0 7 8	
Dunch	7	Jacob	1 1 6¼	13	2 0 0	
Snell	10	Mr Douglas	7 13 10½	13	10 0 0	
	13	D^{s} McGilchrist	10 0 0	13	10 0 0	
	13	D^{s} Murray	10 0 0	12	9 4 7½	
	13	Williamson	10 0 0	13	10 0 0	
Blagdon	13	Silke	3 14 3	13	3 14 3	
	Bibliotheca		1 5 0		1 5 0	
Brown	2	Stephens	0 2 0	3	0 3 0	
Mander	0	Blake	0 0 0	7	0 16 1¾	
			45 19 8½		50 5 3¼	96 4 11¾

Battellae Domus	Quart̃ 1	19 9 0	
	Quart̃ 2	0 5 10	19 14 10

Stipendia Servientium

Communae Promi & obsonatoris	4 6 8
Stipendium Promptuarii	3 6 8
Communae Coqui	2 3 4
Stipendium Culinae	3 6 8
Pro Carbonibus	20 0 0
Pro Purgatione Patinarum	0 3 4
Stipendium Pragmatici	0 13 4

Exhibitiones Scholarium

	Sep̃		Quart̃ 3	Sep̃	Quart̃ 4		
Peryham	0	D^{s} Capel	0 0 0	2	0 3 1	Fletcher	
	13	Mills	1 0 0	13	1 0 0		
	10	Trap	0 15 5	1	0 1 6½		
Senr Soc.	13	Martin	0 10 0	4	0 3 1		
Bell	13	Brooke	0 15 0	4	0 4 7		
Blundel	13	D^{s} Sanford	1 5 0	13	1 5 0		
	13	Skerrat	1 5 0	8	0 15 4		
Dunch	13	Jacob	2 0 0	13	2 0 0		
Snell	0	Mr Douglas	0 0 0	0	0 0 0		
	13	M^{r} McGilchrist	10 0 0	13	10 0 0		
	10	Mr Murray	7 13 10½	13	10 0 0		
	13	Williamson	10 0 0	13	10 0 0		
Blagdon	13	Silke	3 14 3	13	3 14 3		
	Bibliotheca		1 5 0		1 5 0		
Brown	0	D^{s} Stephens	0 0 0	0	0 0 0		
Mander	13	Blake	1 10 0	7	0 16 1¾		
			41 13 6½		41 8 0¼		83 1 7¼

Battellae Domus	Quart̃ 3	4 9 0	
	Quart̃ 4	0 1 11	4 10 11

Reditus & Stipendia Solvenda

Coll. Aedis X^{ti}	1 2 6
Coll. S^{tae} Magd^{ae}	0 4 0
Procuratoribus	0 2 0
Pro Concione	1 0 0
Bursario pro Diligentia	0 13 4
Pragmatico	0 13 4
Stipend̃ Promptuarii	3 6 8

TABLE 2 *continued*

	£	s	d
Stipendium Famuli Magistri			
Tonsoris	0	6	8
Janitoris	0	4	6
Lotricis	0	10	0
	1	5	0
	36	6	2

Expensae Contingentes	£	s	d
Pro Pretio Frumenti	0	1	0
Pro caeno amovendo	0	3	0
Servis Pontificis	0	5	0
Pro purgatione camini Culinae	0	3	0
Pro Lampadᵈ accendᵈ	0	13	0
Mareshallo Mendicorum	0	11	6
Ridge pro Mattis in Sacello pᴸ Billam	0	8	0
Pro Verriculo in usum Sacelli	0	0	6
Pro Paeto in Cam̃ Com̃	0	1	3
Pro Oblatione ad Templus Sᵗᵃᵉ Magdᵃᵉ	0	4	4
Tegulario Teasler pᴸ Bill	25	4	9
	27	15	4

	£	s	d
Communae Promi & Obsonatoris	4	6	8
Communae Coqui	2	3	4
Stipendᵈ Culinae	3	6	8
Pro Carbonibus	20	0	0
Pro Purgatione Patinarum	0	3	4
Pro Linteamentis Magᵣⁱ	0	0	8
Famulo Magᵣⁱ	0	6	8
Lotrici	1	5	0
Janitori	0	10	0
Tonsori	0	4	6
	40	8	0

Expensae Contingentes	£	s	d
Pro Pretio Frumenti	0	1	0
Pro Censu deducendᵈ & Reditu de Abbotsley 1735	4	2	6
Pro Censu deducendᵈ & Reditu de Woodstock 1735	1	16	0
Moderatori infer: Classis Logices	2	0	0
Pro Censu fenestris imposito	1	10	0
Candelario Cosins pᴸ Billᵐ	5	8	0
Mercatori Vicaris pᴸ Billam	6	17	6
Fabro Ferrario Pittaway pᴸ Billam	2	7	5
Doe pᴸ Billᵐ	2	17	0
Holdship pᴸ Billᵐ	0	14	0
Bradgate pro Vino pᴸ Billam	15	18	9
Hallifax pᴸ Billᵐ	0	16	0
Lapicidae Townsend pᴸ Billᵐ	8	5	11
Fabro Aerario Pain pᴸ Billᵐ	9	3	10
Tub pro Candelis in Aula pᴸ Billᵐ	0	6	6
Plumbario Cole pᴸ Billam	5	1	6
Dolario Tub pᴸ Billam	1	2	6
Pro Literis accept̃	0	1	6
Magᵗᵒ Walker pro Gradu	0	13	4
Fabro Lignario Franklyn pᴸ Billam	8	7	6¾
	77	10	9¾

TABLE 2 *continued*

Summa hujus dimidii Anni recipienda	488	7	11½
Summa solvenda	306	16	2¾
Summa recipienda excedit Solvendam	181	11	8¾

Summa hujus dimidii Anni recipienda	600	00	11
Summa hujus dimidii Anni solvenda	343	15	3
Summa hujus dimidii Annie recipienda excedit solvendam	256	5	8
Summa totius Anni recipienda	1088	8	10½
Summa totius Anni solvenda	650	11	5¾
Summa totius Anni recipienda excedit solvendam	437	17	4¾

Mag^r Loci	60	0	0
Mr Sanford	30	0	0
Mr Lux	30	0	0
Mr Wilson	30	0	0
Mr Thomas	30	0	0
Mr Coxe	30	0	0
Mr Godwyn	30	0	0
Mr Quick	30	0	0
Mr Land	30	0	0
Mr Fernyhough	30	0	0
Mr Dagg	30	0	0
Mr Burchinshaw	30	0	0
Mr Walker	30	0	0
Domus	17	17	4¾
Summa total	437	17	4¾

TABLE 3

Computus finalis M^{ri} Wilson et M^{ri} Thomas Bursar̃ pro Anno 1735

Recipienda

Reditus Status	1 Dimid̃ Anni	256 17 7		
	2 Dimid̃ Anñ	262 16 4	519 13 11	
Reditus Frumenti	1 Dimid̃ Anñ	17 2 1		
	2 Dimid̃ Anñ	142 4 9		
	1 Dimid̃ Anñ	214 8 3½	159 6 10	
Proficua	2 Dimid̃ Anñ	193 6 10	407 15 1½	
Pro Caponibus			1 13 0	
Suma recipiend̃ in Redit̃ Profic̃ et Capoñ			1088 8 10½	
	1 Quarter̃	513 4 5		
	2 Quarter̃	461 1 8		
In Battellis	3 Quarter̃	733 11 3		
	4 Quarter̃	590 14 8	2299 12 0	
Remañ in Promptuario in fine Anni			67 17 9	
Sum̃ total recipiend̃ in Redit̃ Profic̃ Cap̃ Batt̃ &c			3454 18 7½	

Computus finalis M^{ri} Wilson et M^{ri} Thomas Bursar̃ pro Anno 1735

Solvenda

M^{ro} et sociis	143 17 7	
Dñae Guise	100 0 0	
Stip̃ Scholar̃ et Exhib̃	200 7 10	
Battellae Domus	24 5 9	
Stip̃ serṽ &c	76 14 2	1088 8 10½
Expensae contingentes	105 6 1¾	
Sum̃a Dividend̃ in fine Anni	437 17 4¾	
Pro Pane	110 16 6	
Potu	216 8 0	
Butyro	49 3 0	
Caseo	74 2 8	
Lanio	297 8 0	
Supra Com̃	158 18 10	
Increment̃	14 17 0	
Bursar̃	1376 9 11	2366 9 9
Remañ in Promptuar̃ in eunte Anno	68 5 10	
Sum̃a tot̃ Solvend̃ M^{ro} Soc̃ &c pro Pane Potu &c	3454 18 7½	

TABLE 3 continued

Recepta

In Redit̃ Profic̃ & Capoñ		946 14 7½
In Battellis		2140 7 5
Suñ tot̃ recept̃ in Redit̃ Profic̃ Cap̃ & Batt̃		3087 2 0½

Recepta in Cautionibus

S. Abbott	5	
C. Bennett	10	
Mʳ Buller	15	
Mʳ Carew	15	
C. Carew	10	
C. Coxe	10	
S. Daddo	5	
C. Daniel	10	
C. Fletcher	10	
S. Gregory	5	
B. Higgins	6	
B. Jones	6	
C. Milles	10	
Mʳ Masters	15	
C. Preston	10	
C. Princeps	10	
Mʳ Rickards	15	
C. Sanford	10	
S. Skinner	5	
D. Edward Turner	15	
C. Trap	10	
B. Watkins	6	
B. Wallis	6	
		219 0 0

Arreragia

In Battellis	a Dⁿᵒ Drake ex parte	30 0 0	4 14 0
In Reditibus	a Dⁿᵒ Beadon	5 0	30 5 0
	Hicks pro Caponibus		

Soluta

Mᵗᵒ Soc̃ Scholar̃ Servientibus &c		1088 8 10½
Pro Pane Potu Caseo Butyro &c		2298 3 11
Suñ tot̃ Mᵗᵒ Soc̃ & pro Pane Potu &c		3386 12 9½

Soluta in Cautionibus

C. Armstrong	7 0 0	
C. Ashton	7 0 0	
Mʳ Barter	7 0 0	
Mʳ Beachcroft	7 0 0	
C. Bound	7 0 0	
Mʳ Gardner	7 0 0	
Mʳ Higford	7 0 0	
Dˢ Haynes	7 0 0	
C. Field	7 0 0	
Mʳ Millchamp	7 0 0	
C. Nevington	7 0 0	
C. Trap	10 0 0	
Dˢ Whitler	7 0 0	
Mʳ Webber	7 0 0	
Dˢ Wheeler	4 0 0	
		105 0 0

TABLE 3 *continued*

Recepta pro Domo

	£	s	d
Dividenδ in fine Anni	17	17	4¾
Pro fiñ Woodstock	1	3	0
a Mᵗᵒ Bree pro Horto	2	2	0
Pro fiñ Heyton	4	0	0
a D Dño Edward Turner	20	0	0
a Mᵗⁱˢ Carew Buller Masters Rickards	40	0	0
Legař Dñae Venn	50	0	0
	135	2	4¾

Comparatio

	£	s	d
Suñ totař recipienda	3454	18	7½
Suñ totař recepta in Rediť Battełł	3087	2	0½
Suñ non recepta ex altera parte Libri	367	16	7
Faciunt suñā recipiendam	3454	18	7½

	£	s	d
Suñ recepta in Rediť Battełł	3087	2	1½(sic)
Cautionibus	219	0	0
Arreragiis Battełł	4	14	0
Redituum	30	5	0
Pro Domo	135	2	4¾
Suñ totař recepť	3476	3	6¼

Soluta pro Domo

	£	s	d		£	s	d
Aedi Xᵗⁱ pro fiñ et feoδ	49	13·	8				
Anñ Taylor	1	1	0				
Coñissař in causa Elsworth pro feoδ Venñ	1	9	2				
Lapicidae Townshend p⁼ Biłł	76	11	2				
Bursař prioris Anni	2	2	5¼				
Legař Dñae Venn	50	0	0				
Pro Literis	0	0	4				
Pro Horto	35	9	8		216	7	5¼

Comparatio

	£	s	d
Suñ totař solvenda	3454	18	7½
Suñ toť soluť Mᵗᵒ Soč &c pro Pane Potu &c.	3386	12	9½
Suñ non soluta ex altera parte Libri	68	5	10
Faciunt suñam solvendam	3454	18	7½

	£	s	d
Suñ soluť Mᵗᵒ Sociis &c et pro Pane Potu &c	3386	12	9½
In Cautionibus	105	0	0
Pro Domo	216	7	5¼
Suñ totař soluť	3708	0	2¾

	£	s	d
Suñ totař recepta	3476	3	6¼
Suñ totař soluta	3708	0	2¾
Suñā totař Soluť excedit recepť	231	16	8

Nov 6 1736 Received of Mr. Thomas
the Ballance of this Account
Thomas Wilson

5   JOHN JONES

---

*Sound Religion and Useful Learning:
the rise of Balliol under John Parsons
and Richard Jenkyns, 1798–1854*

Text with documents

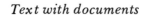

A fuller version of this article is available in typescript in the College Library, together with appendices listing and giving skeletal biographical information about A) The Master and Fellows 1800–1850, and B) Open Scholars 1827–1850.

SOUND RELIGION AND USEFUL LEARNING: THE RISE OF BALLIOL UNDER JOHN PARSONS AND RICHARD JENKYNS, 1798–1854.

It is now generally agreed that the torpor and decline of the University of Oxford in the eighteenth century have been much exaggerated,[1] and Richard Hunt has given some support to this revisionist view in relation to Balliol.[2] But it is still undeniable that the College's affairs were in an unsatisfactory state when John Parsons was elected Master in 1798.

John Parsons was the son of Isaac Parsons, butler of Corpus Christi College. He attended Magdalen College School and then Wadham, whence he was elected a Fellow of Balliol in 1785. Accounts of him do not mention any scholarly works, but in fact he was responsible for the preliminary work on the preparation of the Oxford edition of Strabo.[4] Association with this was not something for later writers to advertise, as it contained many errors which had been seized and enlarged upon by the *Edinburgh Review* in one of its scornful attacks on Oxford scholarship and education.[5] As a young Fellow he was also a regular anonymous contributor to the *Monthly Review*[6] until its political position became more inconsistent with his own (which was Tory through and through[7]) than he could stand. Although frequently incapacitated by gout for weeks on end, he was a dominant figure in the University throughout his Mastership. His main contribution was as a member of the committee which prepared the Statute of 1800 introducing Honours Examinations.[8] It may seem paradoxical to a modern reader that an unshakable Tory should have been behind what appears now as a reforming movement, but it must be remembered that in the thinking of the time laxity in matters of religion and scholarship was associated with revolution. A tightening-up of "academical discipline" was a defence of the established order of things.[9]

At the turn of the century, Parsons presided over a resident body averaging some half a dozen Fellows (about half the total), perhaps three or four B.A. members and twenty-five or so undergraduates, including a single Servitor working his way.[10] The variation of the number of undergraduates in residence between 1700 and 1860 is

shown in Figure 1. Most of the Fellows had been undergraduate
Scholars and had succeeded to fellowships with little or no effort,
as the 1507 Statutes still in force gave Scholars a *ceteris paribus* advantage over *extranei* in fellowship elections, and a series of disputes
and visitatorial appeals had failed to establish clearly the limits of
this advantage.[11] Under the same Statutes each of the Scholars was
appointed to serve a Fellow on the nomination of that Fellow: although the service was by 1800 purely notional, the system of scholarship places being in the gift of individual Fellows had survived. An

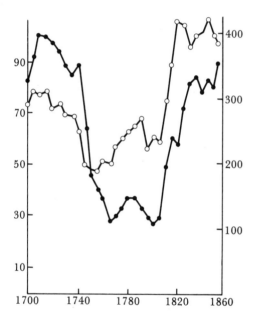

Figure 1. Dots and left hand axis: five year averages of numbers of undergraduates in residence at Balliol, derived from A. Clark's lists in the
Library. Encircled dots and right hand axis: five year averages of
matriculations p.a. in the University as a whole.

in-bred society was the inevitable result. Appointments to the scholarships, which carried the expectation of fellowships in due course, may sometimes have been made on merit, but it is obvious from the registers that family connection was commonly involved.[12] The in-breeding was exacerbated by the fact that two of the Scholars were appointed from Blundell's School, Tiverton, by the Blundell Feoffes, who had acquired this right in return for bailing the College out of financial difficulties in the seventeenth century. These Scholars had an almost inalienable right of succession to Blundell Foundation fellowships, of which there were two with the same voting rights as ordinary fellowships. It was unusual for a Fellow to retain his place for long. A fellowship was for most just a place in a queue for College livings, which were offered on vacancy to the Fellows in order of seniority. The waiting time might be spent in desultory study or with one or two pupils, but few of the Fellows were career academics. George Powell was an exception to this pattern. He was elected as an *extraneus* from Brasenose in 1786, surviving an appeal to the Visitor by the minority, and lived in College, immersed in his Hebrew and astronomy, until he died in 1830.[13] Since, however, he lived as a recluse and took very few pupils, he made little impact.

Richard Jenkyns was admitted a Scholar in 1800, probably as a result of representations by John Randolph, Bishop of Oxford, whose protegé and pupil he appears to have been.[14] When Robert Finch[15] came up two years later he wrote to his father that Jenkyns was one of the few "at all worthy of distinction as being *literally scholars*".[16] In 1803, following an open competition, he was elected to a fellowship.

1. *J. Jenkyns (Richard Jenkyns' father) to R. Jenkyns (Richard Jenkyns' godfather),* *5 Dec. 1803*[17]

Among the many letters of congratulation I have received on my son's success, one from the Bishop of Oxford gave us no uncommon degree of satisfaction. He thus expresses himself.

> I cannot refrain from writing a line of congratulation on your son's success at Balliol. I had my doubts about it, for tho' I knew the Master was his friend I saw he was afraid of a Party in the College not being disposed to do what was best & there was also a powerful competitor or two. It has

turned out however right & there is this additional satisfaction that the Fellowship has been fairly earned by your
son's conduct and diligence. I hope he will go on deserving
of it & derive from it real benefit to himself & comfort to
you & the rest of his Family.

With love &c . . . J.O.

It appears that the Bp. took a particular interest in the event of this
election as he had previously requested him to give him an early acct.
of it. Richard says, that it was honourable & nearly unanimous.   1]

The opposition probably came from George Powell, Thomas Cooke
Rogers and William Warrington, who were friends of Samuel Gamlen,[18]
a disappointed candidate.[19] Although described by Robert Finch as a
"self-sufficient prig" who "retails only the opinions of others",[20]
Jenkyns was straightaway the most effective teaching Fellow and remained so practically on his own for most of the next decade. The
main teaching mode was College lectures: the surviving accounts condemn them as tedious recitations of closely defined and prescribed
material which interfered with any plans a man might have for wider
reading.[21] There is a glimpse of what sounds like a modern tutorial in
1802.

2. R. Finch to T. Finch (his father),   *26 Mar. 1802*[22]

I find Mr. Rogers a pleasant tutor & well-inform'd scholar. Sometimes
an interview takes place between me and himself in which we not only
read, but criticise and descant upon the author before us . . .   2]

But this seems to have been regarded as a novelty and no further
allusions to tutorial-type teaching are found in this period.
   Samuel Gamlen presented himself as a fellowship candidate again
on the next occasion, in 1806, as did his Scholar friends, Robert Finch
and Benjamin Cheese. There were two external candidates and everyone was well aware from the outset that the choice was really between
one of these, William Vaux of Christ Church, and Gamlen. Vaux
was elected by the votes of John Parsons, Charles Wood, William
Marshall, Matthew Hodge, Richard Jenkyns and John Mousley, against
those of George Powell, Thomas Cooke Rogers and William Warrington.[23] The election threw the College into a twelve-month turmoil   .

which culminated in two separate appeals to the Visitor by Rogers and Warrington[24] and by the three Scholars.[25] Powell supported the Fellows' appeal but for some reason did not sign it.[26] The principal basis of both appeals was that three Scholars, whose qualifications were adequate, had presented themselves and one of these should, according to Statute, have been preferred to an *extraneus*. There were also complaints about the conduct of the election. It is clear from Finch's private correspondence that the two sets of appellants were not just trying to get Gamlen in on a technicality: they felt that Parsons "the tyrant" and his party had acted with "interested partiality"[27] to bring in another Fellow of their own persuasion. The three Scholars were widely read and cultivated men, but had no respect for Parsons' regimented system of study and examination, which was "an insult upon sense and learning".[28] Gamlen also suspected that the fact that he had "Tivertonian connections", although he was not on the Blundell Foundation, had counted against him.[29]

Parsons made a vigorous and lengthy answer[30] to the appeals, insisting that Vaux, who had recently been examined publicly, was the better qualified, that the *ceteris paribus* preference for Scholars needed to be applied with caution in view of the fact that Scholars were appointed without competition, and that the election had been properly carried out in every respect. Richard Prosser[31] was called in to assist in the drafting of this answer.[32] Prosser, as a Fellow from 1773 to 1793, had been the earliest of the reforming Tory disciplinarians to appear in Balliol, and the College's fortunes had taken a temporary turn for the better under his influence. He enjoyed a sort of Honorary Fellow status, together with his distinguished pupil Matthew Baillie, the royal physician.[33] The Visitor was Shute Barrington, Bishop of Durham, who was another "vigorous champion of the protestant establishment".[34] Barrington rejected the appeals, and for good measure solemnly rebuked the two Fellows for their conduct and language.[35] Parsons had already seen to it that Rogers had very few pupils, and neither Gamlen nor Finch resided again. Cheese, on the other hand, wrote to Finch that although "The Master, I suppose, would be glad to ferret me out", he was determined to ride the storm.[36] This he did until 1810 by which time he was sufficiently restored to Parsons' favour to be elected a Chaplain Fellow.[37] The affair cleared the air on the openness of fellowship elections, except those on the Blundell Foundation, for ever.

Plate 1. John Parsons, 1808.

The first class list was published in 1802. Balliol names first appeared in the class lists of 1808, the first Firsts were obtained in 1810 and an intermittent trickle continued for the remainder of Parsons' rule. He was appointed Dean of Bristol in 1810 and Bishop of Peterborough in 1813, and after this was often absent. His Vicegerent was generally Jenkyns, whose influence therefore grew, extending even to the control of admissions from 1816.[39] As senior Tutor Jenkyns also ran 'Collections' or 'College Examinations', which had been introduced at about the turn of the century (they are first mentioned by Finch). Towards the end of term all junior members, except those with imminent University examinations, were orally examined by the Master and tutors.

3. R. Finch to R. Roberts, *3 April 1802*[39]

It is customary & indeed obligatory in our college to analyze every author, whom we read, in the same nature as the collections at X:t church. I think this is a good exercise since it facilitates the retention of striking events in the memory & reduces the matter of a book to a skeleton as it were . . .   3]

4. W.S. Hamilton to his mother, *2 April 1808*[40]

I have been so busy with Collections, which are public examinations, at the end of each term, on all the books we have read during the continuance of the term, before the master and public lecturers . . .   4]

It is clear from the log-book which Jenkyns kept from 1812 that these examinations, which were largely if not entirely oral, were far from perfunctory. They have evolved on one hand into the informal College written examinations which are still known as Collections, and on the other into the interviews which undergraduates have with the Master and their tutors (Handshaking) at the end of term.

In 1816, Noel Ellison and Charles Ogilvie, both of whom had been placed in the First class, were elected Fellows. Charles Girdlestone, another First class man, was elected in 1818. Tradition gives this trio the credit for the marked improvement in the fortunes of the College which began at about this time and soon led to a waiting list for admissions. Ogilvie, who was the most important and served longest, was a vigorous and outspoken man who later described himself as "an attached and zealous member of the Church of England as by Law established".[41] He was for many years a correspondent of, and seems to have been much influenced by, Hannah More,[42] the religious writer, who was "much pleased" with Ogilivie's "account of the good discipline and studious character of the College."[43] "Genial, joyous, graceful Ellison", a Corpus contemporary and intimate friend of John Keble,[44] was rigidly High Church: once, when Rector of Huntspill, he refused to bury a Methodist child until required to do so by his bishop.[45] Girdlestone was of a more liberal inclination.[46]

Parsons died of "suppressed gout" on 12 March 1819 and was buried in Chapel a week later.[47] Jenkyns was the obvious establishment candidate to succeed him, but Powell and Rogers were still Fellows and Warden Tournay of Wadham felt it necessary to suggest to Prosser that he should use his influence to procure Jenkyns' election.

5. *W. Tournay to R. Prosser,*   *12 Mar. 1819*[48]

Our excellent Friend Mr. Jenkyns ought assuredly to be the new Master. Such, you know, was the earnest wish of him, whom we have lost. Can you in any way assist to promote his success by applications, direct or circuitous, to any of the Electors? I fear that his claims are not properly acknowledged . . .   5]

In the event Jenkyns was elected on 23 April 1819. The many published accounts of him as Master are dominated by anecdote. A small man — "The little Master" — he was often ridiculously pompous in dress and manner and many bizarre incidents were well-remembered and perhaps a little embroidered by memoir writers long after his death. He was no great scholar but made no pretensions in that direction, writing nothing for publication except obituary notices for the *Gentleman's Magazine.* He was primarily a shrewd organiser and good judge of men who had a clear view of what was right, knew what he wanted to achieve and usually got his way, in part perhaps as a result of his approach to meetings.

6. *From the private notebook used by R. Jenkyns when he was Vice-Chancellor between 1824 and 1828*[49]

N.B. — Never come unprepared to a Meeting — but by previous

enquiry & conversation again a competent knowledge of the business
to be discussed & form an opinion — & a decided one too, upon the
same —   6]

One of the earliest problems faced by Jenkyns as Master was posed
by the will of Thomas How, a former Fellow who left two thousand
pounds on trust for the foundation of two closed exhibitions at the
College. The exhibitions were to be for the sons of Somerset and
Devonshire clergymen respectively, subject to an over-riding preference for any relative of How's who might offer himself. Foundations of this type had been accepted gladly in the previous two
centuries, but closed exhibitions were no longer as respectable as they
had been. Furthermore, the region which would have been favoured
by this particular arrangement was the home ground of the Blundell
Foundation, which had proved a parasitic burden and had yet to
produce anyone of distinction. The College had learned its lesson and
How's proposed benefaction was refused.[50] Little could be done
about the existing Blundell Foundation, but Jenkyns' consistent
policy, which he spelt out much later in his life, was to keep it under
pressure.

7. R. Jenkyns to J. Kaye, (the Visitor, Bishop of Lincoln),
12 Aug. 1848[51]

The Blundell composition, or rather the Foundation resting upon
it, as it ever has been, will continue to be, the very bane of our Society.
Extreme poverty, I suspect, compelled our Predecessors to make so
improvident a bargain . . . My principle, as that of my respected Predecessor, always has been, to deal strict *justice*, but to give no *advantage* (as was formerly the case with an overpowering party in the
College from Devonshire) to the Blundell Foundation. They must in
justice have their *pound* of flesh — but not an *ounce* more.   7]

In 1825, for example, the progression of the Blundell Scholar
Edward Kitson to a fellowship was obstructed, albeit only temporarily.

8. From the English Register,   *29 Nov. 1825*

In the examination . . . Mr. Kitson appeared from habitual neglect
so grossly deficient in the literary qualifications required by the

Statutes of the College (the force and authority of which the framers
of the Blundell composition expressly recognize) that the Society did
not feel themselves justified in proceeding to an election; since the
admission to a fellowship of a Candidate under Mr. Kitson's circumstances seemed to them in their consciences adverse at once to the
letter and spirit of their institution.   8]

Although the College was powerless to change the way the Blundell
places were filled, it had complete freedom of action so far as the
Domus Scholarship places were concerned because they were without
geographical restrictions. All that was necessary was for the Fellows
to surrender their rights of individual nomination, which they agreed
to do in 1827.

9. *From the English Register*[52]
    AD 1828. March 1st
    At a College Meeting, holden this day,
    Present, the Master, Mr. Ogilvie, Mr. Round, Mr. Carr, Mr. Chapman
and Mr. Moberly
Resolution respecting Minutes of a Meeting in May, 1827
    It was resolved that the following Minutes of proceedings at a Col-
lege Meeting, holden in May last, be entered in this Register:

Scholarships of the College
    "At a College Meeting holden in May, 1827, the attention of the
    "Society was directed to the subject of the Scholarships; and
    "to the inconvenience, which had recently been found to arise
    "from long continued vacancies in that essential part of the
    "Body Corporate. To prevent such inconvenience for the future,
    "it was deemed expedient to attempt a slight modification of
    "the letter of the Statute, which might be entirely consistent
    "with its spirit; and, after mature deliberation and a clear
    "statement of the sentiments of the *non-resident* as well as
    "resident members of the Society, it was resolved:

    "I. That the Master and those of the Fellows who possess the
    "right shall relinquish the practice of nominating individually
    "in turn to their own Scholarships and leave them open to a
    "general competition of Candidates, whether members of the

"College or not, subject however to the statutable limitation
"of age &c.

"II. That, in order to give greater importance and notoriety
"to the election of Scholars, one Election only shall take
"place in any one of the Academical Terms, and the Master shall
"give public notice of the day fixed for filling up any vacancy
"or vacancies one month at least before the time fixed for such
"election.

"III. That the Examination of the Candidates shall be
"conducted by the Master and the Senior Dean and shall be
"similar to the Examination of Candidates for Fellowships, due
"allowance being made in the selection of Books, subjects for
"composition, Questions &c for the respective difference of
"age and attainments in the two cases".

Increase of allowance to Scholars
At the same Meeting, it was resolved that the Weekly allowance
to the Scholars during their residence be increased from Five
to Ten shillings.   9]

The first three Open Scholars were elected, after examination at
length, on 29 November 1827.[53]

10. *From the Latin Register,*

Eodem die electi sunt in Scholares Domus, ex antiqua fundatione,
Petrus Samuel Henricus Payne, Edvardus Hartopp Grove et Edvardus
D'Oyley Barwell; quippe qui Magistro et Sociis, jure suo singulos
Scholares nominandi decedentibus (vid. Reg. Angl. Martii 1, 1828)
post Examinationem habitam, prae cunctis Candidatis sese commen-
daverint . . . [54]   10]

Two of the three came from Shrewsbury, and correspondence about
the examination survives in the papers of Samuel Butler, the great
Headmaster.

11. *E. Grove (father of E.H. Grove) to S. Butler*[55]
                          Kings Arms Inn, Oxford, Nov. 29 1827

My dear Sir,
This has been a day of bustle and anxiety but I am unwilling to

bring it to a close without transmitting to you the result of the late
Examination at Balliol which after four days of what has generally been
considered hard work has pla[ced] Payne — Grove & Barwell as the
successful Candidates for the vacant Scholarships of Balliol — Payne
has also got the Exhibition and Mr. Barwell of Winchester has got a
vacant Scholarship which was not declared or known till after considerable enquiry and discussion this Evening — This circumstance has
placed Mr. Barwell with the other two, but I trust you will have an
honest pride & a heartfelt pleasure in finding two of your own Pupils
at the head of the list & not the less so when you know that they were
placed in competition with Ten or Eleven Candidates and some three
or four Members of the University.[56]
    The Dean was pleased to say publicly in my hearing that Edward
had done himself great credit and that Balliol would consider his admission as a member an honour to the Society. I am told that he com-
plimented both Payne and Grove in his public st[atement] but I was
not present . . .   11]

12. R. Jenkyns to S. Butler[57]

My dear Sir,
    In thanking you for your letter & the very candid & impartial testi-
mony which you gave in favour of your Pupils, I cannot deny myself
the gratification of adding a few words on the subject of their merits
— allow me then to assure you that they all acquitted themselves well
& afforded the most satisfactory evidence by their sound & accurate
scholarship of the excellent system of instruction in which they had
been trained, more particularly Messrs. Payne & Grove. The former
indeed pleased us so much by the display of his talents & attainments
that having agreed to give him the more honourable but not most
lucrative distinction of Scholar, we without hesitation adjudged to
him the Exhibition also to which as educated at Shrewsbury School
he was eligible — I hope & trust that by his future diligence & profi-
ciency he will reflect equal credit on our decision & the place of his
early education.
    Should any circumstance bring you to Oxford I shall have much

pleasure in seeing you at Balliol – In the meantime believe me to be, my dear Sir,

Y^{rs} faithfully

R Jenkyns

Balliol College
Nov. 30 1827
Mr. Turner's examination was so satisfactory that should any contingent vacancy occur I shall be disposed to give him the benefit of it without further trial.[58]   12]

The arrangements were an immediate success, attracting a succession of outstanding men. Shortly after the 1833 examination Payne reported to Butler:

13. *P.S.H. Payne to S. Butler,*   *1 Dec. 1833*[59]

I have been for the last week engaged, as one of the fellows, in the examination for our Balliol Scholarships. There were 30 candidates and it was a competition only second in point of severity to that for the Ireland. Most of the public schools sent in some of their best men . . .   13]

It was usual for the examination to begin with a call on the Master.

14. *A.P. Stanley to his sister Mary,*   *27 Nov. 1833*[60]

We went on Saturday to the Head of Balliol to present our certificates, etc. – we were all shown in to the drawing room – and then brought up one by one to him – something like a dentist's operation – I had been cautioned to make as beautiful a bow as I possibly could, as he is very ceremonious . . .   14]

This was followed by a week of written examinations involving translations and composition in Latin, Greek and English and also papers in Divinity and Mathematics.[61] In some respects accounts in memoirs and letters make it sound like a modern examination, although a week including two consecutive days of eight hours' writing would be regarded as punitive now. The week's work came rapidly to a dramatic climax:

15. *A.P. Stanley to his sister Mary,*   *29 Nov. 1833*[62]

We all assembled in the Hall and had to wait one hour — the room getting fuller and fuller of the Rugby Oxonians crowding in from various parts to hear the result. At last the Dean appeared in his white robes and moved up to the head of the table. He first began a long preamble — that they were well satisfied with all — that those who were disappointed were many in proportion to those who were successful, etc., — all this time everyone was listening in the most intense eagerness — and I almost bit my lips off — till 'the successful candidates are Mr. Stanley' — I gave a great jump — and there was a half shout among the Rugby men — (the next was Lonsdale from Eton). The Dean then took me into the Chapel where was the Master and all the Fellows — in white robes. And there I swore that I would not dissipate the property, reveal the secrets, or disobey the Statutes of the College — I was then made to kneel on the steps and admitted to the rank of Scholar and Exhibitioner of Balliol College nomine Patris, Filii et Spiritus — I then wrote my name in a book and so was finished — I am to be matriculated today.   15]

The examination week — always the last in November — was a very busy time for the Fellows. Non-residents returned to Oxford if they possibly could and all present took part in the examinations and elections. The Master's influence on the whole business was considerable. He was effectively Tutor for Admissions. He also had two votes in the election. On one occasion he got his way when in a two against three minority: the doubling of his vote made it three all and the tie was broken by the statutory obligation of the most junior Fellow (who was of the original majority) to change sides.[63] It is pleasing to note that Jenkyns' man, Alexander Grant, had a distinguished career, becoming Principal of Edinburgh University, whereas the majority choice slipped into untraceable obscurity.

In 1834, the scholarship scheme "having been found productive of the best results" was, "with a view of enforcing its perpetual observance", embodied in the Statutes.[64] It was the unanimous view of those who saw its effects at first hand that this reform was the making of Victorian Balliol. To whom is the credit due? Davis tells us that Jenkyns merely concurred "not because he expected any good from the change, but because the tutors were unanimous on the other side'', and oft repeated tradition singles out Ogilvie as the prime mover. Ogilvie certainly played a large part in the affair: the principal minute is in his hand, and he it was who took the new Statute to the Visitor for confirmation.[65] However, Ogilvie was very much the Master's man, and it seems hardly plausible to suggest that Jenkyns, who was ruling all departments of the College with an iron hand at this time, acquiesced weakly in a radical change he was dubious about. There is no hint of this in the immediate documents, and judgements more nearly contemporary than Davis give unreserved praise to Jenkyns.[66]

Another novel notion which took root in the 1820s was the distribution of prizes to members for excellence in academic competition.

16. *From the English Register,*   *20 Dec. 1822*

It was agreed to present a set of Books to Mr. Bazalgette by way of testifying our sense of the distinction lately obtained by him at his Examination in the Schools and of his uniformly meritorious conduct during his residence in College.   16]

The award of a prize for a First was routine thereafter. In his will made in 1827 George Powell established a prize for an English Essay competition,[67] and Richard Prosser's will of 1828 setting up six exhibitions with the objective of encouraging the "Intellectual Improvement of the Undergraduates of Balliol College combined with general good conduct",[68] can be seen as part of the same trend.

The open scholarship examination also attracted candidates who hoped to do well enough to obtain the offer of a Commoner place, and entrance to the College became very competitive. Basevi's new building had been built in 1826 "In consequence of the deficiency of Rooms to satisfy the very numerous & pressing applications for admission",[69] but the College was soon over-subscribed again. During the 'thirties and 'forties Jenkyns had a regular stream of ingratiating letters about admission. The disposal of Commoner places was at the sole discretion of the Master, and even a senior Fellow could not be confident of getting a protegé in "except under the circumstance of his appearing to advantage in a scholarship examination". In 1834 Robert Peel failed in an approach on behalf of a friend's son and several peers and bishops were also gently rebuffed.[70] By the mid 'thirties, Balliol had arrived, and was generally recognised as a leading College. Not only were its open scholarships highly regarded, but its open fellowships were the blue riband[71] of the University, and success bred success. The College's share of the Firsts awarded rose steadily from an average of about 5% of the total in 1807–14 to an average of 20% in 1845–54, overtaking Christ Church whose share fell from nearly 40% in 1807–14 to about 10% in 1845–54.

The tutors in 1828 were *"Ogilvie, Round, Moberly*; also not quite or nearly equal to these three there were *Chapman* for Mathematics and *F. Oakeley*, a weak Tutor".[72] The role of the College tutor was still the delivery of College lectures to classes rather than tutorial teaching, and those who wanted more intimate assistance made their own arrangements with a 'Private Tutor' or 'Coach', although in 1836 and 1837 "a Senior Fellow of the name of Carr, occasionally looked over the weekly Essay, dividing the work with the Master".[73] Nor, it seems, was there much informal social contact between tutors and undergraduates. Round retired from Oxford in 1831, and Ogilvie, who had at one time been "generally designated in public opinion as the future Master of Balliol",[74] dropped out of the teaching in 1830, resigning in 1834. Moberly vacated his fellowship by marriage, also in 1834, but remained as the first married tutor of the College[75] for nearly a year before leaving to be Headmaster of Winchester. Tutorial appointments were the Master's prerogative and Jenkyns invited A.C. Tait to fill Moberly's place.

17. *R. Jenkyns to A.C. Tait*[76]
Dinder, nr. Wells, Somerset, Aug. 26, 1835

My Dear Sir,

You probably are aware that the event of Moberly's honourable appointment at Winchester will deprive Balliol of his valuable services, & subject me to the necessity of endeavouring to supply his place in the tuition.

I cannot but feel <u>extreme</u> anxiety on this point – the credit, the character, which the College has for many years past happily maintained, so mainly depend on the talents, learning & (what is equally if not more important) the <u>habitual</u> & <u>constant diligence</u> of the Tutors in continuing our system of discipline and education, that I am naturally desirous of securing, if possible, the assistance of one who has himself been brought up under it. —

My anxiety is however in some measure relieved by the hope that *your* engagements will allow you to give the College the benefit of your knowledge and experience; & I now hasten to express this hope that if you accede to my wishes, you may have ample opportunity to make such arrangements as may enable you to enter upon your official duties at the end of the present Vacation . . .   17]

Tait was the leading tutor for the next seven years together with, for most of the time, Robert Scott. W.G. Ward was Mathematical Lecturer: J.G. Lonsdale and E.C. Woollcombe came in the early forties. An important development during this period was the agreement, probably prompted by Scott, that "the use of the books in the Library should under certain conditions & the vigilant attention of the Tutors, be allowed to the Undergraduates of the College".[77] This was a magnanimous sharing of what had previously been reserved strictly for Fellows, and was consistent with the marked easing of the formality of the relationships between teachers and taught which also took place.

18. *From W.C. Lake's reminiscences of A.C. Tait*[78]

He gave me at once that impression of strength and spirit which I always associated with him through life. I soon became almost, or quite, his earliest College pupil; and felt at once his genuine kindness and interest in his pupils. In those days at Oxford — I know not how it is now — intimacies between tutors and pupils ripened rapidly. I was his companion on a short tour in Belgium and Germany in 1837, and again in 1839, and during my last undergraduate year in 1838 was constantly with him . . .   18]

Tait was at the centre of an increased earnestness among the tutors about the teaching arrangements and methods,[79] and when he resigned he was concerned that the efficient machine he had established should not be jeopardised.

19. *A.C. Tait to R. Jenkyns,*   *29 July 1842*[80]

I was yesterday elected Headmaster of Rugby. It therefore becomes my duty, with very mixed feelings, to resign into your hands the

Tutorship which I have now held for seven years . . . It is satisfactory
to think, that, in going away thus suddenly, I leave two colleagues in
the Tutorship behind me, who have your full confidence, & of whose
zeal & ability for their work there can be no question. Of Woollcombe,
with whom I am the most intimate, I must speak in the very highest
terms. I never knew anyone more really alive to the importance of the
duties which devolve on him as Tutor, taking a more deep interest in
the welfare both of his pupils and of the College generally or who
would be more ready to make any sacrifice for his duty. Of the
Scholarship and ability of both Woollcombe & Lonsdale, we, who
remember their examination, must always have the highest opinion:
and of the admirable disposition and conciliatory manners of both,
as their colleague, I must speak most highly . . . I should not feel that
I was doing right, if I did not urge you to continue to them your entire
confidence: And, if it is necessary to look out for some fresh assistance for them, I rejoice to think, that, in Lake and Jowett, you have
two such eminent scholars, and two men of such sterling goodness of
character, who, being both old Scholars of the House, so fully understand the system, by which now for so many years the College has
flourished . . . I feel sure that they possess that tact and sound judgement, and full appreciation of the goodness of the system, under which
they have been educated, the want of which, I cannot but fear, would
make Wall but ill-suited for any office in the Tuition . . . Respecting
Wall most highly as I do, I still feel that he is a stranger to the merits
of what I may call the Balliol System. This, with peculiarities of
manner which you must yourself have observed, and the deficiency
in scholarship which struck us all at his examination, would disqualify
him, I cannot but think, for the office of Tutor . . .   19]

The remark about Wall's examination is particularly revealing. He
had been elected a Chaplain Fellow in 1839. There was little competition in such elections as candidates had already to have been
ordained priest and they took place on occurrence of a vacancy rather
than as regular well-publicised events like the ordinary open fellowships. Indeed, there had been two previous cases of also-rans in open
fellowship competitions being elected Chaplain Fellows (Cheese in
1810 and Oakeley in 1827). Jenkyns agreed with Tait about Wall[81] —
who seems to have been a tiresome and litigious man — and, although

Wall was older than Lake and Jowett, they were preferred to him. Temple joined them as Mathematical Lecturer in the same year, and the tutorial method of teaching seems to have taken the lead from about this time.[82]

The academic development of the College between 1830 and 1845 took place against a background of political and religious controversies of which the Balliol Senior Common Room was often a focal point. The grip of the High Church Tories on the College began to weaken in the late 'twenties with the election of men with minds and ideas of their own like F.W. Newman and F. Oakeley. In 1829 Robert Peel resigned his University seat and offered himself for re-election because he had changed his mind and was now in favour of Catholic Emancipation. Oakeley surprised Jenkyns and the others by voting for Peel and relations between him and them became uneasy.[83] Divergence from the old ways suddenly burgeoned, and Jenkyns found himself with Fellows who were either edging towards Roman Catholicism with the Tractarians or moving in the opposite direction with Thomas Arnold. In frustration, Oakeley thought, at the weakening of his influence, Ogilvie withdrew from Oxford in 1830 despite Keble's lament[84] that Oxford "would become a very sink of Whiggery" without him. The Tractarian movement, in which Oakeley and Ward were prominent, was profoundly disturbing to Jenkyns and he struggled to check its advances in Balliol.

20. *From F. Oakeley's reminiscences (op. cit.). c.1836*

The Master began to deal blows against the obnoxious doctrines on the right hand and on the left — some of them effectual, but more of them impotent . . . The criticism of the weekly themes gave the Master many opportunities of dealing his anathemas against the new school; but his most powerful weapon was the terminal examination at collections. He had certain trial passages of the New Testament which he employed as the criteria of the religious tenets of an undergraduate suspected of 'Puseyism'. One of those most frequently produced was that in which the errors of the Pharisees are exposed. When a man had completed his translation of some such passage, the Master would proceed as follows: 'Now, tell me, Mr. ----, of all the various religious sects and parties which exist among us, which would you say corresponds the most with the Pharisees of the Gospel?' If the examinee was not fully up to the import of the question, he would perhaps answer, 'The Puritans, sir'. This was a safe reply, and in quieter times would have been the best for the purpose; but just then a more powerful antipathy even than the dread of Puritanism was uppermost in the academical mind; and he who wished to receive the Master's highest commendation would always answer, 'The Roman Catholics, sir' . . . The fellows, of course, were less tractable subjects of the anti-Tractarian head of the college than the undergraduates. They had their status in the Society, and their rights, which justified them in making a stand against any vexatious or unconstitutional opposition whenever such was seriously contemplated; but matters did not, as a fact, ever proceed to extremities, and stopped short in 'brushes' or 'scenes', which partook rather of the ludicrous than the serious.   20]

The controversies in the Senior Common Room were very tangled, with the relatively liberal Tait opposed to Ward, and Scott pulling with inordinate conservatism against them both. In 1838 these differences intruded into fellowship elections. In the summer of that year Stanley, a rising liberal star, asked whether he would be an acceptable candidate for the forthcoming fellowship election, was discouraged and therefore offered himself to University College which elected him.[85] Tait struggled hard to avoid the loss of a good man but the right wing had their way. Jenkyns said that he regretted losing Stanley but made no positive move in his favour and was probably relieved that the others had in effect black-balled him.

21. R. Jenkyns to A.C. Tait,   3 July 1838[86]

The Election at University takes place tomorrow. The Master called on me today — the purport of his visit you may easily guess — & I expect S. will be elected. I cannot, I must confess, help regretting the loss of a Candidate in many important points very desirable — & who has already reflected, & may still reflect honour on our Society . . .   21]

22. A.P. Stanley to A.C. Tait,   4 July 1838[87]

I cannot help writing to say how much obliged I am to you for your endeavours to keep me at Balliol — if all my friends had done the same, I should probably not be where I am now . . .   22]

Scott was disturbed not only by the prospect of elections throwing up Fellows with dangerous views but also by the established practice of electing Fellows who had no intention of proceeding to ordination but who anticipated resignation before the Statutes obliged them to do so. In 1837 he petitioned the Visitor for clarification, asking whether all fellowship candidates should be required to enter into an undertaking to take orders.[88] In taking this line, he was completely alone. Jenkyns, although accepting the sincerity of Scott's motives, professed his "own entire freedom from doubt" on the matter and successfully defended the practice as being not only statutable but in the interests of the College.[89]

23. *R. Jenkyns to W. Howley (the Visitor, Archbishop of Canterbury)*
14 Aug. 1838[90]

Within my own experience of 38 years, several Persons have been elected to Fellowships who at the time of their Election were professedly studying the Law — Some of them afterwards took orders; while others, pursuing their original intention, retained their Fellowships only till such time as the Statutes Ch-32 (De promotione ad sacerdotium) required them to be ordained — viz. four years after taking the M.A. degree. They have then on account of their non-compliance with the Statutable injunctions been obliged to resign their Fellowships —
Your Grace will permit me to say that under these circumstances, when no such limitation as the Appellant (Mr. Scott) could expect, is enjoined by the Statutes, it would be neither wise, nor just, to impose any restriction on a mode of Election, which from its very freedom has for many years contributed to the interests & credit of the College. The inevitable results would be to impair the competition by excluding Candidates of high character for talents & attainments — nor would it be fair to require of young men at a period of life when their views & opinions are scarcely formed, any declaration of their future intention, or any pledge of their entering upon a Profession which they may afterwards perhaps wish to relinquish . . .   23]

It appears from this letter that Davis was mistaken in putting Jenkyns on the reactionary side over this issue, perhaps because — writing in the 1890's — he relied on oral tradition for what was to him the fairly recent past.

Ward's lead in the march to Rome became a progressively greater embarrassment to Jenkyns and most of the Fellows, and in 1841 Tait, at the instigation of Woollcombe and Scott,[91] persuaded Jenkyns to ask Ward to resign his Mathematical Lectureship on the grounds that he was contaminating his pupils with deviant doctrine. Before the Master could put the question, Ward resigned.

Despite the intense disagreements between the factions among the Fellows, the College held together. Unlike Oriel ten years earlier it did not tear itself apart, as the Fellows mostly stayed on warm personal terms with each other. Jenkyns avoided precipitate interference and remained on reasonable terms with nearly all the Fellows, though his relationships with them were by this time more distant than they had been. The Fellows were a young body: when Chapman was presented to the living at Tendring in 1838 Oakeley was left as non-resident Senior Fellow at the age of only 36, and the average age of the residents was a mere 26. Jenkyns was 55, and although Jowett says he was "very different from any of the Fellows and was held in considerable awe by them",[92] the awe was not universal, and there was a feeling that he might take advantage of divisions among the Fellows for his own ends.

24. *R. Scott to A.C. Tait,*   *Autumn 1841*[93]

It is of no use to mince the matter in a confidential letter like this. Suppose a dispute in Common Room continued from Election to Election, between those whom we may call *Taitians* & *Wardians*. In comes the Master, suspicious of both and of everything which looks like enthusiasm & plays you off one against the other for his own purposes . . .   24]

This fragile peace was seriously threatened in 1843, when there was a rather ludicrous dispute over rebuilding proposals which were controversial because of their religious implications,[94] and Ward stirred. things up again in June 1844 with the publication of his book *The ideal of a Christian Church considered in comparison with existing practice*. In this book he argued at great length in favour of reforms which would have amounted to reconciliation with Rome. His style was deliberately provocative, as in his remark "Three years have passed since I said plainly that in subscribing the Articles I renounce no Roman doctrine; yet I retain my fellowship which I hold on the tenure of subscription, and have received no ecclesiastical censure in any shape." Jenkyns was very disturbed by the book and concerned about Ward's effect on the College. To stop undergraduates being tainted by further contact with Ward, Jenkyns resolved to refuse permission for long vacation residence. Lake counselled otherwise, arguing that the men themselves felt that Ward's influence was "with them a mere chimera".

25. W. C. Lake to R. Jenkyns,   1 July, 1844[95]

My dear Master

I am induced to take the liberty of writing to you by a letter which I received last night from Woollcombe, & I am sure that in your eyes I shall need no other apology than the interest in our joint college, and your own kind & frequent encouragement to speak with openness to you on all that concerns it, will supply. I confess I am very much alarmed and grieved to hear that in consequences of the pain occasioned to you by Ward's book & your dread of its influence you wish not to allow our men to continue in Oxford, & I would venture very very respectfully to submit you some reasons which make me think that while no danger can possibly be apprehended for the men by their staying, their removal may be most injurious to us in the eyes of any who shall hear of it . . . I assure you that not only has Ward (to my entire belief) scrupulously abstained from *any* attempt to influence our undergraduates, but that we are keenly alive to the importance of his not even coming into contact with them, in such a way as might lead to intimate acquaintance. Nay more, I do not believe that since I have been a tutor Ward has through any means formed *the slightest acquaintance* with any undergraduate, and I have more than once particularly avoided asking him to meet them, when I should otherwise have wished for his company. And this because I am most anxious to avoid the least occasion for a charge of proselytism . . . And thus, during the vacation, sure as I feel that Ward would abstain, (as a matter of fact I imagine he will be absent for much of the first part of the time) I may add that you might trust us more implicitly for not bringing the men into his society. And they are not likely to wish it: for as a party they are perhaps some of the most 'Anti Puseyite' members of the most 'Anti Puseyite' college in Oxford . . .   25]

During the long vacation of 1844 Jenkyns studied the book in
detail and decided to prevent Ward deputising for Oakeley in Chapel,
and even went to the lengths of creating a scene at the beginning of
Michaelmas Term in order to stop Ward exercising his traditional
right, as Senior Fellow present, of reading the Epistle.

At about the same time the Hebdomadal Board appointed a committee of six, including Jenkyns, to report on Ward's book and advise
the University on a course of action. The eventual upshot of this initiative was a meeting of Convocation on 13 February 1845 at which it
was agreed by 777 votes to 391 that Ward's book was "utterly inconsistent with the Articles of Religion of the Church of England, and
with the Declaration in respect of those articles made and subscribed
by William George Ward previously and in order of his being admitted
to the degrees of BA and MA". This censure was followed by a further
motion, passed by a much smaller majority — 569 against 511 — de-
priving Ward of his degrees. Jenkyns was no doubt very gratified, as
he had solicited support for Ward's censure and degradation widely
among former Fellows and pupils. He immediately consulted privately
with his own lawyers and drafted a long case for the opinion of coun-
sel as to "whether the Master of Balliol would be justified in declaring
Mr. Ward's fellowship, *ipso facto degradationis*, vacant", but the
question was never tested as Ward vacated his fellowship by marriage
on 31 March 1845 — he had been secretly engaged throughout.[95]
Ward and Oakeley both joined the Roman Catholic Church a few
months later. It is astonishing to find that in subsequent correspondence with Jenkyns they were positively warm and friendly towards
him — they cannot have known about his scheming behind the scenes.

About 1840 Jenkyns began to hanker for ecclesiastical dignity. It
was not that he sought after financial rewards — his circumstances
were "such as not to render the want of Preferment a matter of
pecuniary inconvenience" — but rather that he wanted a position
which would eventually "afford a comfortable & honourable retire-
ment".[96] Not discouraged by his failure to obtain promotion from his
Prebend to a Canon's stall at Wells in 1840, he persuaded his cousin,
Henry Hobhouse, to suggest his name to Robert Peel when the
deanery, which was a Crown appointment, fell vacant in 1845. Peel
made soundings[97] about Jenkyns with the Dean of Christ Church
(who was Jenkyns' brother-in-law) and then offered him the appoint-

ment. More than fifty letters of congratulation from members of the College survive.[98] Peel's nomination was seen by the writers as Jenkyns' reward for his work at Balliol and for making a stand against the Tractarians.

26. *F.D. Foster to R. Jenkyns,*   4 *June, 1845*

Tidings have reached us this morning of your appointment to the Deanery of Wells, & I must avail myself of the first Post to offer you our hearty congratulations on your promotion to so honourable a position — which, however, you seem richly to have merited, by the firm & decided stand you have made against the spread of Romish principles & practices. You were the first to *act* against Tractarianism; by suspending a Jesuitical Tutor, clever & useful though he were, as a mathematical teacher, & you preferred continuing to live in your Master's Lodge without its requisite alterations, rather than be indebted for them to the aid of the Roman Catholic Pugin . . .   26]

27. *R.R.W. Lingen to R. Jenkyns,*   9 *June, 1845*

I have very great pleasure in offering you my sincere congratulations on your nomination to the Deanery of Wells, a dignity which I hope you may long and happily enjoy. I think that the services you have done to the cause of Academical Education in this country by having been one of the earliest, most consistent, and most successful reformers of the old system fully entitled you to some such honourable notice on the part of Government . . .   27]

28 *J. Collinson to R. Jenkyns,*   12 *June, 1845*

I beg to congratulate you on your well-deserved preferment: those who know the depressed state of Balliol Coll. 40 years ago will appreciate your exertions there, & Dr. Parsons's, & my friend Noel Ellison's. The choice is honourable to Sir Robert Peel as well as to yourself,[99] for I understand you voted against him . . . I hope you have no more trouble with Mr. Ward & the gentlemen 'who advocate the doctrines of one Church & secure the emoluments of another.'   28]

Many of the letters seem to assume that Jenkyns was being pensioned off, but it turned out that he was to have another nine years. He had dispensation[100] from his residence obligations which allowed him to be absent from Oxford when decanal business called, but he usually managed to stay up for most of University term time. At any rate he missed only one College Meeting between his appointment to Wells and his death. He tried to retain his control of the College despite spending about two-thirds of his time at Wells and being much engaged there by the aftermath of ecclesiastical reform,[101] theological controversy[102] and extensive building work on the cathedral[103] — to which he subscribed generously. The atmosphere in Oxford was much calmer after 1845 following the secession to Rome of Newman and his followers. In a much quoted chapter of his *Recollections*, Cox[104] tells us that the "controversy had worn out", "speculative theology gave way to speculation in railroad shares" and "instead of High Church, Low Church and Broad Church they talked of high embankments, the broad gauge and low dividends". Certainly we hear no more of *odium theologicum* in Balliol, and the impression given by the College Minutes is one of a relapse into a preoccupation with practical matters to do with estates and livings. This impression is misleading. Several Fellows, but Jowett especially, were becoming deeply involved in the beginnings of a serious University Reform movement. The thrust of this movement was, however, largely directed at the University and other Colleges. A Royal Commission which included Tait and had Stanley as Secretary was appointed to enquire into the University in 1850. Jenkyns' reply to the Commission's first approach to Balliol was that he held himself responsible only to the Visitor.[105] He had defended this position before, in 1837, when an abortive attempt to launch a Commission had been made in Parliament.[106] It was not that he feared what a Commission might say. What worried him was the erosion of the College's independence which might follow if it were once admitted that the state had any right to look into the affairs of a corporation which had been "founded and endowed solely by the munificence of private individuals". The College had been subject only to its own Statutes and the authority of its Visitor for nearly six hundred years. Under the "salutary influence of such Visitatorial power", the College had faithfully and, it was hoped, "successfully laboured to promote the cause of sound Religion & useful learning". It did not shrink from the "strictest examination" of its "own lawful Visitor", but deprecated any "extraneous interference which would supersede the provision wisely made by the Founders themselves for regulating the objects of their bounty." He stuck to this line — as did most other Heads of Houses — and Balliol made no official answers to the Commission's questions. By this time, however, Jenkyns' dominance over his Governing Body was less than it had been ten years before. He was now nearly seventy and absent much of the time, whereas the Fellows into whose hands the actual running of the College fell — Woollcombe, Jowett, Lake and Wall — were by now very experienced in academic politics and full of self-confidence. They also had a greater commitment to the academic life than their predecessors had had — eight of those who were Fellows in 1850 were to serve for twenty years or more instead of going off to College livings or other appointments after a few years.[107] They were the first generation of real career academics in the history of the College. They decided to cooperate fully with the Commissioners on an unofficial basis. Jowett, Lake and Wall felt able to tell them that, although they could not assist in their capacities as College Officers, they would as individuals be glad to help and make available the College books and information which they happened to have in their possession. They each gave evidence at length and so did Scott and Temple. When the Commission reported in 1852 it had little to say that was critical of the College and indeed used it as an example to support the case it made for the general abolition of closed scholarships and fellowships.

29. *From the Report of the Royal Commission,* 1852

Balliol, which now enjoys so high a reputation, was at the beginning of the present century regarded as one of the worst Colleges in Oxford. Its Fellowships and Scholarships, which were long bestowed as matters of personal favour, were, we believe, first thrown open to public competition by the exertions of its late and its present Head . . .

The decree was, indeed, in itself wise and liberal, and having been carried into execution wisely and liberally, it has brought honour to Balliol and the University . . .

It is the most distinguishing characteristic of this Foundation that it is peculiarly free from all restrictions which might prevent the election of the best candidates to its Headship, Fellowships, Scholarships, and even to its Visitorship. The result of this has been that Balliol, which is one of the smallest Colleges in Oxford, as regards its Foundation, is certainly at present the most distinguished . . .   29]

The principal internal business of the College during Jenkyns' last phase was a rebuilding programme. The hall, which is now the main Library, was enlarged, new kitchens were built and the dilapidated buildings at the bottom of the grove by the back gate were demolished to make way for a plain and functional new building. Jenkyns was responsible for the choice of the architect: he engaged Anthony Salvin, who was also working for him at Wells.[108] Jowett was much involved in the actual execution of the work, however, and his hand is clear, for example, in the inclusion of a chemical laboratory[109] in one of the cellars.

Jenkyns died in the Master's Lodgings on 6 March 1854, a few months after completion of the new buildings. He was buried in Wells Cathedral a week later. "He found Balliol a close college among the least distinguished of collegiate bodies at Oxford — he left it almost entirely open, and confessedly the foremost of all."[110]

NOTES

All unpublished material for which no location is stated is in the College Library.

1. L. Sutherland *The University of Oxford in the Eighteenth Century: a Reconsideration* (Oxford 1973).
2. R.W. Hunt Appendix I to Davis (see note 3).
3. H.W.C. Davis *A History of Balliol College* revised by R.H.C. Davis and R.W. Hunt (Oxford 1963).
4. See the notebook of 1786 in which he listed his corrections, his correspondence with T. Falconer (Misc. Bursary Papers 15) who eventually completed the work for publication in 1807, and his letter to R. Griffiths of 14 Mar. 1788, Bodl. MS. Add C.89, fo.276.
5. *Edinburgh Review* 14 (1809), p. 429.
6. See his letters to the editor, R. Griffiths, Bodl. MS. Add.C.89, fos.276–286v.
7. See his *Sermon preached before the Honourable House of Commons* (1811).
8. MS. Jenkyns VIA.12, p. 26.
9. See W.R. Ward *Victorian Oxford* (1965), p. 13 and S. Rothblatt, Ch. 5 in *The University in Society*, I ed. L. Stone (1975).
10. A. Clark's annual College lists. The last Servitor was admitted in 1810.
11. Archives D.3.45–71.
12. We have a glimpse of how things were done a hundred years earlier from the diary of Jeremiah Milles. On 20 Feb. 1701 he recorded "At night I was at the Tavern with Mr. Strong and Mr. Atwood a Bristoll-man"; four days later he noted "The day before I disposed of my Schollarship to Atwood's son".
13. He left his astronomical books to the Radcliffe Observatory (the Museum of the History of Science has a list in MS. Radcliffe 53). He is mentioned in 1802 (Bodl. MS. Finch e.40, fo.150) as having a sort of observatory at the top of the tower in which he lived over the gate. The instrument he used is probably the one the College deposited at the Museum of the History of Science in 1928. It was assumed that it had belonged to James Bradley, the great Astronomer Royal (Balliol 1710) and was until recently proudly exhibited as such. Unfortunately for this legend, a re-examination kindly performed by G.L'e Turner has shown that it was almost certainly made several years after Bradley's death in 1762, and it seems likely that it is the telescope for which the Dean paid 11 guineas on 14 Nov. 1776 (Misc. Bursary Papers 28.a(2)).
14. See the correspondence of Jenkyns' father and godfather in MS. Jenkyns VIA.lb. I have not been able to discover anything about his previous education: perhaps he was taught at home by his father, who was Vicar of Evercreech, Somerset.
15. Robert Finch (1783–1830); Balliol 1802; Collector.
16. R. Finch to T. Finch, 2 April 1802, Bodl. MS. Finch e.40, fo.152.

17. MS Jenkyns VIA. 1b.
18. Samuel Punter Gamlen (1783–1855); Balliol 1801; Vicar of Bossall, Yorkshire, 1826–1854.
19. Archives D.3.101, p. 8.
20. Letters of Dec. 1803 and Jan. 1804, Bodl. MS. Finch e.21, pp. 97 and 159, respectively.
21. W.S. Hamilton to his mother, 15 Nov. 1807, printed in J. Veitch, *Memoir of Sir William Hamilton, Bart.* (1869); J.G. Lockhart to his mother, 4. Dec. 1809, printed in A. Lang, *The Life and Letters of John Gibson Lockhart* (1897). Jenkyns' lecture notes are in MS. Jenkyns VIA.9, 17 and 20.
22. Bodl. MS. Finch e.40, fo.147v.
23. Archives D.3.101, p. 4.
24. Archives D.3.89.
25. Archives D.3.86.
26. B. Cheese to R. Finch, Jan. 1807, Bodl. MS. Finch d.4, fo.141.
27. S. McCormick to R. Finch, 14 Dec. 1808, Bodl. MS. Finch d.11, fo.18.
28. R. Finch to W. McDonald, 25 June 1805, Bodl. MS. Finch e.23, fo. 105.
29. S.P. Gamlen to R. Finch, 9 July 1807, Bodl. MS. Finch d.8, fo.62.
30. Archives D.3.101.
31. Richard Prosser (1748–1839); Balliol 1767; Fellow 1773–1793; Archdeacon of Durham 1808. See the *Balliol College Record* 1980.
32. T.C. Rogers to R. Finch, 6 July 1807, Bodl. MS. Finch d.14, fo.201.
33. Matthew Baillie (1761–1823); Balliol 1779; Physician to George III.
34. Shute Barrington (1734–1826); Merton 1752; Bishop of Durham 1791; Visitor 1805.
35. Archives D.3.102–108.
36. B. Cheese to R. Finch, 7 Dec. 1807, Bodl. MS. Finch d.4, fo.198.
37. B. Cheese to R. Finch, 24 Jan. and 2 Mar. 1810, Bodl. MS. Finch d.4, fos. 202, 210.
38. 'Memoranda respecting Rooms and Applicants for admission', MS. Jenkyns VIA.8.
39. Bodl. MS. Finch e.40, fo.159.
40. J. Veitch *op. cit.*
41. Bodl. MS. Eng. th. d.39, fo.2.
42. His letters from her are in Bodl. MS. Eng. Lett, d.124, fos.97–138.
43. Hannah More to C.A. Ogilvie, n.d. (c.1816), Bodl. MS. Eng. Lett. d.124, fo.105.
44. J.M. Chapman *Reminiscences of three Oxford Worthies* (Oxford 1875).
45. Personal communication from the present Rector, the Rev. A.M. Virgin.
46. See C. Girdlestone *A third letter on Church Reform: on a comprehension of the dissenters with the established church* (1834).
47. English Register, 1819. Burial in Chapel was a rare honour at the time and there have been only two since - Elizabeth Parsons and George Powell in 1827 and 1830 respectively (Archives D.10.6).
48. Hereford and Worcester Record Office, Belmont Papers, XII, 1.

49. MS. Jenkyns VIA.3.
50. English Register, 29 Nov. 1819.
51. Misc. Bursary Papers 3.
52. The reason for the delay in recording the decision — a unique irregularity — is not clear.
53. Davis and others give the date of the opening of the scholarships as 1828, which was when the decision was minuted. In other places the date is given as 1834, which is when the change in Statute was sanctioned. In fact, it is quite clear that the decision was taken and the first open examination was held in 1827.
54. An entry dated 19 Jan. 1822; "Magister Ogilvie nominavit Gulielmum Dunn in Scholarem Domus sibimet ipsi inserviturum" — is a typical example of the form of words used in previous scholarship appointments.
55. BM. Add. MS.34586, fo.430.
56. Matriculated members of the University were acceptable candidates even if they were from another College, provided they were not over the statutory age.
57. BM. Add. MS.34586, fo.434.
58. R.P. Turner (1811–1888); Shrewsbury School 1824–1828; admitted as a commoner 1828. B.A. 1831. Rector of Churchill near Kidderminster 1841–1888.
59. BM. Add. MS. 34588, fo.416.
60. A.P. Stanley to Mary Stanley, 27 Nov. 1833. Temple Reading Room, Rugby.
61. A few scraps of the early examination papers and questions survive in MS. Jenkyns VIA.11.
62. A.P. Stanley to his sister Mary 29 Nov. 1833, Temple Reading Room, Rugby. James Lonsdale's account (in R. Duckworth *A memoir of the Rev. James Lonsdale* 1893) coincides minutely.
63. W. Pugh and R.G. Chapman 'Henry Wall's notes 1844', *Oxoniensia* XXIV 1959, p. 83. The original document on which this article is based is said to have been in Keble Library, but neither the document nor any trace of it can be found there now.
64. English Register, 1 Feb. 1834.
65. Archives D.9.8.
66. *The Times* 7 March 1854; congratulatory letters to Jenkyns on his appointment as Dean of Wells, 1845, MS.Jenkyns VIA.15; letters of condolence to Mrs. Jenkyns, 1854, MS.Jenkyns VIA.6.
67. English Register, 1 March 1830. Powell specified that the prize was to be for the best performance "in transcribing a paper of Addison as read once slowly and distinctly, in transcribing a short passage of Tully, & in transcribing a similar passage of Plato & translating both, & in composing an English Essay." Great importance was attached to accuracy in receiving dictation and in transcription at this time: see A. Lang, *Sir Stafford Northcote* (Edinburgh 1890), I p. 26, for an account of dictation tests in the scholarship

examination. Despite Powell's precise instructions the prize was from the first award (C. Marriott, 1832) given for "English Composition". The George Powell Essay Prize is still awarded annually.

68. English Register, 15 Feb. 1841.
69. English Register, 2 June 1824.
70. Early Nineteenth Century Balliol Miscellany, 2.
71. A.C. Tait to C.A. Ogilvie, 9 Dec. 1834, Bodl. MS. Eng. Lett. d.124, fo.161.
72. Reminiscences of E.D. Wickham in *Our memories, shadows of Old Oxford* ed. H. Daniel (Oxford 1893).
73. H.S. Escott's reminiscences, Jowett Papers, E.
74. F. Oakley's reminiscences in *Reminiscences of Oxford* ed. L.M. Quiller Couch (Oxford 1892).
75. C.A.E. Moberly *Dulce Domum* (1911), p. 55.
76. Lambeth Palace Library, Tait Papers 76, fo.99.
77. English Register, 6 April 1838. There was a small "Undergraduates' Library" at least as early as 1700: accounts for it and frequent references to it survive from throughout the eighteenth century (see the *Balliol College Record*, 1980).
78. R.T. Davison and W. Benham *Life of Archibald Campbell Tait* (1891), p. 102.
79. See Lambeth Palace Library, Tait Papers, especially 76, fos.245–273, and E. Abbott and L. Campbell *Life and Letters of Benjamin Jowett* (1897).
80. Early Nineteenth Century Balliol Miscellany, 1.
81. Lambeth Palace Library, Tait Papers 77, fo.232.
82. E. Palmer's reminiscences in Abbot and Campbell *op. cit.*, p. 102.
83. F. Oakley's reminiscences, MS. 408 (typescript), Part A, fo.5.
84. J. Keble to C.A. Ogilvie, 22 Jan. 1830, Bodl. MS. Eng. Lett. d.124, fo.25.
85. R.E. Prothero and G.G. Bradley *The Life and Correspondence of Arthur Penrhyn Stanley* (1893), I ch. VII.
86. Lambeth Palace Library, Tait Papers 76, fo.140.
87. Lambeth Palace Library, Tait Papers 76, fo.142. See also P.H.S. Payne to H.H. Vaughan, 10 Nov. 1838, Bodl. MS. Eng. Lett. d.436, fo.35.
88. Archives D.3.118.
89. Archives D.3.121.
90. Archives D.3.123.
91. A.C. Tait to R. Scott, 12 Oct. 1841, Pusey House Library, Scott Letters, packet 2.
92. Jowett's reminiscences, Appendix D in W. Ward *William George Ward and the Oxford Movement* (1889).
93. Copy in Pusey House Library, Scott Letters, packet 2.
94. A full account of this affair — the 'Civil War' of 1843 — is given in the *Balliol College Record* 1978.
95. MS. Jenkins VIB.
96. R. Jenkyns to E. Goodenough, Dean of Wells, 5 April 1840, and other letters in MS. Jenkyns VIA. 30.

97. R. Peel to T. Gaisford, 27 May 1845, copy in Early Nineteenth Century Balliol Miscellany, 7. See also MS. Jenkyns I.2. An account of the making of the appointment is given by Bishop F. West in *Country Life* 20 Oct. 1977, p. 1104.
98. MS. Jenkyns VIA.15.
99. This is presumably an allusion to the parliamentary election of 1829 when Peel resigned his University seat and offered himself for reelection because he had changed his mind on Catholic Emancipation: he was defeated, and it was well known that Jenkyns had been a leading member of the party in the University which had opposed him.
100. The dispensation given by the Visitor (W. Howley, Archbishop of Canterbury) in 1846 is in Misc. Bursary Papers 4.
101. This touched his own pocket: see his petition to the Ecclesiastical Commissioners and letter to Lord John Russell of 1849 in MS. Jenkyns VIA, 26b. In the same year he congratulated Tait on his appointment to the Deanery of Carlisle, this "being one of the new foundation" having "escaped from the fangs of the Ecclesiastical Commissioners". The deanery of Wells, he complained, had "been stripped of *all* the Estates formerly attached to it" and there had been no settlement "in lieu of the spoliation". Lambeth Palace Library, Tait Papers 78, fo.71.
102. In particular the case of G.A. Denison, Archdeacon of Taunton: see MS. Jenkyns VIA, 26b.
103 See MS. Jenkyns VIA, 26a.
104. G.V. Cox *Recollections of Oxford* (1868), p. 338.
105. *Report of Her Majesty's Commissioners appointed to enquire into the State Discipline Studies and Revenues of the University and Colleges of Oxford, together with the Evidence and an Appendix* (1852).
106. Draft by Jenkyns of a petition to the House of Lords against a threatened Commission, 1837. Misc. Bursary Papers 4.
107. College livings which fell vacant around this time were mostly "severally declined by each of the Fellows in succession", e.g. English Register, 4 Mar. 1851.
108. There is an account by Jenkyns of this building programme inserted at the end of the English Register 1794–1875.
109. T.W.M. Smith, 'The Balliol-Trinity Laboratories', Chemistry Part II thesis, Oxford 1979.
110. *The Times* 7 March 1854.

124   BALLIOL STUDIES

ACKNOWLEDGEMENTS

I have had a great deal of assistance in tracking down material from librarians, archivists and others, who are too numerous to list without spreading my gratitude too thinly. Special thanks however, are due to Vincent Quinn for tolerating me under his feet with such helpful kindness, and to Henry Jenkyns (Balliol 1936), whose family papers have been deposited at Balliol since 1951, for his enthusiastic interest and encouragement.

Benjamin Jowett and the Church of England: or 'why really great men are never clergymen'

BENJAMIN JOWETT AND THE CHURCH OF ENGLAND: OR "WHY REALLY GREAT MEN ARE NEVER CLERGYMEN."

Jowett is famous as the archetypal master of Balliol — architect of the educational patterns of modern Oxford, enthusiast for the opening of universities to able young men from less than privileged homes and, above all, superb picker, trainer and placer of the future leaders of government, the public service and the imperial edifice. That he was also a clergyman and a theologian is not often remembered. His contribution to *Essays and Reviews*, written when he was about forty and not yet Master, is something which every historian of the nineteenth century Church of England is compelled to notice. It was a theological landmark, the subject of violent controversy and made Jowett a somewhat suspect figure in ecclesiastical circles. But apart from that one episode he is not usually treated as someone who made a significant mark upon the Church. He made no further major contribution to theology nor is he remembered as the founder of a school of thought.

On the face of it this is, perhaps, surprising. One might have supposed that a man who devoted himself to training the young and advancing their careers, and who was himself a clergyman of strong and radical opinions, might have fostered a whole generation of Balliol bishops and divines. The College did indeed produce some eminent ecclesiastics in the nineteenth century — four Archbishops of Canterbury among them — but few of them were undergraduates during Jowett's mastership and fewer still can be described as in any sense Jowett's protegés. He was, in other words, a respected and influential establishment figure, the creator of the establishment of the future, except as regards his own profession where he seems to be a maverick without obvious heirs.

One might think to explain this by saying that Jowett tried his hand at theology, got into trouble and then turned to more secular activities. But that would be an anachronistic misreading of the late nineteenth century in terms of the late twentieth century. Even after 1871 Oxford was not really a secular place. Religion occupied a great deal of the time — and of the minds — of the university community. Nor

127

was Jowett really a secular person. He did not regard his clerical role as an empty formality. He neither moderated his radical theological opinions nor tried to hide them. Right up to the end of his life he had plans for writing theological works. In any case a head of house who took his clerical profession as seriously (or almost as seriously) as his duties as an educator, and who turned from theology to the business of running the College, would not be abandoning religion for the secular. Jowett certainly thought that the Christian religion was a very important part of a proper education and of the life of the College. Yet he does not seem to have had any overwhelming desire to leave his mark upon the leading churchmen of the future in the same way that he shaped the rising generation of laymen. One is tempted to wonder whether he thought that ecclesiastical leaders were not going to be very important or would cease to count for much in the world of affairs.

In 1867, before he became Master, Jowett asked himself the question "Why really great men are never clergymen?" and moved towards the conclusion that the truly great "don't like to submit to the gêne of a received creed".[1] Since Jowett was clearly fascinated by greatness, success and importance, other people have been equally fascinated by Jowett's own claim to greatness. Sir Geoffrey Faber's biography contains a lengthy introductory section on this point. One might have thought that Jowett – the clergyman – had already answered the question. But he posed it in an interesting form: not "Why are clergymen never really great men?" but "Why are really great men never clergymen?" And his answer – the dislike of the constraint of a received creed – points up the really interesting issue. Jowett was an academic and an educator at a time when received creeds were coming under attack from new academic scholarship. How far was he able to combine successsfully the potentially conflicting roles of clergyman and scholar? Faber, who did not really understand the religious and ecclesiastical world of the nineteenth century[2] and sometimes made very obvious mistakes about it[3] hardly deals with this point.

In the very year after Jowett amused himself with the conundrum about clergymen and greatness, his friend and former tutor – Archibald Campbell Tait – became Archbishop of Canterbury. Tait has been described as the most powerful archbishop since the seventeenth century[4] and it would be interesting to know whether Jowett would have regarded him as a great man. He was plainly fond of him. Even his more formal letters to his old tutor contain flashes of reminiscence which recall their relationship of half-a-century before in affectionate terms. When Tait was made Bishop of London in 1856, Jowett wrote to say that he believed he would be a good bishop "because you are tolerant and keep your eyes open to what is passing round you; because I believe you will not suffer yourself to be surrounded by unfair men".[5] But he probably thought Tait fell short of greatness because he spent too much time on ordinary things. When the see of Canterbury was vacant in 1862, Jowett hoped Tait would be offered it. In fact, Longley was translated from York and Tait declined to move to the northern archbishopric. Jowett then wrote to say how glad he was that Tait was not "to be shelved" (in York) and, in a somewhat roundabout manner, hinted that his friend might busy himself with major matters of ecclesiastical administration which would be "of more real use than preaching to cabmen".[6] The everyday round of pastoral concerns was evidently not, in Jowett's mind, a vehicle for greatness. By this time, also, Jowett had reason to suspect that Tait might be willing to submit to the "received creed".

Tait, like Jowett, is usually reckoned a Broad Churchman[7] but it is difficult to define precisely what it was that Tait and Jowett — let alone they and the others usually numbered as Broad Churchmen, like Thomas Arnold, F.D. Maurice, R.D. Hampden, A.P. Stanley, J.W. Colenso and Frederick Temple — had in common. One of Jowett's letters to Tait contains an affectionate and humorous postscript asking the bishop to tell Mrs. Tait "that 'Latitudinarian' is a tremendous long name to call a fellow . . .".[8] It looks as if Mrs. Tait had called Jowett a Latitudinarian as a (joking?) term of opprobrium — a case of the pot's wife calling the kettle black.

In fact the Broad Churchmen were not a 'party' like the High Churchmen or the Evangelicals. The term was, and is, loosely applied to people with a wide range of opinions and it was just as possible for one of them, in their own day, to dismiss another as 'Latitudinarian' as it is for a member of the Labour Party to describe a Trotskyite as a 'Lefty'. Tractarians had a well-defined policy and objective. They wanted to recover for the Church of England its "catholicism", its sense of being part of the ancient and universal church, and an emphasis on sacraments and priesthood. Evangelicals believed passionately in the necessity of real, serious personal religion focussed upon faith in the atoning death of Christ. Opposed to each other they may have been — and often violently were. But both parties had clear, strict standards of orthodoxy. Both believed that the very words of the Bible were divinely inspired. Both regarded 'liberalism' as the greatest enemy of truth.

Broad Churchmen were bound together by negatives rather than positives. They were uneasy about rigid doctrinal standards because they believed in the sanctity and indivisibility of truth. If scientific discoveries were true then it was not simply a matter of being required by honesty to accept them. It was a necessity of conscience, because all truth was part of the divine nature. If these discoveries conflicted with dogma or with what appeared in the Bible they had either to reconcile the two or, if satisfied that science *had* discovered the truth, modify or abandon what conflicted with it.

The Broad Churchmen also believed in tolerance and in making the national Church as comprehensive as possible. They believed that religion had a role in unifying the nation — and this was another reason for regarding doctrinal formularies with suspicion. The establishment, most of them believed, enabled the common sense and fairness of English law to be the judge of what was permissible. This naive trust in lawyers' unprejudiced good sense made them prefer secular courts to ecclesiastical tribunals (which they believed would all too easily become the instruments of narrowly partisan clergymen whether High or Low.) Above all, they were liberal in the sense that they would passionately defend a man's right to speak his mind even when they did not agree with him.

This, together with their suspicion of doctrinal tests, meant that they were individuals and individualists. They could not be a 'party'. They disagreed among themselves with a vehemence that is surprising in the light of their conscientious liberalism. Bishop Colenso believed himself to be a disciple of Maurice and was shattered when Maurice dismissed his biblical criticism in savagely sarcastic terms.[9] A.P. Stanley's courageous willingness to defend persecuted 'liberals' was matched only by his instinct for dissociating himself, in advance, from their opinions and enterprises.[10] And Tait's willingness to join the other bishops in condemning *Essays and Reviews* led to a bitter quarrel with Temple.[11] Relations between Broad Churchmen were not always characterised by sweetness and light. If Mrs. Tait did indeed call Jowett "a Latitudinarian" that was a relatively mild as well as a tremendous long name to call a fellow. Jowett himself, though he was strongly opposed to the attempts to prevent Hampden from becoming Regius Professor and, later, Bishop of Hereford, privately described him to Stanley as "a Janus" about whom "I could not say anything in his favour".[12]

The first major ecclesiastical controversy in which Jowett was involved, albeit indirectly and peripherally, was the attempt to persuade the University of Oxford to censure the leaders of the Tractarian movement. The Balliol Senior Common Room contained not only W.G. Ward, one of the Tractarians under fire, but also Tait, one of the protagonists in the attack upon them. The ninetieth of the *Tracts* which gave the movement its name, published in 1841, was an attempt by Newman to demonstrate that the *Thirty-Nine Articles*, the doctrinal formularies of the Church of England, could be interpreted in a sense entirely consonant with strict Roman Catholic orthodoxy. Tait was one of four tutors of Oxford colleges who published a joint letter condemning the tract. He found himself in an uneasy alliance with a former friend of Newman's called Golightly who took upon himself the task of whipping up antagonism to the Tractarians by methods of which Tait did not always approve.[13] Newman was censured by the Hebdomadal Council and publication of the tracts ceased. The furore, however, did not die down. In 1845, by which time Tait had succeeded Thomas Arnold as Headmaster of Rugby, Ward was stripped of his degrees by convocation and Newman only escaped the same fate by the interposition of the Proctors' veto. Like Newman, Ward became a Roman Catholic.

The effect of the controversies upon Senior Common Rooms was very like the effect in the 1960's of the student power movement. There was the same heady sense, for some people, that an entire younger generation was committed to revitalising society. For others there was the deep suspicion that the young were being manipulated by unscrupulous older men. There was the same feeling, on both sides, that what was going on in the University was directly linked with the whole future of the country. Moreover, there was the same curious interplay of personal relationships and controversial opinions. Old friends held violently opposed views and old enemies found themselves on the same side. Sometimes neither the friendship nor the enmity was much affected. In other cases amity was totally destroyed by the fierceness of the debate about principles and policies.

In the small society of the Balliol Senior Common Room personal friendships seem to have survived remarkably well considering the extremes to which public and official action was taken. Ward, the mathematics lecturer, was a compelling figure, dynamic, Chestertonian and lovable. A brilliant intellect and a clever logician, he was all too often carried, by the force of his arguments and the cleverness of his own wit, far beyond the point at which more sensible men would have rested their case. Tait was a much more solid, down-to-earth, even dour, character. His role in 1841, as prosecutor of unorthodoxy, was an unusual one for a Broad Churchman, though the disciplining of ritualists was to be a major preoccupation of his archiepiscopate.[14] Faber suggests that Tait was really an Evangelical beneath his liberal veneer and that Jowett did not perceive this at the time, if at all.[15] But this is to misunderstand Tait's personal religious position and to underestimate Jowett's perceptiveness.

Tait is probably not really to be understood in terms of English and Anglican religious parties at all. He had been brought up in Scotland as a Presbyterian (though with Episcopalian leanings). What made him a liberal were the characteristics Jowett listed in the letter, already quoted, which he wrote to Tait in 1856 — tolerance, an awareness of the world, an unwillingness to be controlled by a clique. The well-known story of the tragic deaths of his children illustrates his spiritual strength and discipline.[16] Probably his personal religion and piety had not changed greatly since his Presbyterian youth. He was no English Evangelical but a somewhat eighteenth century Scot, devout, common sensical, theologically acute but not an outstanding intellectual, basically very orthodox, a firm believer in a national establishment and solidly opposed to popery.

Jowett, who had become a Fellow while still an undergraduate and who was only twenty-four at the time of the great excitements of 1841, actually understood the situation very well. His role in the affair was not that of a protagonist. He was one of the young men to be influenced one way or another by the more powerful personalities around him. He was, at one stage, pulled towards Ward and the Tractarians. He described himself as having virtually become a Puseyite,[17] a danger — if danger it was — that he himself took seriously. Long afterwards he wrote to Tait, "Supposing that the Tutors of Balliol had been all like Ward, where should I have been? [I] . . . remember with gratitude that at the time of my election to the fellowship you helped to keep up some light of common sense in me".[18] It was probably Tait's down-to-earth Protestantism Jowett was referring to.

Jowett seems, indeed, to have understood Tait very well — to have perceived that there were limits to his liberalism and to have sensed the reality of his personal piety, for all that it lacked the open fervour of Evangelical religion. In the earliest surviving letter from Jowett to Tait (written from Paris in the summer of 1842 and chiefly to ask Tait to arrange for some money to be sent to a somewhat impoverished Jowett) there is a revealing short paragraph on the state of French religion. Jowett obviously knew that Tait would sympathise with his own dislike of deism and of much conventional Roman Catholic religious observance.[19]

Even more revealing was Jowett's advice to Stanley in 1845, when the latter had drafted a pamphlet which might have exposed him to charges of "Latitudinarianism" and wished to have Tait's opinion of it. "Concerning your pamphlet", Jowett wrote, "I have spoken to Tait, who thinks that he cannot possibly judge without reading it. I do not think his opinion of much value in such a matter."[20] It was a curiously prophetic remark. Twenty years later, during the controversy over Colenso's biblical criticism, Tait was to use the same excuse to get out of an awkward situation but was to use it in a form which was quite openly biased. It was not his business, he told his brother bishops, to condemn a book he had not read, adding "when I do read, I wish to read good books."[21]

In the decade after 1845 Jowett was concerned with many things other than theology. He became a tutor and discovered an enthusiasm for teaching. He made a systematic attempt to master the philosophy of Hegel, one of the first English scholars to do so, and embarked with Frederick Temple on a project to translate Hegel's works into English. He became interested in the reform of the University and the improvement of provision for proper teaching. And, in 1854, he failed to be elected Master of the college: Robert Scott was the successful candidate.

In this decade he was, however, also working with A.P. Stanley on a set of commentaries on the Pauline epistles. Stanley was the friend to whom, perhaps above all others, Jowett was most deeply attached. They had been undergraduates together at Balliol and Stanley had become a Fellow of University College. There is no real reason to suppose, as Faber did, that Jowett's feeling for Stanley was a repressed and unacknowledged homosexual one.[22] Faber made a great deal out of an episode in 1849 when Stanley's father died and Jowett wrote to offer to be with his friend to support him through a difficult period. Stanley's reply was an undoubted rebuff, refusing Jowett's offer and saying that he and his family were sufficient to themselves in the crisis.[23] Stanley seems also to have found Jowett's devotion rather stifling to his own intellectual development and his personal independence. He and Jowett were in almost daily touch with each other at this time and Stanley appears to have felt restricted and overwhelmed. Jowett took the rebuff with surprisingly good grace, too good a grace to have been possible (one would have thought) if Faber were right in his interpretation of the friendship. It is true that Jowett reverted to addressing Stanley by his surname, rather than as "Arthur" which he had used in his letter of condolence.[24] But he was to use Stanley's Christian name from time to time on future occasions when he wished to express particular happiness or sorrow for his friend.[25] And if the episode was really of such tremendous significance, then it seems almost unbelievable that when Stanley's mother died in 1862, Jowett should have made *precisely the same 'mistake' all over again.* He wrote a letter which began "My dearest friend" and contained the sentences "I wish I could be with you" and "Please write to me if you are able, and tell me whether there is anything you would like me to do for you".[26] This time, apparently, there was no rebuff.

It is fairly clear that Jowett never occupied the place in Stanley's affections that Stanley occupied in his. It is possible that social differences had something to do with that. The son of a bishop, product of Arnold's Rugby, with his aristocratic marriage and important connections, Stanley would tend to think of his own circle of family and friends as rather different from Jowett's. Jowett was the person from whom he had "learned more than any living man"[27] and it may be that that gives the clue to the real basis of the friendship. Stanley was a fore-runner of the young men who were to pass through Jowett's hands, a sort of quasi-pupil. The letters between them throughout their lives are full of Stanley's wonderings and Jowett's hopes and advice about the next preferment likely to come Stanley's way. They never discussed what was to happen to Jowett. If Stanley felt stifled sometimes by Jowett's instructions and plans, no doubt many of the Balliol young men would feel the same. Jowett was the preceptor who watched what Stanley got up to, hoped to see him in a position of influence, and wanted to prepare him as fully as possible for that moment. Stanley would probably not at any time have described Jowett as his closest friend. C.J. Vaughan (Dean of Llandaff and Master of the Temple) who was at school with him, married his favourite sister and was chief mourner at his funeral, was probably always that. Conversely Jowett, no matter how much Stanley meant to him personally, could remain very detached from Stanley's enthusiasms, like an adult from a child's.

In the 'forties Stanley was campaigning furiously against the law that required clergymen to subscribe the *Thirty-nine Articles* at ordination. Jowett might have been expected to be equally vigorously opposed to subscription, which was also required of everyone matriculating at Oxford. In fact he seems to have remained fairly detached and had not himself objected to subscribing the *Articles*, though he thought that the requirement encouraged dishonesty.[28] In 1854, just before the commentaries were published, he became very angry when an attempt was made to require scholars of the College to declare that they were members of the Church of England. It is possible that his anger was really a consequence of his resentment at Scott's election, for Scott was behind the proposal, rather than an expression of his objection to doctrinal tests in principle. He was, at any rate, prepared to vote for an amendment, proposed by H.J.S. Smith on the grounds that "old chains are the best", to require scholars to subscribe the *Articles* (presumably for a second time).[29]

The commentaries appeared in 1855. Neither Stanley on *I* and *II Corinthians* nor Jowett on *Thessalonians, Galatians* and *Romans* would now be regarded as significant contributions to the study of Pauline theology, but there is no question that Jowett's was, at the time, the more scholarly and important of the two. For one thing, Jowett abandoned the *textus receptus*, the Greek text of the New Testament (substantially that of Erasmus and Béza) used by the translators of the Authorised Version and by most English scholars until Westcott and Hort produced their critical edition of the New Testament in

1881. Jowett's was a courageous as well as a scholarly action for pious sentiment had given a kind of sanctity even to the errors and inaccuracies of the received text. Jowett preferred the version edited by the German philologist Lachmann and published in the 'forties, which used the oldest known Greek manuscripts and aimed at restoring the text as it had been in the fourth century when those manuscripts circulated.

Jowett became Professor of Greek in the very year in which his commentaries were published and his approach to the Greek of the New Testament was essentially that of the classicist who wanted the best text possible. He paid little attention to its background in Judaism, the occurrence of Aramaisms or the differences between Greek and Hebrew thought. This is not surprising. Trying to unravel the Pauline epistles as the attempts of a first century non-Palestinian Jew, trained in the rabbinic schools, to express his Hebraic theology in Greek terminology, is comparatively recent. Nevertheless, Jowett showed some sympathetic understanding of Paul as a human being. He was criticised by J.B. Lightfoot for refusing to treat Paul's Greek as if it were precise and accurate, to be interpreted in strict accordance with grammatical and lexicographical rules.[30] It is so obvious that the epistles are often almost incoherent, when the vehemence or fervour of the author takes command, that Jowett's less pedantic approach must be the right one.

But it was not Jowett's performance as Greek philologist or textual critic that drew most fire: it was his theological opinions. These appeared in essays scattered through the volumes, rather than in the commentary itself, and particularly in five appended to the volume on *Romans*.[31] These hardly help to uncover the theology of St. Paul: they are comments on contemporary orthodoxy. A quite clear and coherent theological position is set out. For all that Jowett has the reputation of not regarding natural science as a very serious academic discipline — or at any rate as unlikely to broaden the mind and thus contribute to genuine education — he took the results of scientific enquiry seriously. What is known to be true must not be denied simply because dogma requires it. His essay 'On Natural Religion' points out that far too many people live as if there were two different worlds — a religious world and the world of actual experience — each with its own kind of truth, which seem never to touch each other. Religion and the real life of common sense are treated, with different sets of words and ideas, as if it would be bad taste to allow them to intermingle. But science, he thinks, is not something to be feared even by the religious. It may be that all things do not equally exhibit marks of design but all things are equally subject to the operation of law. Now that man knows that nature operates in terms of laws, there is no need to fear nature. It would be immoral as well as foolish and retrograde to try and draw men to God by ignoring the scientific understanding of nature and attempting to revert to a state of ignorance and fear "when men cowered like animals before the storm."

For a generation brought up on the natural theology of William Paley this was shocking stuff. Paley had elaborated the argument from design, as a proof of God's existence, until he was prepared to maintain, for instance, that the precise amount of poison in a snake's bite was proof of the divine goodness.[32] Jowett would have nothing to do with that kind of intermingling of the scientific and the religious way of thinking. Instead he advocated an acceptance of a scientific understanding of a universe which operates regularly and predictably and which could, therefore, be understood in its own terms. The problem was, when you did that, to find a way to assert the centrality of God and the importance of a religious understanding of reality. Ten years earlier he had written to Benjamin Brodie, "What appears to me to make the greatest gulph between us is not your taking a rationalistic or mythic view of the Bible, or difficulties about miracles, or even prayer, but that you do not leave any place for religion at all, so that although you may hold the being of God as the Author of the Universe, I do not see how you would be worse off morally if Atheism were proved to demonstration."[33] The acceptance of natural explanations for things would all too easily become naturalism in which there was no real place for God at all.

From the insistence that man's moral dimension required belief in God Jowett never deviated. In a sermon preached in College chapel in 1871 on 'Darwinism and Faith in God' he was to argue that the advances of physical science in no way diminished "the voice within us which is always repeating. . .that we must avoid the evil and choose the good."[34] And in 1893 he wrote to T.H. Huxley, on hearing that he was to give the Romanes Lecture on 'Ethics and Evolution',

No one has yet represented adequately the antithesis of

the moral and the physical. Is not the word 'evolution'
rather unfortunate? There are so many kinds of progress in
the world and in human nature and it does not distinguish
them. I do not think that we can give up the great traditions of the world respecting truth and right and respecting
divine and human perfection. When simplified and purified
all religions agree on them; and all good men and the better
part of all philosophies. We cannot do without that necessary basis of morality, nor can we imagine how natural
science (though it transforms the destinies of man in various
ways, and may do so yet more in the future) can possibly
supply it.[35]

Nevertheless there remained the problem that science seemed to
challenge many of the things that Christians had been taught to believe. People who accepted the discoveries of science could not believe
that creation happened as *Genesis* described it or that the sun stood
still at Joshua's command. If faith was a matter of believing a number
of *things*, then there was a problem. At the time of his letter to Brodie,
Jowett seems rather naively to have thought that the way to deal with
this problem was to compensate for reduced quantity by increased
intensity. In another letter of about the same date he wrote, "I feel
very deeply that one cannot live without religion, and that in proportion as we believe less, that little, if it be only an awful feeling about
existence, must be constantly with us; as faith loses in extent it must
gain intensity. . .".[36] The phrase "constantly with us" is the key to
the passage. Eventually, perhaps through the influence of Hegel,
Jowett was to develop a theological understanding of the constant
presence of God, in history and in the universe. This was not yet
achieved in the commentaries of 1854 but he had moved some way
from the naivety of ten years earlier. He was as passionately convinced
as ever that accepting natural explanations must not eliminate faith,
morality and devotion but he had, at least, abandoned the crude idea
of faith as something that could be quantified.

It was this, indeed, which brought his commentaries under fire and
led to the first accusation that his opinions were heretical. His critics,
like his biographers, simply ignored the essay 'On Natural Religion'
and concentrated upon the essays on justification by faith, predes-

tination and, above all, on the atonement. If Jowett's abandonment of the apologetic arguments beloved of eighteenth century proponents of a rational Christianity, shocked the conventionally religious, what he had to say on the subject of justification and predestination aroused the fury of the Evangelicals. His essay 'On Righteousness by Faith' bluntly set aside the whole tangled controversy about whether men are saved by their faith or their works, which had been going on since the Reformation. Luther, he admitted, had an instinctive sympathy with Pauline ideas; an emphasis upon simplicity, true inward religion, faith, humility and dependence upon God. But the reformer's theology, he thought, distorted the meaning of Paul's language, and this distortion had been made worse by subsequent generations. St. Paul did not define faith as meaning faith in the blood or even the death of Christ, nor did he suggest that the person who is justified would have any sense of assurance or consciousness that this was so. But, Jowett thought, that that was what the doctrine had come to mean.

The truth is that Jowett no longer thought of "faith" as "believing a set number of things." It would have been impossible for him any longer to talk about more or less faith, judging it in terms of the amount that one found it possible to believe. Faith had become, for him, an attitude of mind, a "spirit", "a return to God and nature", "a living communion with God". Such a conception of faith has little to do with how *much* one believes. To speak of having *more* faith, in the sense in which Jowett now used the term, would be to speak of intensity not quantity.

The essay 'On Atonement and Satisfaction' attracted most of the wrath of Jowett's critics because of the obvious and direct challenge the author was issuing. The essay on natural religion planted its barbs almost in passing. The essay on righteousness, though plainly taking a line very different from Evangelical orthodoxy, did not actually deny that orthodoxy in so many words. The essay on the atonement quite clearly and specifically pronounced the conventional belief of the day to be wrong. And it did so in terms which not only attacked the penal substitutionary theology of the Evangelicals but also the satisfaction language of the medieval theologians and thus offended High Churchmen, too. There was no possibility that Jowett's purpose might be overlooked. He described the conventional explanation of the atonement as revolting to men's moral feelings. God, he said, is represented as angry with us for what we never did; he is ready to inflict a disproportionate punishment on us for what we are; he is satisfied by the vicarious sufferings of his own son. In place of this, Jowett offered an alternative view, hesitantly and with a repeated insistence that any theological formulation must fail to capture the essential religious mystery. He thought that communion with Christ, in part a mystical sense of his presence, in part a more down to earth determination to identify with his moral standards, was the way to understand atonement.

Even those, like Lightfoot, who were not entirely unsympathetic, found Jowett's attempt to formulate an alternative theology less convincing than his attack on the conventional view. In a sense they were justified in doing so. Jowett had, in effect, advanced a purely subjective and exemplarist theology. He had, indeed, come very close to admitting this himself, saying in the closing section of the essay, "We know nothing of the objective act on God's part by which He reconciled the world to Himself."[37] Jowett tried to defend himself against the attacks of his critics by revising the essay in subsequent editions. He refused in any way to modify his opinion but attempted to make his argument clearer and more watertight. The effect of this was merely to make his onslaught on conventional theology seem the fiercer. The revised essay opened with what was almost a caricature of the penal substitution theory which was then bluntly rejected. And Jowett abandoned his attempt to remain agnostic about the objective aspect of the atonement, summarising instead the attempt of German philosophers and theologians from Kant to Hegel to expound alternative views. Those, he believed, Englishmen would find too remote and theoretical, substituting the metaphysical for the practical and reflecting "at too great a distance what ought to be very near us."[38] His own view was manifestly subjectivist, arguing that Christ's death is to be understood as the greatest moral act ever performed and, thus, as setting the seal upon what his life had stood for. It moves men and women to perceive their own imperfection and their need for greater closeness to God while at the same time assuring them of God's love. They are then able to use the knowledge of that love, as real as the love of an earthly friend but with the power of the divine, to become like Christ, to be reconciled to God and pass into the relationship of sons of God.

Even the milder first edition was too much for unsympathetic critics. Jowett was denounced to the university authorities for holding views contrary to the teaching of the *Thirty-Nine Articles*. Golightly, who had embarrassed Tait by the fervour of his attacks on Newman in 1841, now became one of the prime movers in this campaign against Jowett. The Vice-Chancellor summoned Jowett and asked him to subscribe the *Articles* again, undoubtedly a degrading experience. Jowett signed. It was "the meaner part", as he told Stanley, ". . .I could not do otherwise without giving up my position as a Clergyman."[39]

It is possible, of course, that this last remark merely meant that Jowett felt obliged to sign in order to retain his position at Balliol. It is also possibly surprising that he was willing to submit, in view of what he was later to say about greatness, clergymen and the received creed. But there is no reason to believe that Jowett was other than sincere. He took his clerical duties seriously till the end of his life. Theology, religion, personal devotion and his preaching office were always important to him. But equally he always stressed the impossibility of treating theological statements as if they were precise and exhaustive definitions. He seems to have believed — with some reason — that the *Articles* were originally intended to be inclusive rather than exclusive and that the attempt to require subscription to the *plain and literal sense* of the formularies was an innovation.[40]

This requirement was the real heart of the problem for the conscientious clergyman. He was required to teach a truth which is expressed in several different ways. Faith, religious belief, theology and doctrinal formularies are not precisely the same thing. Faith — at least as Jowett defined it — is a committed attitude of mind. Religious belief is an intuition about the nature of reality. Theology is the systematic attempt to express that belief intellectually. Formularies try to summarise the main essentials of belief in a concise theological language. The boundaries between them are not hard and fast and it is not always clear at what level any given statement is being made.

The Articles were produced in the sixteenth century. The controversial issues of the reformation era — free will, predestination, grace, justification, faith and works, the papacy, ecclesiastical authority and the authority of the Bible, sacraments, ministry and the nature of the Church — all naturally loom large. So, inevitably in a document emanating from Tudor England, does the question of civil obedience. But the *Articles* also incorporate much of the language of the classical Christian creeds, influenced by doctrinal controversies of the fourth and fifth centuries about the Trinity and the Incarnation. Merely to understand what any given article is asserting may involve a considerable historical and philological, as well as theological and philosophical exercise. Moreover the *Articles* themselves do not claim an ultimate authority. Several of them imply that the Christian tradition and the pronouncements of the great councils of the early Church have an important – though not an over-riding or infallible – authority. And the Bible is treated, throughout, as the one final authority, containing "all things necessary to salvation: so that whatsoever is not read therein, nor may be proved thereby, is not to be required of any man, that it should be believed as an article of the Faith. . ." (Article IV). But the Bible is not a collection of theological propositions. It contains narrative, poetry, exhortation, parable and history (or what was thought to be history) as well as a relatively small amount of directly theological writing. Most Christian theology has been an attempt to work out the logical consequences of the commitment and belief evoked by the Bible. If new knowledge (of a scientific or historical kind) or a new understanding (resulting from research in the textual or philological field) leads to a different and more accurate interpretation of some key passage of the New Testament, the implications of the *Articles* themselves would seem to be that theology would have to be brought into line with the Bible, not *vice versa*.

The nineteenth century was becoming acutely aware of these problems in a way that had never happened before. Issues related to the truth of and authority for theological statements were becoming more and more prominent. For someone who was both a clergyman and an academic the whole question of integrity and truth was uncomfortable yet inescapable. There is plainly no point in holding a religious belief unless one believes it to be true. But one may honestly, sincerely and deeply believe something to be true and yet ask all sorts of critical questions about the *sense* in which it may be true. As scientific discovery began to suggest, for instance, that the Old Testament account of the origin of the world could not be literally a description of what actually happened, men like Jowett had to ask themselves, In what sense is the story true? If it is an assertion of a relationship between

God and the universe rather than a quasi-scientific description of an event, in what sense did God *make* the world?

The question of the nature of religious truth began to seem enormously subtle and complex. The relative authority of Bible, doctrinal formularies, the general Christian tradition and the prevailing contemporary notions of what constituted orthodoxy, would cause all sorts of conflicts, within oneself and in controversy with others. Even when one signs an income tax declaration to the effect that "the particulars given on this form are correct and complete", one does so with the saving clause, "to the best of my knowledge and belief." And those particulars, though possibly complicated, are factual. To be asked to subscribe something as complex as the *Thirty-Nine Articles*, without reservation or saving clause, and in a plain and literal sense, was to be asked to do something totally unreasonable.

On the other hand it is not unreasonable to require a clergyman (and especially a clergyman engaged in teaching theology to other prospective clergymen) to make a public declaration that he holds to the teaching of the Church. However much he may say to himself that his questionings and his divergence from conventional orthodoxy are not about *whether* the teaching is true but *in what sense* it is true, there may come a point at which it is dishonest to pursue his private understanding of truth and at the same time continue to hold an ecclesiastical office. For a clergyman who is also an academic, a rigorously self-critical mind and an uncompromising integrity are essential. If Faber is to be believed, Jowett thought that only someone capable of a first in Greats possessed the necessary resource for such a life-long struggle![41] But it is not surprising that Jowett, when writing his notes on "Why great men are never clergymen", said that it might be better "for a great man in a high Ecclesiastical station . . . to drop all dogmatic theology — and to fill his mind with great schemes for the regeneration of mankind . . .".[42]

It is not surprising either that Jowett felt compelled to tackle seriously the whole question of the interpretation of scripture. He had first begun to draft an essay on the subject in 1847, intending to include it in the Pauline commentaries. It was still incomplete when the manuscript went to the publishers and had to be left out. Jowett hoped that it would be ready for the second edition of 1859 but again

failed to complete it. It finally became his contribution to the notorious volume called *Essays and Reviews*.

It was intended that the contributors to this volume should deal
with theological subjects critically, in accordance with new knowledge,
but "reverently" and within the framework of the tradition of the
Church of England. The prime mover in the project seems to have
been H.B. Wilson who had been, with Tait, one of the four signatories
of the tutors' letter which had led to the censure of Tract XC and the
degradation of Ward. The champion of orthodoxy of 1841 was on
the path to becoming the heretic of 1861. Stanley, characteristically,
did not become involved in the project. The other Balliol contributor
to the volume, besides Jowett, was Frederick Temple. Enormously
hard-working and energetic, intellectually able and also very practical,
Temple was rather younger that Jowett and had been his pupil.
Having been an undergraduate at Balliol, he became a Fellow in 1842.
From 1848 to 1857, though a clergyman, he was attached to the
department of the Committee of the Privy Council on Education,
precursor of the Board of Education. For most of this time he was
Principal of Kneller Hall Training College, a new institution for training schoolmasters to teach pauper children in workhouses. He succeeded Tait at Rugby in 1857, presumably a very sharp contrast to
Kneller Hall, and became Bishop of Exeter in 1869. Like Tait, too, he
was to be Bishop of London and eventually Archbishop of Canterbury.
To him Jowett had dedicated his two volumes of the commentaries
"in grateful acknowledgement of numberless thoughts and suggestions and of the blessings of a long and neverfailing friendship." There
were many things that these two shared: background, circumstances,
interest in the education of the underprivileged, and in Hegel and in
radical theological ideas.

Essays and Reviews appeared in 1860 and was rapidly reissued in
several new editions in the next few years. It was the centre of a theological controversy more violent than anything before it in the nineteenth century. The essays were varied and uneven. Frederick Temple
revised and extended a sermon, 'The Education of the World', in an
attempt to expound a theory of development or progress in revelation
and the knowledge of God. It was neither very radical nor very
rigorous. Rowland Williams wrote on the critical biblical study of
Baron von Bunsen. Baden Powell's essay on the 'evidences' of Chris-

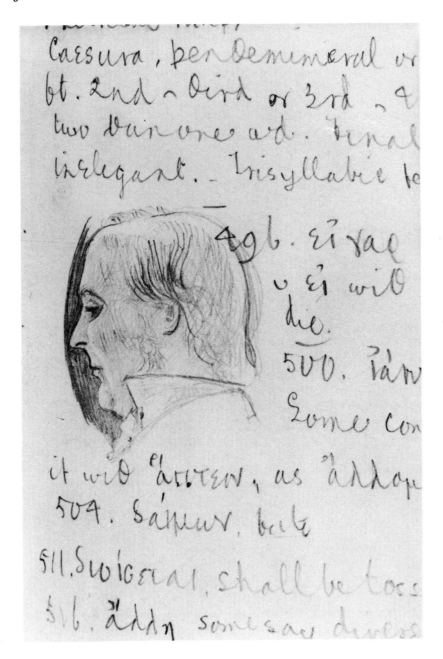

Plate 1. Benjamin Jowett, sketched by Gerard Manley Hopkins.

tianity and Charles Goodwin's 'On the Mosaic Cosmogony' also dealt
with themes in which natural science and Christian faith were thought
to be in conflict. But Mark Pattison wrote on 'Tendencies of Religious
Thought in England, 1688–1750' and H.B. Wilson himself contributed
an essay on the national church. There was neither plan nor editorial
policy. Nor was there an agreed theological perspective. It was a typically Broad Church production. Every man spoke for himself: outraged conservative opinion – if not the devil – did its best to take
the hindermost.

Jowett's essay, the last in the book, was a long one, almost double
the length of most of the other contributions. For the modern reader
it is also rather tedious, not just because of the somewhat verbose
style but also because Jowett uses so much space to argue a case which
would now be readily conceded. For Jowett's own day, no doubt, it
needed to be argued step by step. There was little in the argument
that the author had not already adumbrated, touched on or hinted at
elsewhere. But it was set out fully and systematically. Jowett argued
that it was essential that the results of scientific enquiry and critical
scholarship be taken seriously and the Bible be treated as any other
book would be treated, in its context and as expressing the minds of
men of a particular historical era and cultural setting. He wanted to
get rid of the complex patterns of symbolic, traditional and allegorical
interpretation which had been read into, rather than out of, the actual
text. He thought that trying to 'prove' doctrinal positions from scripture was an ill-conceived and impossible task. He had some, but not
much, sympathy with genuine tradition but his was essentially the
approach of the textual critic who believed that truth was to be discovered primarily by getting back to the original document and behind
the centuries of theological debate. He perceived clearly, of course,
that the New Testament world was very different from that of classical
Greece. He made some attempt to recapture the feel of that world
but had few of the necessary tools for doing so. First century Judaism
was largely a closed book to him. All its complexity, its inheritance
of thousands of years of religious tradition, its grapplings with the
impact of Hellenism, did not really interest him. Getting back to the
sense of the New Testament itself appeared to be essentially a process
of simplification and the benefits, he believed, would be those which
result from simplicity. It would be easier, for instance, for Christians

to agree, to unite, and to engage in mission together, if they could get back to the original meaning of the gospels.

Jowett's summary of his own argument was masterly:

> That Scripture, like other books, has one meaning, which is to be gathered from itself without reference to the adaptations of Fathers or Divines; and without regard to *a priori* notions about its nature and origins. It is to be interpreted like other books with attention to the character of its authors, and the prevailing state of civilization and knowledge, with allowance for peculiarities of style and language, and modes of thought and figures of speech. Yet not without a sense that as we read there grows upon us the witness of God in the world, anticipating in a rude and primitive age the truth that was to be, shining more and more unto the perfect day in the life of Christ, which again is reflected from different points of view in the teaching of His Apostles.[43]

This summary comes about two-thirds of the way through the essay. The last third is taken up with various *obiter dicta* and includes, significantly, a gentle warning that the intending clergyman may not be the best person to tackle these problems unless he has "clearness of mind to see things as they are, and a faith strong enough to rest in that degree of knowledge which God has really given . . .". This touch of the patronising does not altogether disguise the fact that Jowett still partly shared with his critics the feeling that religion and an open mind do not really go together.

Samuel Wilberforce, Bishop of Oxford and a leading High Churchman, attacked the book and urged his fellow bishops to take concerted action against it. After a meeting at Lambeth, the archbishops and twenty-four bishops issued a letter expressing their disapproval of the views expressed by the essayists. In what seemed to Jowett, and even more to Temple, to be an act of near-treachery, Tait was one of the signatories. It *seemed* that he had submitted to the gene of the received creed. The Convocation of Canterbury formally debated whether to pass synodical judgement upon the book. The lower house voted to proceed to judgement in June 1861 but the upper house, the bishops, took no immediate action because Williams and

Wilson were about to be prosecuted for heresy before the ecclesiastical tribunals. The book was, however, eventually condemned by
Convocation in 1864.

Meanwhile the prosecution of the two essayists proceeded. Williams
and Wilson were the most vulnerable of the essayists because their
views seemed clearly unorthodox and they were also without doubt
subject to the authority of the Church courts. The Court of Arches,
the Archbishop of Canterbury's court, found them guilty, but the Ju-
dicial Committee of the Privy Council, acting as court of appeal in
ecclesiastical causes, reversed the judgement. The whole process took
nearly three years. Meanwhile Jowett himself came under attack in
the university. His salary as Professor of Greek became a matter of
controversy which was used by his opponents, led by Dr. Pusey, as
an opportunity to attack his theological orthodoxy. Pusey also ini-
tiated a prosecution of Jowett before the Vice-Chancellor's Court for
teaching doctrines contrary to and inconsistent with the doctrines of
the Church of England. The Vice-Chancellor's assessor (effectively
judge in the case) decided that his jurisdiction was, at best, doubtful
and refused to proceed. For all that Jowett used to talk of the per-
secutions he had suffered in the years following his disappointment
over the mastership, he had really escaped very lightly.

There was to be no more public theology. He continued courage-
ously, in typical Broad Church fashion, to defend theological freedom.
After he had become Master and when Colenso's Old Testament criticism had succeeded *Essays and Reviews* as the theological storm
centre, Jowett defended the bishop and provided him with an opportunity to preach in Balliol chapel. But, academically, he concentrated
on the Greek philosophers and particularly on Plato, and the College
occupied more and more of his time and thought. He became Master
in September 1870, just ten years after the publication of *Essays and
Reviews* — apparently as a result of the direct and deliberate inter-
vention of Gladstone who offered Robert Scott the deanery of
Rochester and thus created the vacancy to which Jowett was elected.

Gladstone's action was, on the face of it, odd. He approved neither
of Jowett nor his theology. The pencilled comments he wrote in the
margins of Jowett's essay — Gladstone was in the habit of annotating
the books he read — were virulent in the extreme. His remarks are
ad hominem. Where Jowett had written "Everyone . . . has need to

JOWETT AND THE CHURCH 149

make war against his prejudices . . .", Gladstone remarked, "None more need than the writer of this essay." And his final comment on the essay as a whole was, "A cold vain barren Philosophy, ending with the Grave here. The sport and Triumph of devils hereafter." None of the other essays was annotated, except Temple's and, in that case, there were as many approving underlinings or ticks as there were disapproving "ma"s. The only articulate note was "Homer! Dante!" written against Temple's assertion that a modern child of twelve stood at the intellectual level once occupied by a full grown man. No other book he read seems to have provoked Gladstone as Jowett's essay did. Even Colenso (of whom Gladstone disapproved very severely) did not receive the sort of treatment meted out to Jowett. The bishop's *Pentateuch and the Book of Joshua, critically examined* (or rather the first Part of it, for Gladstone seems to have become less and less interested in the later more technical volumes) was favoured with the usual onomatopoeic noises but no real comment.[44] Nevertheless Gladstone was a fair man and, even when appointing bishops, did not allow unorthodox theological opinion to outweigh other qualities. He had sent Temple to Exeter in the year before Jowett became Master.[45]

Though Temple's nomination to Exeter provoked an outcry among both Evangelicals and Anglo-Catholics, Temple had already dissociated himself from the other contributors to *Essays and Reviews*. Even in the rather muffled account given by his biographer, who tried very hard to present Temple in the best possible light, his action hardly appears very creditable.[46] He seems to have done three things – asked the boys not to read the book, asserted that as Headmaster of Rugby he would not have contributed to it, and stressed that he had had no idea what was in the other essays. Subsequently, after he had become a bishop, and once again in circumstances which are difficult to sort out, he "withdrew his essay from further publication."[47] Temple *had* submitted to the gêne of the received creed. The dedication in Jowett's commentaries must have acquired an ironic overtone. The "long and never failing friendship" came to an end. All Jowett's close theological friendships with Balliol men of the 1840s were fading. He remained on good but not intimate terms with Tait till the latter's death. He continued to count Stanley as a close friend and preached regularly for him in the Abbey. Even Florence Nightingale was not allowed to denigrate him. But Stanley had this knack of being never quite in the front line and had "behaved strangely" at times.[48] There was no one who could be trusted absolutely and no one with whom to strike the old theological sparks. His close friends of later years were not theologians or clergymen. After he became Master his interests were primarily in public affairs and the men who figured in them.

Neither bishopric nor deanery would have tempted Jowett.[49] One simply cannot imagine him being lured away from Balliol as Scott had been. "I am where I wish to be", he replied to Tait's letter of congratulation after his election, "My desire here is not to be leader of a party but to educate the young men or get them educated."[50] It was the height of his ambition and one suspects that he would not have regarded a bishopric as a step up from the mastership. It would also have required a degree of submission which he would have found difficult to accept.

The fact that there was no more public theology and that he was where he wanted to be, getting young men educated, does not mean that his theological thinking stopped. He had asserted in *Essays and Reviews* that the study of scripture ought to be part of a "liberal education" because there is "a sense of things into which we must grow as well as reason ourselves, without which human nature is but a truncated, half-educated sort of being."[51] He became a preacher. Sermons in college chapel were a relatively recent innovation. Earlier there had been a system of catechetical lectures at which the undergraduates, who attended chapel compulsorily, were questioned about what the lecturer said. Jowett had been unwilling to undertake these lectures though he, like other tutors, regularly gave religious addresses to his own pupils gathered once a term in his own rooms. In 1869 he was asked to preach a course of sermons in chapel and after he became Master in the following year he preached regularly twice each term.[52] His language and style were simple, direct and straightforward, rather a contrast to his other writings. It would, no doubt, be absurd to suppose that they were the most exciting moment in every undergraduate's week, but — allowing for the fact that one had to be in chapel — they appear to have been genuinely appreciated by a good many. What he said seemed to be about real things, about life as it actually was, and to derive from a genuine conviction and a courageous determination to say what he believed to be true.[53]

In Jowett's sermons and in the theological or religious ideas he wrote down in his note books — some of which were notes for sermons — it is possible to detect a theological position which is clearly derived from the views he had already set out in the commentaries and his essay. There are three main points. First, it is impossible to defend or protect Christianity by being obscurantist or to try and overcome the truth by adopting an ever more rigid theological position. One has to meet the temptation to take refuge in dogma by having confidence in history.[54] With this there went, secondly, a concept of God which was strongly influenced by Hegel and by Plato — "God as goodness and wisdom, tending ever to realize itself in the world" — and a belief that the essence of religion was self-sacrifice and self-denial, the greatest moral power in the world.[55] The third aspect, and one which saved his position from being simply barren and minimalist, was his personal devotion to Christ as the ideal, not located in some historically and geographically remote context, but the present focus for life. *Imitatio Christi* was something that always fascinated Jowett and plans to write a life of Christ figured again and again on his lists of projects to be undertaken. Here, too, the influence or example of Hegel may be guessed at. But he was always, as he had hinted in the revised essay on the atonement, concerned to be practical where Hegel was metaphysical, to make things seem intimate rather than remote. And if, through Plato's influence, he thought of God as "Law" or as "Ultimate Truth" he saw these not as abstractions but as embodied in the person of Christ.

What Jowett failed to see was that much of what he dismissed as mere dogma enshrined a vital part of the Christian tradition based, in turn, upon Christian experience. Prayer, sacraments, worship and doctrine can all be ways of conveying a richness and depth of belief which are lost if everything is pared down to the irreducible minimum. Morality, as he had said to Brodie thirty years previously, was the one thing he really felt *compelled* to maintain. Inevitably, in consequence, his sermons often read as if they were chiefly concerned to urge a sense of moral endeavour rather than to convey hope and forgiveness or evoke love. Coupled with Jowett's admiration of greatness and success, the effect may sometimes have been somewhat crushing. An irate clergyman wrote to Tait (after he had become Archbishop) saying that the laity needed to be protected from the clergy and retailing, in support of this claim, gossip he had heard from the younger generation about Balliol sermons. Miracles were sneered at, the literal truth of the scriptures questioned and, after the suicide of an undergraduate, it had been said that "when a man found himself beaten in the battle of life it may pehaps be better that he should give it up." "All this offensive talk", said Tait's correspondent, "is owing to the Essays and Reviews Judgement."[56]

There is no necessity to suppose that it was Jowett who said those particular words about suicide. If he did, he may have been trying to defend the man's action in an era when suicide was regarded as a crime and a sin. But achieving something with one's life was a favourite theme of his sermons, though he was always careful to insist that by achievement he did not mean worldly success. As in a sermon on the text "It is finished"[57], which Tait always remembered as helpful and striking[58], Jowett meant to convey to his hearers that they ought to make their lives morally valuable, beautiful and creative.

It is simply not possible to estimate how much Jowett's views, expressed in his regular sermons, may have influenced parish clergymen up and down the country who had been educated at Balliol. His reiterated opinion that it was better for such men not to engage in theology presumably meant that he had no conscious desire to disturb their orthodoxy. But he did not hide his dislike of obscurantism and his ideas, no matter how moderately expressed, were bound to leave some mark upon them. For those who were potential leaders in the Church, the ambivalence of Jowett's attitude would create an even more difficult dilemma. On the one hand he did not think that run-of-the-mill pastoral activities (like "preaching to cabmen") were a proper vehicle for greatness. On the other, he believed that theological speculation was as dangerous for them as for parish clergymen. What he thought they ought to engage in was the government and adminis-tration of the Church or "great schemes for the regeneration of man-kind". Yet, if they then conformed to conventional orthodoxy, there was always the risk that he would regard them as having betrayed the truth and submitted to the gêne of the received creed. It must have been an impossible ideal for a bright young aspiring clergyman to live up to and perhaps it is not surprising that Jowett created no obvious group of disciples. His typically Broad Church individualism would also make it difficult for him to found a school of theological thought.

What had happened to Tait and Temple would incline him against grooming Balliol men for bishoprics.

It is possible, however, that this is only part of the answer to the puzzle with which this essay began — why someone who influenced the rising generation in every other sphere seems to have left so little mark upon his own profession. There is a sense in which Jowett's *indirect* influence has not been recognised as it ought.

The two most eminent ecclesiastics produced by Balliol during Jowett's mastership were Charles Gore and Cosmo Gordon Lang. Both were undoubtedly famous and influential. Of the two, it was Lang, much the younger, who came closest to fulfilling Jowett's prescription for an important churchman. Lang's distinguished ecclesiastical career culminated in his becoming Archbishop of Canterbury from 1928 to 1942. He was a statesman and administrator of considerable skill. (He was the archbishop of the abdication crisis.) And he did not concern himself, at least for most his life, with what Jowett called "those great questions which lie on the threshold of the higher study of theology . . .". Jowett would have thought that entirely right and proper in an important clergyman but he would not have approved of Lang's High Church tendencies and he might well have thought of Lang as too comfortable within the constraint of the received creed to be a great man. It is certainly difficult to regard Lang as a disciple of Jowett's in terms of his ideas and thought.

Charles Gore, leading Anglo-Catholic theologian in the first quarter of the twentieth century, ascetic, founder of a monastic community, and successively Bishop of Worcester, Birmingham and Oxford between 1902 and 1919, was almost everything of which Jowett would have disapproved. Nor can Gore really have been at home in Jowett's Balliol. Yet ironically a collection of essays, *Lux Mundi*, edited by Gore and published in 1889, was almost as much of a cause of scandal as *Essays and Reviews* had been thirty years earlier. In that volume, as in much of his later writings, Gore's object was to reconcile Anglo-Catholic theology with the results of critical and scientific investigations. He was often suspect in the eyes of older Anglo-Catholics but even this did not win him much sympathy from Jowett who when he read *Lux Mundi*, commented that he was "a good deal disappointed in it. It has a more friendly and Christian tone than High Church theology used to have, but it is the same old haze and maze — no nearer approach of religion either to morality or to historical truth."[59] Any influence Jowett may have had on Gore himself was probably mediated through T.H. Green, who had been a pupil of Jowett's and become a Fellow of the college in 1861. Green had developed a much more systematically Hegelian philosophy of religion and this, in turn, influenced the whole *Lux Mundi* school, though they rejected his extreme immanentism.

Jowett also exercised an important indirect influence through another neo-Hegelian, Edward Caird (who was also his pupil and eventually succeeded him as Master) upon the thinking of William Temple. Frederick Temple's son, William was an undergraduate at Balliol after Jowett's death and was eventually to succeed Lang as Archbishop of Canterbury. He was, perhaps, the most influential Anglican theologian of the twentieth century. Between the two world wars, indeed, most Anglican clergymen were brought up on Gore and Temple and it could be said that the prevailing orthodoxy of the first half of the century was a theology influenced by philosophical idealism and a desire to take the results of the natural sciences seriously. It may be that Jowett's ideas were genuinely seminal in a way that has never been fully recognised.

NOTES

1. G. Faber *Jowett: a portrait with background* (1957), p. 136. Archbishop Benson's son, Arthur, used a curiously similar phrase, when it was suggested to him that if he were to "take orders" he might become Headmaster of Eton; "Prominent position and great work are so bound up in my mind with *gêne* and odious publicities and bonds of all kinds that I do not desire them . . ." D. Williams *Genesis and Exodus* (1979), p. 128.

2. Faber *op. cit.*, p. 236, completely misunderstood Rowland Williams's use of the term "fiction" as applied to certain explanations of the doctrine of justification by faith. In his contribution to *Essays and Reviews* Williams used the word not to imply that Christ's atoning death was fictional or mythical but as a way of pointing out that righteousness cannot be *transferred* from one person to another, except in a very notional (or *fictional*) sense.

3. Faber *op. cit.*, p. 277, evidently thought that Bishop Samuel Wilberforce, like his more famous father, was an Evangelical.

4. P.T. Marsh *The Victorian Church in Decline* (1969), p. 9.

5. Lambeth Palace Library: Tait Papers: Personal Letters: vol. 79, fos.25 ff., Jowett to Tait, 19 September 1856.

6. *Ibid.*, fos.305–308, two letters from Jowett to Tait, 12 and 21 October 1862. The letters are principally about permission for Jowett to administer holy communion to Florence Nightingale who was ill at her home in Hampstead in Tait's diocese: "her views", Jowett warned Tait, "are not what some would call orthodox."

7. See e.g. the article on Tait in *The Oxford Dictionary of the Christian Church* ed. F.L. Cross (reprinted with corrections 1958).

8. Tait Papers: Personal Letters: vol. 79, fos.25ff.

9. "To have a quantity of criticism about the dung in the Jewish camp, and the division of a hare's foot, thrown in my face, when I was satisfied that the Jewish history had been the mightiest witness to the people for a living God against the dead dogmas of priests, was more shocking to me that I can describe." F. Maurice *Life of F.D. Maurice* 2nd edn. (1884), I p. 174.

10. Stanley declined to contribute to *Essays and Reviews* on the grounds that it was an ill-advised venture but was incensed by the attempts to prosecute some of the contributors. As Dean of Westminster he refused to allow the first Lambeth Conference to use the abbey in case there might be an attempt to condemn Colenso, but dissociated himself strongly from some of Colenso's writings.

11. Faber *op. cit.*, pp. 253ff.

12. Balliol College MS.410: an undated and incomplete letter from Jowett to Stanley.

13. Tait Papers: Personal Letters: vol. 77, fo.54. A very curt letter from Tait to Golightly on the impropriety of using anonymous letters to the press.

14. J. Bentley *Ritualism and Politics in Victorian Britain* (Oxford 1978), pp. 46ff. and p. 113.

15. Faber *op. cit.*, p. 253.

16. R.T. Davidson *Life of Archibald Campbell Tait* (1891), I p. 190. Five of
    Tait's six daughters died of scarlet fever within one month. That he was able
    to surmount this tragic experience in spite of his love for his children appears
    to have been due to his deep faith.
17. E. Abbott and L. Campbell *Life and Letters of Benjamin Jowett* (1897), I
    p.74.
18. Tait Papers: Personal Letters: vol. 78, fos.268–71. Part of the letter is illeg-
    ible because of the way it has been bound in the volume.
19. *Ibid.*, fo.178.
20. Abbott and Campbell *op. cit.*, I p. 115.
21. P. Hinchliff *John William Colenso* (1964), p. 104.
22. Faber tended to interpret most Victorian friendships in this fashion, see
    Oxford Apostles 2nd edn. (1963), pp. 215ff. There is a sermon of Jowett's
    on the subject of friendship (in *Sermons on Faith and Doctrine*, 1901, an
    additional sermon printed as an appendix) which draws heavily on Plato,
    refers to David and Jonathan, Achilles and Patroclus, and is difficult for a
    modern to read without putting some such interpretation on it. But no mod-
    ern could *preach* it innocently either and the fact that Jowett could do so is
    itself significant.
23. G. Faber *Jowett*, pp. 152ff. Nearly twenty years later Jowett was to write
    "He Stanley has behaved strangely to me at times and I have always imagined
    there to be explanations." (Balliol College: Copies of letters from Jowett to
    Florence Nightingale: 28 November 1865). The explanation, Jowett thought,
    was the influence of Stanley's sister.
24. Jowett wrote Stanley a letter from Bonn on 1 January 1849 the first page
    and a half of which is in German and which opens with the rather arch
    "Lieber Prinz Arthur" but the letter itself deals with politics, the nature of
    university education and other entirely unembarrassing matters. (Balliol
    College MS.410).
25. Balliol College MS.410: in a letter from Torquay, probably of 1862, written
    when Jowett had heard that Stanley had been summoned to Osborne prob-
    ably in order to be "requested to accompany the Prince of Wales to the East",
    he begins the letter "My dear Arthur".
26. *Ibid.*, letter dated 9 March 1862, written when Stanley was actually on tour
    with the prince in Egypt and Palestine.
27. Apart from the period in which they were working together on the commen-
    taries, Jowett is hardly mentioned in R.E. Prothero and G.C. Bradley *Life
    and Correspondence of Arthur Penrhyn Stanley* (1893). There is one brief
    earlier mention of him (vol. I p. 212) as one of Stanley's friends at the time
    of their election to fellowships.
28. Faber *op. cit.*, pp. 152f.
29. Balliol College MS.410, an undated letter from Jowett to Stanley giving the
    names of Fellows voting on either side. Cf. Lambeth Palace: Tait Papers:
    Personal Letters: vol. 78, fos.267f., Jowett to Tait, 10 November 1854. The
    resolution imposing the test was carried only because the Master's vote coun-
    ted as two votes. The matter was taken to the Visitor who disallowed the

imposition of an additional test.

30. In *Journal of Classical and Sacred Philology* II, (1856) pp. 104ff (see article on Jowett in *Dictionary of National Biography*, first supplement). Lightfoot was the friend and associate of Westcott and Hort, and was to be Westcott's predecessor as Bishop of Durham.

31. *The Epistles of St. Paul to the Thessalonians, Galatians and Romans* (1855), Vol. II, particularly the essays on 'Natural Religion', 'Righteousness by Faith', 'Atonement and Satisfaction' and 'Predestination and Free-will'.

32. William Paley *Natural Theology* bound with *Horae Paulinae* (American Tract Society "from a late London edition"), pp. 304f.

33. Faber *op. cit.*, p. 140.

34. *Sermons on Faith and Doctrine* (1901), p. 18. These and other of Jowett's sermons were edited for publication after his death by W.H. Fremantle, Fellow and Chaplain of Balliol from 1882 to 1894, afterwards Dean of Ripon and perhaps the nearest thing there ever was to a Jowett protegé in high ecclesiastical office. His son, Sir Francis Fremantle, bequeathed a sum of money to the college to endow the Fremantle lectures on the congruity of science and religion in memory of his father.

35. Imperial College London: The Huxley Papers: Scientific and General Correspondence: vol. VII, fo.91: 18 April 1893. There is a copy of the letter in Balliol College: Jowett Letters Box 3, 'B. Jowett, Copies of Letters'.

36. Abbott and Campbell *op. cit.*, pp. 114f.

37. B. Jowett *Epistles*, II p. 422.

38. In the second edition (1859), p. 585.

39. Faber *op. cit.*, p. 226.

40. *Ibid.*, pp. 152f.

41. *Ibid.*, p. 138.

42. *Ibid.*, p. 136.

43. *Essays and Reviews*, the final paragraph of section 4 of Jowett's essays 'On the Interpretation of Scripture'. Because there were so many editions and the essay was reprinted so many times, it seems better to refer to sections and paragraphs rather than to page numbers. Since this article was written a very thorough study of *Essays and Reviews* has been published: Ieuan Ellis *Seven against Christ: a study of Essays and Reviews* (Leiden 1980).

44. Gladstone's copies of *Essays and Reviews* and of Colenso's works are now in St. Deiniol's Library, Hawarden. I am indebted to John Prest for drawing my attention to the comments on the last few pages of Jowett's essay.

45. On the fly-leaf at the back of Gladstone's copy of *Essays and Reviews* there is pencilled a list of names which includes those of Jowett, Stanley, Maurice, Temple, Pattison and even Colenso (*Pentateuch and Joshua* did not appear till two years after *Essays and Reviews*) along with others of a less radical reputation. One is tempted to wonder whether Gladstone was making a list of names for Palmerston to consider, perhaps as a counterweight to' the Evangelicals whom Shaftesbury usually suggested to him.

46. *Memoirs of Archbishop Temple* ed. E.G. Sandford (1906), I pp. 219ff.

47. *Ibid.*, pp. 301ff.

48. See note 23 above.

49. Balliol College: Copies of letters from Jowett to Florence Nightingale: in a letter probably written in January 1865, at a time when Jowett felt that Balliol had treated him badly and that he was being generally persecuted, he said that no mitre had ever been made that would fit his head. Deaneries were better, but even they were not what he really wanted.

50. Tait Papers: Personal Letters: vol. 88, fo.163, Jowett to Tait, 10 October 1870.

51. 'On the Interpretation of Scripture', 6.2.iii.

52. B. Jowett *College Sermons* (1895), p.vi.

53. *Ibid.*, p. ix. Not everyone found his sermons helpful, however, at least in earlier days, see E.G. Sandford ed. *op. cit.*, I p. 91.

54. Balliol College: Jowett Papers: 'Descriptions of the present state of theology' - notes written in a small notebook marked 'F' and cf. 'Criticism and Dogma' in Abbott and Campbell *op. cit.*, II p. 310.

55. Cf. the almost despairing notes on 'Changes in Religion', 'The New Christianity' and 'The Two Great Forms of Religion' in Abbott and Campbell *op. cit.*, II pp.311ff.

56. Tait Papers: Personal Letters: Vol. 90, fos.199f: the Reverend G.R. Portal to Tait, 13 October 1872.

57. No.XIX in *College Sermons*.

58. Abbott and Campbell *op. cit.*, II p. 237.

59. *Ibid.*, p. 377.

7 CARL SCHMIDT

Classical Studies at Balliol in the 1860's: the undergraduate essays of Gerard Manley Hopkins

Plate 1. Hopkins' staircase — his rooms were on the ground floor, to the left.

CLASSICAL STUDIES AT BALLIOL IN THE 1860's: THE UNDERGRADUATE ESSAYS OF GERARD MANLEY HOPKINS

I

Gerard Manley Hopkins came up to Balliol from Highgate School as an Exhibitioner in Trinity Term 1863 and took the Final Honour School of *Literae Humaniores* in Trinity 1867. The Balliol undergraduates of 1860/1–1866/7 included Edward Caird (Master 1893–1907) and J.L. Strachan-Davidson (Master 1907–16). Hopkins' own immediate contemporaries provided Balliol with two distinguished Fellows, Evelyn Abbott, co-biographer of Jowett, and Baron Francis de Paravicini; a junior was R.L. Nettleship, whose works include an admirable memoir of T.H. Green, one of Hopkins' philosophy tutors. These seven years reveal Balliol classical studies at their high point, with Robert Scott (Master 1854–70) and Benjamin Jowett, Regius Professor of Greek, both active in the tuition of undergraduates, and an accomplished team of tutors including Edwin Palmer, W.L. Newman and T.H. Green. Balliol classics was the best in Oxford: there were some seventy Firsts in Mods during these years, and of the thirty-five men who got Firsts in Greats, twenty-two were elected to Fellowships at Oxford, as were another ten who did not get Firsts. In Easter Term 1860 the whole of the First Class consisted of three Balliol men. The special status of *Literae Humaniores* in Oxford generally is affirmed with particular force in Balliol by the following fact: of the one hundred and fifty men in residence during these years (some of whom took more than one Final School, some of whom took none) ninety-three took Greats.

A good deal is known about the substantive content of studies from such works as A.M.M. Stedman's *Oxford: Its Life and Schools* (1878), and the general background of Victorian Hellenism has been brilliantly illuminated by Richard Jenkyns in *The Victorians and Ancient Greece* (Oxford 1980). Between these two types of account, purely factual and broadly interpretative, there is room for a closer look at the texture of studies as revealed in the undergraduate essays of a single Balliol man of this period. We are fortunate in having preserved for us nearly all the Greats essays of Gerard Manley Hopkins, which the

161

Society of Jesus keeps, along with the other Hopkins papers, at Campion Hall, Oxford.[1] With the help of the Master's Report Book, kept in the Balliol Archives, we can examine the character and trace the growth of a distinguished undergraduate classical career.[2] For ease and brevity of reference to the body of this essay, I have printed at the end two appendices containing 1) a full account of the contents of the essay-notebooks and some related manuscripts, and 2) all the Report Book entries relating to Hopkins in continuous sequence. This will make it easier for those whose main interest is Hopkins rather than Balliol classics to find the information they want.

Hopkins' Balliol tutors were E.C. Woollcombe, James Riddell, who died in 1866, Riddell's successor T.H. Green, W.L. Newman, the Master, and Jowett. Through the last he was sent in Trinity 1866 to Walter Pater, Fellow of Brasenose, for "coaching". This was the name for specialist teaching from an outside tutor. As J. Wells, Fellow of Wadham, remarks in his chapter on the *Lit. Hum.* Schools in Stedman's *Oxford*, "down to about 1870, it was almost an invariable rule for the future first class man to 'coach' ",[3] and the fact that an undergraduate whom Pusey called the "Star of Balliol"[4] should have been sent to Pater for his fifth term of Greats work (see Appendix One, notebook D.III) does not imply that he did not get on with Jowett, but rather the contrary. (According to Fr. Vassall-Phillips, who knew Hopkins when the latter was curate of St. Aloysius', Oxford, in 1878, for the Greek professorship at Dublin Hopkins "was recommended by Dr. Jowett, who wrote of him as one of the finest Greek scholars he had ever known at Oxford".)[5] I do not know where this comment on Hopkins is to be found *apud* Jowett; but it serves to confirm the truth of the (un-Balliolish) expression "Star" and is warmer than the "Extremely satisfactory" which is the highest commendation accorded by the Master in his reports.[6] Hopkins' own opinions of his tutors, in so far as he voiced them, have long been known from his published correspondence and journals;[7] but the only tutor's comment on him, one by T.H. Green (discussed below), was not occasioned by an academic matter.

The single most important event in Hopkins' undergraduate life was his conversion to Roman Catholicism in July 1866, an event of which there are distinct anticipations in essays written for Pater in the Trinity

Term preceding. But if it was as a Catholic that he wrote his essays for Green in Hilary 1867, it was as a High Anglican that he entered Balliol. It is therefore interesting to read the Pascal-like journal entry on his inner religious state, "A day of the great mercy of God",[8] in the light of Scott's comment in the Report Book for Easter and Act (= Trinity) Term 1865: "Very industrious but not quite regular at Chapel" (Appendix Two). The subject of this essay is not, of course, Hopkins' religious development at Balliol; but it should not be forgotten that *all* Balliol men, not just the especially religious, studied Scripture along with Classics for about three of their four years' course. Without comparing the Greats essays of his contemporaries, if such survive, it is not possible to say whether Hopkins was exceptional in relating his religious convictions to the topics of moral philosophy in hand, as he occasionally did. What we can say is that his conversion, with all the personal upheaval it involved, did not diminish but rather intensified the seriousness with which he carried out his philosophical studies. It has even been claimed by Professor Zaniello that "Hopkins' deep investigations into a theory of perception [in the *Journal* observations of the 1870's] are based on his philosophical studies" and "His vocabulary reflected his study of philosophy at Oxford and his careful re-working of the materials of the English empiricist tradition".[9]

II

The elements of Logic formed a part of the work for Honour Moderations *In Literis Graecis et Latinis* and it is interesting to note that four of the six essays in notebook D.I are on logical topics. Item 6 is a 'Master's Essay' (of the type still written by first-year Balliol undergraduates) and only one essay, 'On the rise of Greek Prose-writing', seems directly related to literature studies for Mods, in this case Thucydides and Demosthenes. What we should think of as criticism of classical literature seems hardly to have existed in the university examinations as yet, and presumably the student was taught to argue with a view to his later efforts in philosophy for Greats. The choice of books seems a little severe (see Appendix Two), with no Greek or Latin lyric or pastoral poetry, though there is a good deal of drama, as well as Homer, Virgil and Juvenal. Freshets of literary criticism could spring forth later even in so austere a terrain as a Greats essay on *phronesis* and *prohairesis* ("judgement"; "choice") (discussed below); but for Hopkins' response to classical literature at Balliol we have to turn to the miscellaneous comments in Notebook B. II. Most of the contents clearly date from the Mods period, and we have on folio 140 the title of a tutorial essay which was either not written or has been lost (it might have been in notebook D.I, the opening leaves of which have been cut out): 'Cf. pop. ideas of Greece as to its early hist. with those of historians – philosophers. Or how far the influences wh. meet us in ancient hist. are evolved fr. within. Cf. this with mod. hist.' (Hopkins freakishly uses the Greek letter *theta* for *th*.) Possibly this was not a Mods essay at all, but is to be related to the Greats Ancient History work done in Trinity 1865 and was jotted down here because Hopkins had the notebook to hand. It is frustrating not to have even the title of a single essay on classical literature proper.

What we do have, amongst many comments showing close attention to philological detail, is the occasional critical remark suggesting that Hopkins found Greek literature lacking in imaginative quality (though sometimes his tone can be positive). Thus he finds perverse the tendency of editors to consider Aeschylus a perfect writer: "The truth is that he was utterly deficient in a sense of the ridiculous of which this [*Choephori* 205–11][10] is not the only instance, not to speak of common sense" (f. 27). And even when praising as "excellent" the smile of the corks that buoy up the net (*Choeph.* 506–7) he thinks it "very much above the usual flats of Greek tragedy" (f. 36). Or he decides that "the story of Agamemnon's murder is very unpoetical – the bath etc." (f. 57). To judge by the often-quoted letter to A.W. Baillie of 10 September 1864, his implicit criterion here is Shakespeare – the murder of Duncan in *Macbeth*, say, or the account of the murder of King Hamlet – for of Shakespeare he writes with glowing enthusiasm, "all after admiration cannot increase but keep alive this estimate, make his greatness stare into your eyes and din it into your ears".[11] (Here we have that Victorian worship of Shakespeare, originating with Coleridge, which climaxed in the *Shakespearean Tragedy* of A.C. Bradley, who came up to Balliol two years after Hopkins took Schools.) On the other hand, the last stricture quoted above occurs in the same sentence praising *Choephori* 973ff as 'a splendid speech, the finest in the play'. In *Agamemnon* 1461 he marks the wordplay in *eris eridmatos* ("a deep laid cause of strife") observing judiciously that "the greater part of the dramatic beauty is

lost to us through our imperfect knowledge of Greek" (f. 72). Hopkins
senses, as reader, the want of that close intimacy one is granted towards even the older forms of one's native tongue. Yet there is clearly
a foreshadowing of his own later technical experiments in his awareness in Aeschylus of "curious alliterations and assonances, which have
not been sufficiently noticed in Greek tragedy": he gives none himself, but *ie, ie, diai Dios* (*Agam.* 1485; *io ie* in Fraenkel's edition)
would be an example (cf. "Pure *fast*ed faces draw unto this *feast*" in
'Easter Communion', written just after Hopkins took Mods).

Hopkins' most complimentary remarks on Aeschylus in B.II may
belong to the period before he came up to Oxford, at any rate if the
lines translated from the *Prometheus Desmotes* on f. 39 are the
original from which he quoted in a letter to E.H. Coleridge of 3 September 1862, in which he remarks "what stilted nonsense Greek
tragedy usually is" but qualifies "[*Prometheus Bound*] is really full
of splendid poetry".[12] He notes how in the phrase *tracheia pontou
Salmodessia gnathos* (*Prom.* 726) "this word *gnathos* applied, as it is
here, to the sea is very descriptive, it paints the way in which the sea
seems to *gnaw* or *grip* at the land" (f. 44), and of *kyknomorphoi,*
used of the Phorcides in *Prom.* 795 (f. 52), he writes:

> this cannot be literally swan-shaped . . . nor again can it
> mean *long-lived as swans* since the word *morphè* in the
> compound could only refer to bodily shape: in point of
> fact it is a very good descriptive epithet; these three old
> hags were overgrown with white down like swans: they
> were, I see it is said, born with white hairs.

The words "descriptive" and "paints" represent a peculiarly visual
preoccupation, one satisfied, of course, in generous measure in the
poetry of Shakespeare. We could conclude that Hopkins found Greek
poetry wanting by comparison with English because it was not pic-
torial enough; when he found "one of those poetical touches which
cannot be reduced to exact explanation but *convey a fine image
nevertheless*" (my italics), as in *Choeph.* 186–7, he became excited
and absorbed: "*dipsioi* as an epithet of *stagones* is a difficult word . . .
It *may* mean *eager,* or else perhaps *thirsty* is put for *thirstily-drunk*
as the first large drops of a thunder-shower would be. I would try *salt*
in something of the same sense; because salt excites thirst" (both

quotations on f.26). Fanciful the last sentence may be, but the quality of concentrated attention is impressive; and did Hopkins in proposing *"eager"* remember half-consciously *Hamlet* I v 69, "eager droppings into milk"?

Even if these critical jottings are strictly pre-Oxford, there is no sign anywhere else that Hopkins' imagination was aroused and stimulated by his studies for Moderations. Neither Homer nor the tragedians spoke directly to his lyric sensibility as did the poetry of his native language.

III

Although many distinguished contributions to literary and philogical scholarship continued to be made by Balliol classicists, Honour Moderations were increasingly coming to be seen as mainly a preparation for Greats, the latter itself regarded as a preparation for life in public service and administration. While in some respects the *Lit. Hum.* school was broader than it is today, covering Political Economy, which is now part of 'PPE', and including, as I have already said, continuing study of Scripture (at least in the third year), it contained relatively little Ancient History.[13] Of the thirty-eight surviving Greats essays by Hopkins, twenty-eight are philosophical, and even those on 'Authenticity', 'The Philosophy of History' and 'Is history governed by general laws?' support the conclusion that Greats was overwhelmingly a school of philosophy. 'Authenticity' is an exercise in method, distinguishing between the "artistic or dramatic unity" of early and the "scientific or critical unity" of later historiography. 'The life of Socrates' is mainly a study of ethics. The great historians of Greece and Rome were read, along with the moderns Grote, Arnold and Mommsen; but the chief interest was in general political ideas, especially in their bearing on modern issues. There was no minute scrutiny of coinage, monuments or inscriptions, no use of material evidence to check literary sources, and no comparison of major with minor authorities.

Great generalising modern authorities like Maine and Buckle were used, and the essays in D.V, the most 'PPE'-like of all the notebooks, reflect the 'progressive' atmosphere which prevailed in Balliol then as now. In 'On Representation' Hopkins sees the role of *a priori* political reasoning as being to "correct" political principles established by *a posteriori* reasoning from history. Equally 'liberal' is his favouring votes for women and education of the lower classes to enable them to vote (the College at this time had in T.H. Green a member of the Royal Commission enquiring into the endowed grammar schools of England). 'Is history governed by general laws?' acutely analyses the notion of a historical law as a generalisation about what is and not about what must be: Hopkins is resolutely anti-determinist. But for students of the poet, as well as of Jowett, the chief interest of this piece is a pencilled note vividly evoking a (?tutorial) discussion with the future Master. Hopkins had argued that the Elizabethan Age would have been much the same without Shakespeare as with him (since his individual influence was "incredibly small"), on which he notes, "Jowett thought this about Shakspere was quite untrue. . . the whole of subsequent literature deeply influenced by him".

If the echoes of such discussions now seem to us a little naive in their generality, we should perhaps remember that the purpose of Victorian Greats was the analysis of argument, not the amassing and ordering of factual detail. In that analysis, the substance and method of Plato figured prominently, and a wide acquaintance with Plato's writings is only to be expected among the undergraduates of Jowett's college. An essay on virtue and vice (in D.X) cites the *Sophist*, the *Phaedrus* and the *Parmenides*, while another, on 'Plato's view of the connection of art and education', refers to the *Philebus*, section 15D of which Hopkins translated as an exercise. The essays, it must be said, are not the less readable (for someone untrained in Greats) for their almost exclusive reference to primary authorities. However idiosyncratic its metaphor, the tart comment on an unspecified group of philosophical writers is probably typical of what Hopkins' fellow students produced: "those who are quite grimed with the concrete, like the lesser Positivists" (D. XII., f. 2). Certainly, modern philosophers were read: 'The Autonomy of the Will', written for Green, shows knowledge of Kant; but one is struck by what seems a personal note of vexation in the conclusion to this essay: "unchecked analysis is wearisome and narrows and dies away into unimportance". We know that as far as Hopkins was concerned, it was not until 1872 that he found, in Duns Scotus, a philosopher who could "sway [his] spirits to peace" (see 'Duns Scotus's Oxford'). Yet he could find, even in so unlikely a source as Comte (without, unfortunately, a precise reference) a notion that had a personal force for him — the view of feelings

as having a logic of their own ('The relation of Plato's dialectic to
modern logic and metaphysics'.)[14] His acquaintance with Hegel was
probably indirect (see Appendix Two, final entry), and the fact that
Hegel was read at all may be attributed to the influence of Green and
Jowett.[15] It seems doubtful whether many undergraduates – Edward
Caird may have been an exception – had enough German to read
Hegel in the original.

To judge by Hopkins' essays, the *centre* of the Greats course was
moral philosophy, a subject which (to borrow phrases from 'Henry
Purcell') "finds him" and "fans fresh his wits". This is not to deny a
perceptible enthusiasm for the historical interpretation of Greek cul-
ture revealed in a passage such as the following:

> Up till then [the time of Plato] creative impulse had [been]
> concentrated in the grace and limit of a statue, in archi-
> tectural proportions. . .or in the calculable counteraction
> of two speakers in a play. As this began to wear out, the
> reflective and melancholy spirit arose, the passing beyond
> limits and proportions, the feeling for the infinite and the
> suggestive   ('The Sophists').

A quickening of interest is also evident in two lively passages on the
Idea from the notebook D.XIII (folios 2–3). They have already been
printed by Zaniello ('Tonic of Platonism') but are so characteristic
thay they deserve to be published again:

> . . . no doubt, taking the Idea for a hand and the name
> for its glove left behind, then although to handle it by the
> concrete may leave it a dry crumpled piece of skin, abstrac-
> tion may as injuriously blow it out into a graceless bladdery
> animation; in either case the charm is gone.
> . . .The figure shewing how the Idea can be one though it
> exists in many is that of the sun in broken water, where
> the sun's face being once crossed by the ripples each one
> carries an image down with it as its own sun; and these
> images are always mounting the ripples and trying to fall
> back into one again. . .

(It is interesting to reflect that the second of these passages, written
in 1867, is almost contemporary with the experiments with colour

then being carried out in France by Monet and Renoir.) As Zaniello's studies have shown, Hopkins was greatly influenced in the formation of his mature views of perception and individuation by his Oxford work in epistemology and metaphysics. But to get to the *heart* of Hopkins we have to recognise the merely provisional quality, for him, of such aesthetic terms as "grace" and "charm"; the function of "mortal beauty" is that it *can* lead to virtue and truth and "keeps warm / Men's wits to the things that are"; and even in the undergraduate essays we trace foreshadowings of Hopkins' later preoccupation with "God's better beauty, grace" ('To what serves Mortal Beauty?').

It is particularly when he is comparing ancient with Christian ethical values that Hopkins writes with force and feeling. In 'The pagan and Christian virtues', one of three essays on moral topics written for Pater, he declares that the Greeks saw morality as based on relations to others, whereas Christianity bases it on "the all-important relation. . .to God" (f. 10). He locates "almost all the peculiar forms of Christian morality" in "Catholicism, the consistent acceptation of Christianity", using here a phrase which indicates the part played by reasoned belief as against emotion and aesthetic preference in his conversion to Catholicism a few months after this essay was written. He concludes by contrasting Christian with pagan humility. 'The relation of the Aristotelian *phronesis* to the modern moral sense', written after his conversion, was read to T.H. Green, in a tutorial the charged atmosphere of which is not hard to imagine. Hopkins uncompromisingly rejects what he sees as the Greek notion of morality (the attempt to approximate to an ideal of behaviour) for that of Christian theology, in which

> . . . one rather says that merit lies in the energies themselves and turns upon their strength, so that the outer life must not indeed contradict the forces within but can only rudely register them and will become less and less their adequate expression. (D.X,3, f. 11).

Implied in this statement is the view that Christian virtue is grounded in divine grace and is nourished by prayer, the moral state of a man's soul being ultimately knowable to God alone.

We can judge Green's reaction from a letter of 9 January 1869, part of a discussion occasioned by Hopkins' decision to become a Jesuit. Opposing the 'new' Christianity to dogmatic (and especially Catholic) Christianity, Green declares:

> A morality that reflects on itself must needs refer itself to God, i.e. be religious. If there seems now to be a reflective morality, which yet is not religious, this is not really unreligious, but its religion is for the time dumb; and this dumbness mainly results from the action of philosophy upon the dogma of the revelation of God in Christ. When it is found that this dogma (tho' in a wrong, because dogmatic, form) embodies the true idea of the relation of the moral life to God, the morality of speculative men will find its religious tongue again.[16]

Tense the atmosphere of the tutorial might have been, but the cordiality between these two intensely serious men probably survived. Hopkins' only negative comment occurs in a very early letter attributing the cutting down of a beech in the Garden Quad to W.L. Newman and Green, a man "of a rather offensive style of infidelity" who "naturally dislikes the beauties of nature".[17] At this time he was much closer to being, in his aesthetic High Anglican way, one of those who, in a letter of Green's of 29 December 1868, "hugs his own 'refined pleasures' or (which is but a higher form of the same) his personal sanctity".[18] But in the same letter the philosopher declares "I never had his intimacy, but always liked him very much", a statement alongside which we may place this from Hopkins' letter to Baillie of 6 May 1882, after his former tutor's death in March of that year: "I always liked and admired poor Green. He seemed to me upright in mind and life".[19]

The essential difference between the two men is not, as may seem to transpire from Green's remarks, one of viewing morality as personal rather than social (the religious as against the philosophical), though Green's opposition (in the letter of 29 December) of "true citizenship" to "saintliness" seems to imply as much. It is rather a difference over whether true Christian religion is possible without a tradition of dogma and an authoritative Church to uphold it, the difference between, roughly, the Christianity of Jowett and that of Cardinal Newman (see further below). It is especially interesting to compare what

Green wrote on this subject when *he* was an undergraduate of twenty-two, the same age as Hopkins when he wrote 'The life of Socrates'. Green's long 'Essay on Christian Dogma' was read to the Old Mortality Society in 1858. In it, he criticises the exponents of dogmatic theology as "witnesses against themselves that they are the children of them that stoned the prophets" and insists that "The true philosopher can find room for the saint, though not the saint for the philosopher. . . The latter's 'ideology', which the dogmatist anathematises, enables him at once to retain dogma in its essence and to account for its form".[20] The very language here reveals the depth to which the classical philosophical training penetrated: *ideology, dogma* and *anathematise* are transparently Greek, while even *essence* and *form* hint an implied contrast between *ousia* and *eidos*. Hopkins could hardly have read this paper, yet his essay 'The life of Socrates' (possibly written for Green) almost adopts the opposing standpoint to Green's, though it is not true that he cannot *find room* for the philosopher:

> [Socrates] was what the Romans meant by *vir sanctus et fortis.* Yet his goodness is without sanctity. The want of sanctity, holiness, the quality wh. gives the most delicate self-respect or what looks like self-respect, was of less importance in Greece necessarily than it has been since, and yet self-respect was a prominent virtue with the ancients, in the *megalopsychos* of Aristotle, in the form of self-assertion in the defence of Socrates. . . [but] Alcibiades and Critias were not the companions of a saint. (D. II, 6)

Whether or not Hopkins, in writing this, was preparing himself for a direct engagement with Green, he is aware of a challenge to his own values and is quick to go on the offensive, willing, indeed to *be* offensive in face of his tutor's "offensive style of infidelity" (see p. 170 above): "[Socrates'] belief in his mission witnessed to by his familiar spirit was medieval, *but without the depth and the grace"* (my italics). His avowed preference in this essay for St. Francis and (prophetically, in 1865) St. Ignatius over Socrates is closely connected with his conviction that "the great fault of the ancient ethics" is "that it makes goodness motiveless and merely objective". Just as Hopkins would have rejected the equation of "delicate self-respect" with the refined self-regard Green seems to have in mind, so he would have rejected

Green's characterisation of Newman in that same letter of 29 December 1868: "I imagine him [i.e. Hopkins] to be one of those, like his ideal J.H. Newman, who instead of opening themselves to the revelation of God in the reasonable world, are fain to put themselves into an attitude – saintly, it is true, but still an attitude." It is not entirely plain what Green particularly objects to here, but one suspects that he is substituting a modern and (to him) timely "reasonableness" for an untimely, anachronistic, even "medieval" saintliness, without being aware that the "citizenship" he prefers is as open to being called an attitude as is "saintliness". If "attitude" implies pretence, it is hard to see what is the concession being made by "saintly, it is true".

The characterisation of Newman here Hopkins would have rejected, but probably not the naming of the man as his "ideal".[21] The source of Hopkins' distinction between Christian morality as "subjective" and classical morality as "objective" is the Newman who declared in a sermon 'On Justice, as a Principle of Divine Governance' (8 April 1832) that

> we must never say that an individual is right, merely on the ground of his holding an opinion which happens to be true, *unless he holds it in a particular manner* [my italics] ; that is, under those conditions, and with that particular association of thought and feeling, which in fact is the interpretation of it.[22]

Hopkins' concern with a man's inward spiritual disposition, his motive, his conscience, known in their fullness to God alone, authoritative for the individual but incapable of being rendered "objective", finds expression in a note written opposite D. VI, 4, which probably dates from just before his conversion:

> the essence of conscience is that its approval or dissent shd. be expressed together with and at the moment of every act of the mind wh. is concerned with morals.

The closeness of this to the passage quoted from Newman needs no arguing; for Hopkins there can be no "objective" morality, pagan *or* Christian: it is not enough to *hold* the true opinions even in theology; what matters is *how* they are held, how, in association with thought and feeling, they are "interpreted". Hopkins never, of course, quotes

Newman in these essays on moral philosophy; but it is not always the writers we quote most often who have influenced us most deeply. And yet it was more than Newman's *writings* that made him for Hopkins, as Green put it, his "ideal"; reading Newman's *Apologia*, published in Hopkins' second year at Balliol (April 1864), would have placed before him the image of a man, not just a set of arguments for leaving the Church of England. It was accordingly to Newman at the Birmingham Oratory that Hopkins travelled in the summer of 1866 when he had reached his decision.

As I have been arguing, there are echoes of Hopkins' inner debates in some of his formal work for Greats. His conversion brought all the personal disruption that could have been foreseen — loss of friendships, pain to his family, disapproval from his tutors, some measure of alienation from college society. But Hopkins had clearly determined that a poor performance in Schools was not going to provide occasion for adverse comment on his religious change. He worked with an intensity that is echoed in a question he addressed to Robert Bridges before the latter took Finals: "Is not the thought of Greats like a mill-stone round your neck now? It was to me".[23] As is well-known, he came out in the First Class as, in the words of his examiner, Prof. J.M. Wilson of Corpus, by far the best man "for form".[24]

It seems appropriate to end with two unpublished passages from one of the most interesting of the essays Hopkins wrote for T.H. Green, possibly in the term before he took Schools. Bearing the austere title 'The relation of the Aristotelian *phronesis* to the moden moral sense and *prohairesis* to Free Will', it perfectly typifies Balliol Greats in the 1860's, while Hopkins' personal involvement is attested by the idiosyncratic vigour with which he writes in the first passage and by the perceptive use of poetry in the second as illustration of that language of morals that has been even more intensely cultivated in modern Balliol than in his day:

> We may well consult common speech, which is healthy and disinterested, upon this. We say for instance there is a want of something, I cannot tell what it is, and we have longings and cravings — children especially do, and we do in seeing a pathetic landscape or hearing such music — which we do not know what will satisfy: the pain is in fact in not knowing what to wish.

The double discipline of philosophy and religion proved insufficient to help Hopkins cope with the pain of knowing what he *did* wish. As the second passage shows, only a third, and no less exacting *technè*, poetry, written and read, could enable him finally to do that:

> There is an instance of all that one can say about longing and wishing in Wordsworth's poem *The Forsaken*. What the man's craving is for is the dead Barbara, but the impossibility of her return is so full that he does not shape a wish for it. Yet since a blind craving is always engendering a wish, he does utter his prayer for the cottage to move 'from behind yon oak', because although the thing is impossible yet the cottage and tree being before his eyes he can manage to picture them otherwise and thus give in his thought the conditions to the impossible. Then since the sense that there is no power to move the cottage cannot be kept out of sight for long, he passes from one wish to another, because their existence is only possible by not dwelling on them.[25]

Jowett remarks somewhere that if Balliol produced a poet, it would not be able to hold him. Certainly one cannot imagine the Governing Body of the College in the 1860's electing Swinburne to a tutorial fellowship; but Hopkins, even if he had wanted it, had lost forever his chance of an Oxford career not through his activity as a poet but through his becoming a Catholic. He was, however, to return to classical scholarship when the Society of Jesus sent him to Dublin in 1884 to become Professor of Greek in the Royal University, to which the Catholic University College was affiliated. There is perhaps a pleasant irony in reflecting that the initiative of the Jesuit order combined with a reference from Jowett in Hopkins' appointment to an institution which Newman had tried to make into a "Catholic Oxford". But his career there was one of frustration and despondency, terminated by his early death in 1889 through typhoid and exhaustion caused by overwork. None of his scholarly projects, which included a study of Greek lyric art, came to anything.[26] The Society of Jesus had proved no more capable of 'holding' its most illustrious poet than had Jowett's college; yet I believe that the peculiar *ascesis* of each played a necessary part in helping to produce the forty-seven *Poems 1876–89* which

make Hopkins a "star" of his Order, his College, and the literature of
his century. But whereas there is a good deal about Balliol in books
on Hopkins, there is very little about Hopkins in books about Balliol.
It has been the aim of this essay in part to remedy that neglect.

Standing from left to right: L.T. Rendell, Earl of Kerry, W. Hulton, M.W. Ridley,
W.A. Brown, G.M. Hopkins, R. Entwistle, F.A. Reiss, G.M. Argles,
T.L. Papillon, A. Anderson, R. Doyle, [W.A.] Harris,
Seated from left to right: E.J. Myers, R.A. Hull, C.M.B. Clive, J.F.L[angford]
S.J. Fremantle, A. Barratt, A.E. Hardy, E.M. Sneyd-Kynnersley.

Plate 2. Hopkins (back row, sixth from left) among a group in Balliol, 1863.

APPENDIX I

A Descriptive Catalogue of the Undergraduate Notebooks of Gerard Manley Hopkins at Campion Hall, Oxford and at Balliol College, Oxford

The Hopkins MSS are described in *The Journals and Papers of Gerard Manley Hopkins*, ed. Humphry House, completed by Graham Storey, 2nd edn. (Oxford, 1959) pp. 529–35 (*JP*); by A. Bischoff, 'The Manuscripts of Gerard Manley Hopkins', *Thought* 26 (1951), pp. 551–80; see also T.A. Zaniello, 'Note on the Catalogue of the Manuscripts of Hopkins' "Oxford Essays" ', *Papers of the Bibliographical Society of America* 69 (1975), pp. 409–11. Storey errs in the Preface of *JP* in giving the source of 'The Position of Plato to the Greek World' as MS D.X (p. xxiii); in fact it is item 5 in MS D.II the only MS not in Campion Hall. This was given to Balliol by the Society of Jesus in 1963 to mark the septcentenary of the College. That date was also the centenary of Hopkins' entry to Balliol, a point made by the Librarian, Mr. Vincent Quinn, in expressing the College's thanks to the then Master of Campion Hall, Fr. Deryck Hanshell, S.J. I have grouped the MSS into (A) Books of notes (B) Books of essays. Tentative dates are assigned to some of the essays in the light of the Report Book record printed below as Appendix Two.

The following items are printed in *JP*: D.I,6; D.II,3, 5; D.III,1; D.IV; D.IX,3; DXI,1; extracts from D.XII beginning "All words mean either things or relations of things" and on Parmenides. Some of these are reprinted in G.G. Castorina, *GMH: Journals and Papers* (Bari, 1975), along with items D.V,1 and D.IX,2. T. A. Zaniello, 'The Sources of Hopkins' Inscape: Epistemology at Oxford, 1864–1868', *Victorian Newsletter* 52 (1977), 18–24, prints D.VI,2 and D.XI,2. Zaniello errs in claiming that the word *taking* on f.3 of D.VI,2 was intended by Hopkins to be "lacking" (p. 23). The tutor who read the essay has underlined the word and on the facing folio Hopkins has written "American. Say *seductive*". The tutor was wrong and Hopkins right (see *OED* taking *ppl. a.* 2). Two interesting extracts from D.XII are printed in Zaniello, 'The Tonic of Platonism: The Origins and Use of Hopkins' "Scape" ', *The Hopkins Quarterly* V (1978), 5–16.

A. *Book of Notes*
B.II. Dated 23 May 1862 (see *JP* p. 529). Contains what may be school notes on *Prometheus Desmotes* and Thucydides II 87ff. (but note that the latter was a set book for Honour Moderations; see Appendix Two) and notes on lectures by Riddell and Jowett, including a profile sketch of the latter (f. 90).
M.2. Notes on Aristotle's *Nicomachean Ethics*, perhaps from 1865–6, when he worked on this for Greats.
D.VII. 'Extracts &c'. Dated 27 Jan. 1866. Described in *JP* p. 530. A reference to Ellis on Bacon relates this to work done in the following Lent term, which included the *New Organon* I, 1–60 (see below).
D.VIII. 'Plato's Philosophy - R.W.' Notes on lectures by R. Williams covering the antecedents, Plato, and Aristotle's criticism of Plato (1865–6). See also D.XI.
D.XII. 'Notes on the history of Greek philosophy etc.': the items 'All words mean. . .' and 'Parmenides' are preceded by the date 9 Feb. 1868. The summary of Pater on early Greek philosophy that opens folio 1 may refer to lectures attended in connection with work done in Michaelmas 1866 and Lent 1867 (see App. Two below).

B. *Books of Essays*
D.I. Six essays written for E.C. Woollcombe, W.L. Newman (?) and the Master (Robert Scott). The four on logic probably date from Michaelmas 1863 (see App. Two). The last is a 'Master's essay' (?1864).
  1. An explanation and criticism of Subject, Predicate, Copula and Attribute, with an especial reference to the import of propositions (3pp).
  2. Distinguish between the *clearness* and *distinctness* of concepts and state the method by which each is attained (2pp).
  3. On cumulative and chain evidence (2pp).
  4. Distinguish Induction from Example, Colligation of facts and other processes with which it has been confounded (2½pp).
  5. On the rise of Greek Prose-writing (5pp).
  6. On the signs of health and decay in the arts (12½pp; pr. in *JP*).
D.II. Six essays, 1 and 2 initialled R.S., 5 initialled T.H.G. (T.H. Green).

(?1865, Lent or Trinity, to judge from refs to Grote in 2,4; see App. Two).
1. Credit and the causes of commercial crises (3½pp).
2. Authenticity: why do we believe some things in ancient writers and not others? (3pp).
3. Poetic Diction (2½pp; pr. in *JP*).
4. The Sophists (4½pp).
5. The Position of Plato to the Greek World (4pp).
6. The Life of Socrates (3½pp).

D.III. Six 'Essays for W.H. Pater Esq.' Presumably Trinity 1866 (see *JP* p. 133).
1. The origin of our moral ideas (5½pp; pr. *JP*).
2. Plato's view of the connection of art and education (2pp).
3. The pagan and Christian virtues (6pp).
4. The relation of Plato's Dialectic to modern logic and metaphysics (2pp).
5. Shew cases in wh. acts of apprehension apparently simple are largely influenced by the imagination (1½pp).
6. The history and mutual connection in ancient ethics of the following questions – Can virtue be taught? Are virtue and vice severally voluntary and involuntary? (4pp).

D.IV. 'On the Origin of Beauty: A Platonic Dialogue'. Dated 12 May 1865. Very probably a paper written for the Hexameron, an Oxford High Church Society. See *JP*, pp. xxii–xxiii.

D.V. Five 'Essays - Sculpture &c' dated 22 May 1865. Written presumably in the Trinity Term along with D.IV, though item 5 may belong to Michaelmas, when Hopkins was working on Political Economy (see App. Two below). (Item 2 may have been written for Jowett, since a note by GMH opposite f.8 seems to record a discussion with him). Item 3 is initialled RS; the initials AS after item 4 (see also D.VI 6) belong to no one who taught for Balliol from 1862–8, and they are almost certain to be those of Scott, who sometimes formed his R's very like A's (I am grateful for this information to the College Archivist, Dr. John Jones).
1. On the true idea and excellence of sculpture (5pp; pr. Castorina).
2. Is history governed by general laws? (6pp).
3. On the Rights and Duties of Belligerents and Neutrals (3½pp).
4. On Representation (4pp).

5. On the nature and use of money (3pp).

D.VI. Eight essays, items 3 and (?) 6 written for Scott, possibly the others also. Item 8 is *post* Trinity 1866, when H. went to Pater (see D.III above) and read *Republic* V–X (item 8 is on Bk. VII). Item 3 and the two logic essays point to Hilary, 1867, but Michaelmas 1866 is probable (see App. Two).

1. Is the difference between *a priori* and *a posteriori* truth one of degree only or of kind? (2¼pp).
2. Causation (2½pp and notes) (pr. Zaniello, 'Sources', 22–3).
3. How far may a common tendency be traced in all pre-Socratic philosophy? (3pp and notes).
4. Account of the dialogue of Plato's *Republic* fr. the end of the introduction to the beginning of the discussion of mythology (II, x–xvi) (1½pp; *unfinished*).
5. The Connection of Mythology and Philosophy (3pp).
6. The contrast between the older and the newer order of the world as seen in Caste (2pp).
7. Translation of *Philebus*, 15D.
8. The Education of the Philosopher as set forth in bk. VII of Plato's *Commonwealth*, with the exact service rendered by each science as far as the introduction of dialectic (2¼pp).

D.IX. Four 'Essays Hilary Term '67'. Tutor uncertain; see App. Two below.

1. Distinguish exactly between deduction, induction, analogy and example (2pp).
2. The tests of a progressive science (1½pp; pr. in Castorina).
3. The probable future of metaphysics (7pp; pr. in *JP*).
4. *Exetastikè gar ousa* (sc. *he dialektikè*) *pros tas hapasôn tôn methodôn archas hodon echei.*

['For being investigative it [Dialectic] possesses a path towards the first principles of all methods' (Aristotle, *Topics* I, 2, 101 b 3). I am grateful to Mr. Jonathan Barnes for identifying and translating this quotation.]

D.X. Four 'Essays for T.H. Green Esq.' Most probably Hilary 1867 (see App. Two).

1. The history and mutual connection in ancient ethics of the following questions — can virtue be taught? Are virtue and vice severally voluntary and involuntary? (6pp).

2. Anticipations in Plato of the Aristotelian doctrine of the syllogism (4pp).
3. The relations of the Aristotelian *phronesis* to the modern moral sense and *prohairesis* to Free Will (8pp).
4. The Autonomy of the Will (3½pp).

D.XI. Six 'Essays [for] R. Williams'. Either Hilary 1867 (like D.X) or Trinity 1867 (Hopkins' Finals Term). Item 5 points to Hil. 1867 or later (App. Two).

1. The possibility of separating *èthikè* from *politikè epistèmè* (6pp.; pr. in *JP*).
2. Connection of the Cyrenaic Philosophy with the Cyrenaic Morals (2pp; pr. in Zaniello, 'Sources').
3. The moral system of Hobbes (4pp).
4. Connection of Aristotle's metaphysics and his ethics (3½pp).
5. The Philosophy of History — what is meant by it?
6. Arguments for and against the progressiveness of morality (3pp).

APPENDIX II

Extracts relating to Hopkins from a Report Book on Balliol Undergraduates kept by Robert Scott (Master of Balliol, 1854–70)

The entries are in Scott's hand and run from Michaelmas 1863 to Hilary 1867. They contain a list of subjects/books studied and brief comments on progress. There is no entry for Trinity 1863, Hopkins' first term in residence, or for Trinity 1867, his last. At the head of the entry for 'Easter and Act Terms' (i.e. Trinity) 1867 we read "N.B. An alteration having been made this term in the plan of the Collections, the Master only received Reports of those Gentlemen whom the Tutors considered to require special warning or remark". For Easter and Act 1864 the subjects are omitted. The comments are in italics here for clarity.

Michaelmas 1863
    St. Matthew. Dem: de Cor; Thucyd: II, III; Aesch.: Agam. Virg: lib: Georg.; Juvenal. Logic. Catech[etics] *Fair. very Fair except in Divinity.*
Lent Term 1864
    St. John. Dem: de Cor.: I–VI; Soph: Ajax. Trach. Aeneid I–VI. *very satisfactory.*

Easter and Act Terms 1864
  satisfactory.
Michaelmas 1864
  The Gospels. Dem: de Cor.; Aristoph. 4 Plays; Sophocles 5 Plays;
  Homer. Cic: Philippics; Tacitus Histories; Virgil; Juvenal. Logic.
  Extremely satisfactory.
Scott adds at the end: "In this Term . . . Scholar de Paravicini, Exhib^{nrs}
  Hopkins, Myers were in the first [i.e. in Honour Moderations] in
  Litt. Gr. et Latin."
Lent Term 1865
  Ep. to Romans. Republic I–IV. Grote Vol. II. *very steady &*
  creditable.
Easter and Act Terms 1865
  Gospel according to St. Mark. Plato's Republic; Herod. Bk. I. pt.
  [*sic*]. History of Greece (Grote). *Very industrious but not quite*
  regular at Chapel.
Michaelmas Term 1865
  B. of Joshua, Judges, Ruth. Ethics I–III. Livy I–V. Polit: Eco-
  nomy. *very creditable.*
Lent Term 1866
  II B. of Samuel; I,II. Kings. Ethics IV–VI. III. IX. X; Republic
  I–IV. Livy VI–X. N. Organon 1–60. *working hard.*
Easter and Trinity Terms 1866
  Ep. to Hebrews; Gospel St. John. Republic V–X; Ethics V. VIII.
  IX. VI. Arnold III Vol; Mommsen II Vol. *Satisfactory.*
Michaelmas Term 1866
  Herodotus. Rom: history. Preller's Fragments of Early Greek
  Philosophy. *Fairly satisfactory.*
[Lent Term 1867]
  Ethics. History of Greek Philosophy; Hegel's Phil. of History. Ro-
  man History; Arnold Vol. 3; Mommsen v 2, 3. Logic. *Satisfactory.*

NOTES

1. Passages from Hopkins' writings are printed by kind permission of the Society of Jesus. I wish to express here my gratitude to Fr. Paul Edwards, S.J., Master of Campion Hall, Oxford, for his great kindness in making the Hopkins papers available for me to consult on several occasions in the preparation of this study.
2. I am grateful to Mr. Vincent Quinn, Keeper of the Special Collections at Balliol, for answering many enquiries and especially for drawing my attention to the Report Book, which recently came to light in the Bursary archives of the College. (This is the "big book" referred to by Sir William Anson in a letter of 1865; see H.H. Henson *A Memoir of the Right Honourable Sir William Anson* (Oxford 1920), p. 57; Anson was Hopkins' senior by one year).
3. Hopkins uses the term himself, in a diary entry of 2 May 1866; see *The Journals and Papers of Gerard Manley Hopkins*, 2nd edn. (Oxford 1959), p. 133. A.M.M. Stedman's *Oxford: Its Life and Schools* I have consulted in the second edition (1887); coaching is described on p. 262.
4. *Letters and Notices* (April 1910), p. 391. This private publication of the Society of Jesus is cited by Alfred Thomas, S.J., *Hopkins the Jesuit: the Years of Training* (Oxford 1965), p. 42 n.1, as the source of the phrase attributed to Pusey.
5. Fr. O.R. Vassall-Phillips, C.SS.R. *After Fifty Years* (1928), p. 81. The author of this memoir, who knew Hopkins as priest at St. Aloysius', Oxford, records his somewhat unexpected interest in another Balliol man who went down five years before him: "It used to be said of him that he expressed surprise at not being allowed to keep by him Swinburne's *Poems and Ballads* whilst he was in the novitiate at Manresa" *(ibid.).*
6. The report book's main value for us is twofold: it gives us the prescribed studies to which the essays in the notebooks may be related with fair chronological accuracy, and it reveals the steady industry which won Hopkins his Firsts in Mods and Greats. Even if Robert Bridges' remark "He had not read more than half of the nine books (of Herodotus) when he went in for 'Greats'" *(The Poems of Digby Mackworth Dolben, with a Memoir* ed. Robert Bridges, Oxford 1915, p. ci) is literally true, and does not rather mean that Hopkins had not studied all the books with the same punctilious thoroughness, there is no sign in the Report Book that his tutors ever complained of unfinished work.
7. See especially the letter to his mother of 22 April 1863, Letter XL in *Further Letters of Gerard Manley Hopkins* ed. C.C. Abbott, 2nd edn. (Oxford 1956), pp. 73–4: "Jowett . . . advised me to take great pains with this [the weekly essay] as on it would depend my success more than on anything else". The Latin essays written alternatively with those in English (?only in the undergraduate's first term) have not survived among Hopkins' papers. His impression of Pater is in *Journals and Papers,* p. 133.
8. Entry for 12 March 1865, in *JP*, p. 58; see further the valuable notes of the editor on pp. 325–6, which throw light on this entry.

9. T.A. Zaniello, 'Sources', p. 24; see headnote to Appendix One for full ref.
10. Line-references are to the Loeb editions for convenience; I do not know which editions Hopkins used. Greek quotations are transliterated.
11. Abbott *Further Letters*, p. 217.
12. *Further Letters*, p. 6.
13. See Appendix One for the exact manuscript sources of the essays discussed.
14. The remark attributed to Comte seems itself an echo of Pascal's famous "Le coeur a ses raisons que la raison ne connait point", *Pensées* ed. L. Brunschvicg, 5th edn. (1909), IV p. 277.
15. Geoffrey Faber *Jowett: a portrait with background* (1957), pp. 178–83, discusses Jowett's introduction of Hegelian thought to Oxford. On Green at Balliol, see the splendid Memoir in *Works of T.H. Green*, vol. III (1889), pp. lii–lviii by R.L. Nettleship, a junior of Hopkins and evidently a friend; see *The Letters of Gerard Manley Hopkins to Robert Bridges* ed. C.C. Abbott (Oxford 1935), p. 18, and *Henry Scott Holland: Memoir and Letters* ed. Stephen Paget (1921) (cited again below). Nettleship, Fellow and tutor of the College from 1869 to his tragic death while mountaineering in 1892, left *Philosophical Lectures and Remains*, the first volume of which was edited with a biographical sketch by A.C. Bradley (Fellow of Balliol, 1874–81) in 1897. Bradley came up two years too late to know Hopkins; it might have been an interesting relationship. On Bradley at Balliol, see Katharine Cooke *A.C. Bradley and his Influence in Twentieth-Century Shakespeare Criticism* (Oxford 1972), pp. 19–29.
16. Paget *Scott Holland*, p. 31.
17. Abbott *Further Letters*, p. 83.
18. Paget *Scott Holland*, pp. 29–30.
19. Abbott *Further Letters*, p. 249.
20. T.H. Green *Works*, III p. 185.
21. For Newman's influence on Hopkins see N.H. MacKenzie 'The Imperative Voice - An Unpublished Lecture by Hopkins', *Hopkins Quarterly* III (1975), pp. 101–116, esp. pp. 106–8; M.D. Moore 'Newman and the "Second Spring" of Hopkins' Poetry', *Hopkins Quarterly* VI (1979), pp. 119–37.
22. *Sermons, Chiefly on the Theory of Religious Belief* (1843), p. 88.
23. Abbott, *Letters of GMH to Robert Bridges*, p. 18.
24. Bridges *Poems of Dolben*, p. ci.
25. The extracts are on folios 15 and 16 of notebook D.X. Hopkins mistakes the title of Wordsworth's poem. 'The Forsaken' is in fact the poem numbered XII in the sequence of 'Poems founded on the Affections', the arrangement made by Wordsworth himself in the Collective Edition of 1815. The immediately following piece, no. XIII, which begins " 'Tis said that some have died for love", is the poem intended; since it has no title, Hopkins presumably confused it with the preceding piece (in which the words "wish" and "pain" occur).
26. He declared excitedly to Bridges in October 1886, three years before his death: "I have made a great and solid discovery about Pindar or rather about the Dorian and Aeolian Measures or Rhythms and hope to publish something when I have read some more. But all my world is scaffolding" (*Letters to Bridges*, pp. 228–9).

8   TOM SMITH

The Balliol-Trinity Laboratories

This article is based on a thesis submitted for Part II of the Final Honour School of Natural Sciences (Chemistry) in June 1979. A copy of the full thesis, which contains as an appendix a bibliography of publications from the Balliol-Trinity laboratories, is deposited in the Balliol Library.

THE BALLIOL-TRINITY LABORATORIES

Balliol was the first College in Oxford to undertake the building of a chemical laboratory for its students. The Daubeny Laboratory, opened in 1848 on Magdalen land, had actually been built by Dr. Daubeny, who held the Chair of Chemistry from 1822 to 1855, with the College making some contribution, and the laboratories at Christ Church were not used for the teaching of chemistry until 1866.

On 10 July 1851 the Master and Fellows agreed "that the opinion of some eminent Architect be taken . . . respecting the demolition of the present old buildings at the bottom of the Grove, and the erection of new rooms in their place."[1] The architect engaged was Anthony Salvin. A tender for the building from a London builder, Mr. Kelk, was accepted on 27 April 1852 and work was begun after the end of term in July that year. The new building was primarily residential, and is still so. At a College Meeting on 8 November 1853, however, it was revealed that "the Plans for fitting up the Lecture Rooms and Laboratory having been exhibited, it was Agreed that Estimates should be obtained previously to the work being undertaken . . ."[2] Then, on 2 December, "it was Agreed that a sum not exceeding £165 − viz. £87.10s on Mr. Kelk the Builder's Estimate and £77.10s for certain apparatus stated to be absolutely necessary for the study of Chemistry be granted for the fitting up of the Laboratory."[3] Located on the staircase now numbered XVI this laboratory consisted of two cellars, today used as a students bar.

Chemistry was not a popular subject at Oxford in the first half of the nineteenth century. The structure of the examination system, with its emphasis so firmly on classical literature and philosophy, meant that lectures by professors such as Daubeny were attended only by those whose interest was sufficiently great. Moreover, those few who did attend were often not undergraduates but senior members who could afford the time for such amateur pursuits.

But in an age both of reform and of growing interest in science, this situation was not to continue long. B.C. Brodie, later Aldrichian Professor of Chemistry, predicted change in a letter to H.H. Vaughan, later Regius Professor of Modern History, dated 1 November 1846:

I cannot but think that it will not be long before some
public protest will be made against the present state of
things as regards knowledge. It may come next year or ten
years hence. It may shake the present system to its foundations or the inert mass may be too strong for it. But I
can see a fermentation of mind at Oxford, an introduction
of new books, and new ideas and an entering on new tracks
of inquiry, which I feel assured must result in some such
effort.[4]

Other men, including Henry Acland, Dr. Lee's Reader in Anatomy
at Christ Church, A.P. Stanley, Fellow of University College, Francis,
Jeune, Master of Pembroke College, and Jowett were pressing for reform. They wanted to broaden the examination system in order to
encourage the study of less popular subjects, especially natural science.
In 1849 Convocation did pass a new Examination Statute and a
Natural Sciences School came into existence. Under the new scheme
there were three examinations and all candidates were to graduate in
Greats as before and one of three other schools; mathematics and history being the other two designated subjects. The Statute of 1849
made no mention of any practical requirements in the Natural Science
School, and it was not until 1857 that the Examiners warned that no-
one should be held worthy of honours in a subject unless he could
show knowledge of its practice.

At the inception of the Examination Statute there was no home
for the Natural Science School. Following the establishment of the
school, a meeting was held in New College to raise funds for the creation of a Museum to house existing collections and to provide laboratories, lecture rooms and a library under one roof. But it was not
until ten years later that the University finally erected a Museum for
the study of natural sciences.

In 1852 the Royal Commission of Inquiry into the state, discipline,
studies and revenues of the University and Colleges of Oxford published its report. In response the Hebdomadal Board, in June of the
same year, appointed a Committee to consider the recommendations
of the Commissioners. As regards the question of natural science at
Oxford this Committee was in sympathy, if not complete agreement,
with the Royal Commission. It conceded that

the University ought to employ what Funds it can command, and which are not wanted for purposes of still greater
utility, in building a great Museum for all departments of
Physical Science, with proper Lecture-rooms, Laboratories,
and apparatus for Lectures.[5]

The committee was aware of the need for practical instruction, in
chemistry at least, for it

inquired particularly into the need there was for an Assistant to the Professor (of Chemistry) for the purpose of
teaching 'Practical Chemistry' to Pupils in the Laboratory,
— a department of teaching which had scarcely become
systematic until within the last fifteen years, but which is
now considered essential to anyone who would study
Chemistry with a view to examination for honours.[6]

Balliol was highly praised in the Report of the Royal Commission:

It is the most distinguishing characteristic of this Foundation that it is peculiarly free from all restrictions which
might prevent the election of the best candidates to its
Headship, Fellowships, Scholarships, and even to its Visitorship. The result of this has been that Balliol, which is one
of the smallest Colleges in Oxford, as regards its Foundation,
is certainly at present the most distinguished. The measures
which we recommend would, indeed, enable other Societies
to carry on a generous rivalry with it; but on the other hand
this College would enter on the contest still more unshackled
than at present, with the advantage of its well-earned reputation, and with the command of the services of some of
the ablest persons in the University.[7]

Richard Jenkyns, a Master for whom the success of his College was
all important, would have been keen that Balliol students should do
well in the newly created Honour School of Natural Science. But
teaching facilities for the new school were limited. It is not, therefore,
surprising that the College, which was embarking on a building programme, should wish to make provision for undergraduates intending to read for the new school; and a purpose-built laboratory for

teaching was the ideal means of doing this.

With the new laboratory the College also required a chemical lecturer. Henry Smith, the mathematical lecturer, was chosen. He was a man of brilliant intellect. He took a double First in 1849, having won the Ireland University scholarship the year before. Following his election to a fellowship at Balliol in November 1849 he gained the Senior Mathematical scholarship in 1851. In order to learn some chemistry he became a pupil of Nevil Story-Maskelyne, the Deputy Reader in Mineralogy, who was at that time occupying the Laboratory formerly used by Daubeny in the basement of the Ashmolean Museum, in Broad Street. He also went to the Royal College of Chemistry for a few months to study under Dr. Hofmann,[8] the famous German chemist. Definite records of his attendance are not available, but it seems likely that he enrolled as a casual student in the summer or autumn of 1853. A great ambition of his life was realised when, in 1860, he was elected to the Savilian Professorship of Geometry. As a teacher of mathematics he was very successful; and as a teacher of chemistry he was, at the least, successful enough for his first-ever pupil, A.G. Vernon Harcourt, to become one of Oxford's most distinguished chemists.

In 1855 Benjamin Collins Brodie the younger was elected to the Aldrichian Professorship of Chemistry in succession to Daubeny. Brodie had been at Balliol and was a close friend of Jowett, with whom he had been an undergraduate in the 1830s. He graduated B.A. in 1838, taking a Second in mathematics, and entered his uncle's chambers as a barrister. After a short period he turned to science and went to Giessen to study chemistry in the school of Liebig. He stayed there until 1845, working, at Liebig's suggestion, on the chemical constitution of beeswax, which investigation he continued in a private laboratory in London on his return. His work led to the discovery of cerotic acid and a number of solid alcohols, and was recognised by his election as a Fellow of the Royal Society in 1849, and the award of a Royal Society Medal in 1850. His formulation of cerotic acid as $C_{27}H_{54}O_2$ was very close to the empirical formula accepted today, $C_{26}H_{52}O_2$. It was an important discovery because it confirmed the existence of homologous series.

When Brodie came to Oxford as the new Professor there was no laboratory for him to use. The mineralogist Story-Maskelyne occupied the basement of the Ashmolean, although this was ostensibly the home of chemistry in Oxford. Construction of the University Museum had by then been sanctioned, but the building had not been started. He therefore inquired whether he might be allowed use of Balliol's lecture room and laboratory for purposes of teaching and research. On 12 December 1855 the Master, Robert Scott, who had succeeded Jenkyns the year before, wrote in reply to Brodie:

My Dear Brodie,

I have consulted the College on the subject of your application which was considered as twofold, referring to the Laboratory and to the Lecture-room. It was resolved as follows:-

1. That the Laboratory be lent to the Professor of Chemistry for two years; — saving the rights of the Mathematical Lecturer —

2. That the Upper Lecture-room be lent to the Professor of Chemistry for two years; provided that

1. The room be at any time available for such College purposes as it may be required for —

2. That care be taken that no chemical preparations be used there which may cause inconvenience to the neighbours —

I may explain, that although the reservation referring to the requirements of the College was added, yet that it would only become practice if an extreme case of need, in the judgement of the College, arose —

Any arrangements which you wished to make in the Lecture-room, not being inconsistent with your giving the room back to us again in the same condition in which you received it, would be left to your discretion —

We do not ask for any rent for either Lecture-room or Laboratory —

Believe me, my dear Brodie,
very truly yours,
Robert Scott.[9]

Syllabus of a Course of Lectures on Chemistry to be
delivered in Michaelmas Term 1856, in the Lecture
Room of Balliol College, on Tuesdays and
Saturdays, at *One* o'Clock.

Chemical notation.

Classification of certain elemental bodies according to the
form of their combination with Hydrogen.

   a. Elements of which 1 atom combines with 1 atom of Hy-
     drogen : Chlorine, Bromine, Iodine, Fluorine.
       Combinations of these elements respectively with Hy-
     drogen, with Oxygen, and with Oxygen and Hydrogen.
     Chemical analogies of this group of elements.

   β. Elements of which 1 atom combines with 2 atoms of Hy-
     drogen : Oxygen, Sulphur, Selenium, Tellurium.
       Combinations of these elements respectively with Hy-
     drogen, with Oxygen, and with Oxygen and Hydrogen.
       Combinations of Chlorine and Sulphur. Analogy of
     Sulphur to Oxygen.
       Combination of Carbon and Sulphur. (Bisulphide of
     Carbon.) Sulphur Salts. Analogies of the group.

   γ. Elements of which 1 atom combines with 3 atoms of Hy-
     drogen : Nitrogen, Phosphorus, Arsenic, Antimony.
       Combinations of these elements with Hydrogen, with
     Oxygen, and with Oxygen and Hydrogen.
       Combinations with Chlorine and Iodine. Combinations
     of Arsenic and Phosphorus with Sulphur. Analogies of
     the group.
       Observations on Carbon, Boron, and Silicon.
       Comparative view of the chemical relations of the above
     groups of elemental bodies.

The atomic weights used in these Lectures will be those of
Gerhardt, in which (the atomic weights of all other elements
being the same as those usually adopted) the atomic weights of
Oxygen, Sulphur, Selenium, Tellurium, and Carbon, represented
respectively by the letters O, S, Se, Te, and C, are taken

$$
\begin{array}{ll}
O & 16 \\
S & 32 \\
Se & 79.2 \\
Te & 128 \\
C & 12
\end{array}
$$

*Gentlemen who wish to attend these Lectures are requested to enter
their names with Mr. Rowell at the Ashmolean Museum, between the hours
of Eleven and Four, and to pay the fee of One Pound. This fee gives a
permanent admission to all Public Lectures of the Professor of Chemistry.*

Plate 1. Brodie's lectures.

By comparison with the periods before and after, the years 1856–8, covering the period when he was installed in the Balliol laboratory, were among Brodie's most unproductive. The lack of good laboratory facilities was no doubt partly responsible. During the years 1848–54 he had been engaged in a variety of researches apart from the investigation of beeswax, including some work on graphite.

Graphite was one of Brodie's two major research interests over the next three years, culminating in a paper of 1859 'On the Atomic Weight of Graphite.'[11] He used a 1:4 mixture of nitric and sulphuric acids to oxidise graphite. Analyses on the product and its salts (which were later confirmed) led him to

> the remarkable inference that carbon in the form of graphite functions as a distinct element; that it forms a distinct system of combinations, into which it enters with a distinct atomic weight, the weight 33. Analogy would lead us to a similar conclusion with regard to the elements boron and silicon. How far this inference is to be extended to the allotropic forms of other elements experiment alone can decide.

Brodie termed the element graphon and experimentally verified its existence using the rule of Dulong and Petit. He accepted this as confirmation of his theory despite the fact that the law was known to be unreliable in a number of cases.

Organic peroxides were his other principal interest at this time, and he published his findings in a paper entitled 'On the Formation of the Peroxides of the Radicals of the Organic Acids.'[12] He prepared benzoyl and acetyl peroxides by treatment of the acid chloride or anhydride with hydrated barium peroxide. It seems probable that at least a part of this work, which he extended some years later,[13] and of the work on graphite were done in the laboratory at Balliol.

In the same year that Brodie became Professor, the foundation stone was laid for a Museum to house the Natural Science School. From the very start Brodie agitated for his department in the Museum to be completed and fitted rapidly, although he was informed that he could not have priority over the other Professors. He demanded £600 for additional accommodation in 1855, and in 1858 Hebdomadal Council learnt that, although £1,650 had been spent on chemistry fittings (cf. Balliol's £77 10s.), the Professor still required more.

Brodie was finally recognised as a special case, and the completion of the Chemistry Department was accelerated, so that he was able to give his first course of lectures there in 1858, albeit in a room without gas, with unpainted doors and windows, and in a building which had not been fully roofed.

With the move of Brodie to the Museum the chemical cellar in Balliol fell into disuse. There is no precise date for its closure. Scott, in evidence given in 1870 to the Royal Commission on Scientific Instruction and Advancement of Science, said that following the foundation of the Museum it was 'so much more convenient for students to work in the University laboratory that the thing has dropped.'[14] He told them furthermore that the old laboratory was not used for any other purposes of science.[15]

The third report of the Devonshire Commission,[16] which dealt exclusively with Oxford and Cambridge, was thorough and comprehensive. A good deal of it was drafted by Henry Smith, who was on the Commission. The Commissioners felt that the Colleges could do much to promote science by endowing more scholarships for natural science and by electing Fellows who were scientists on a more regular basis: since the throwing open of many fellowships at Oxford nearly twenty years previously, only nine out of one hundred and sixty-five had gone to scientists. On the subject of College laboratories, they felt it was unnecessary for each College to have a laboratory, however useful that arrangement might be as regards original research. A laboratory shared by a group of Colleges would be a good thing, in the same way that existing College Lecturers were shared by three or four Colleges. For example, Balliol, Trinity and Exeter had an agreement on the mutual availability of College lectures, as did Magdalen and Merton. The Commissioners made it plain, however that they would prefer to see such lectures open to the whole University.

At Balliol there were already scholarships in natural science, thanks to the benefaction of Miss Hannah Brackenbury, by which three scholarships tenable for three years were founded and endowed in 1866. One was awarded in each alternate year for natural science or for law and modern history. When Jowett became Master he negotiated changes with Miss Brackenbury, embodied in the Trust Deed of 1 July 1872, so that there was a total of eight scholarships tenable for four years, one a year to be awarded for natural sciences and one a year for law and modern history. The only other Colleges to offer awards in natural science at this time were Merton, Magdalen and Christ Church. Of these, Merton possessed a science lecture room and both the other two had laboratories.

The first sign of Balliol's intention to build another laboratory appeared on 21 March 1874, when it was agreed at a College Meeting "That the Architect be authorised to introduce a Laboratory into his plans."[17] The plans mentioned were for a large new Hall and other buildings which were to be built on the site of some old stables, to the design of the architect Alfred Waterhouse. The Hall is the only part which remains unchanged. The laboratory was constructed below ground level at the north-east corner of the Hall, and exists today, much changed, as a music and exhibition room (see Appendix, Plan, and Plate 2). The Hall was officially opened in June 1877 with a large banquet, but it was over two years later, at the start of Michaelmas Term 1879, before the laboratory was finally ready for use.

As with the earlier laboratory, there is little evidence to suggest reasons for its construction. The timing of the project is curious for it was in 1877 that a new block of buildings was begun on the southern side of the Museum. Completed in 1879, it increased considerably accommodation in the Chemistry Department.

The Report of the Devonshire Commission may have influenced the College in deciding to build a laboratory, particularly the point concerning the sharing of facilities. In the summer before the laboratory was opened "A communication from the President of Trinity was read, proposing united teaching of Chemistry and Elementary Physical Science in the two Colleges of Balliol and Trinity."[18]

The scheme then worked out contained the following essential points:[19]

1. The lecturer was to be engaged by Trinity (with Balliol's approval) on the Millard foundation, and would receive a stipend of £250 p.a., £150 from Trinity and £100 from Balliol.
2. The laboratory and lecture room were to be provided by Balliol, which was also responsible for their upkeep.
3. The lecturer would be required to act as tutor to all natural science undergraduates in the two Colleges, and was personally responsible for the teaching of preliminary chemistry, preliminary physics,

Plate 2. The Balliol teaching laboratory in the 1930's, looking East.

honours chemistry and pass school chemistry and physics. Furthermore, he would teach preliminary physics to Exeter men; Exeter
was to pay £50 p.a. to the joint fund.
4. The lecturer was not to hold any post at the Museum or to undertake any other educational work, but he was to be allowed to continue his own researches.
5. A maximum sum of £100 p.a., contributed equally by both Colleges, was to be allowed for apparatus, assistance and working
expenses in the laboratory.
6. Men from other Colleges could attend lectures, on payment of a
terminal fee of £2 (or £3 for two terms) but could not use the
laboratory.

This latter resolution was in fact dropped, for at the start of the
Michaelmas Term 1879 it was agreed that

> the fees to be paid to the Laboratory by out-College men
> (including Exeter) were to be determined by the Master
> and Professor Smith after consultation with the President
> of Trinity and Mr. Dixon.[20]

Harold Dixon, who had taken a First in natural science at Christ
Church in 1875, was the first man appointed to the joint lectureship.

The financial position of the laboratory and lecturer were greatly
helped when, in 1882, "It was announced that the Duke of Bedford
had promised £5,000 towards the foundation of a Physical Science
Lectureship."[21] The Trust Deed is dated 29 March 1882 and Article I
states that:

> A Lectureship in Physics that is to say, in Chemistry and
> Natural Philosophy or both those branches of Science shall
> be and is hereby established in connection with Balliol
> College . . .[22]

The Duke of Bedford, who had two sons who had recently been at
Balliol, stipulated that the lecturer should not receive less than £150
p.a., but otherwise the College was free to invest the money as it
wished, to arrange for lectures as it wished, and even to alter the regu-
lations, so long as such alterations were not "contrary to the general
scope and intention of these presents."[23]

Dixon was appointed Duke of Bedford's lecturer from the start of the academic year 1882–83. This new endowment caused the arrangements with Trinity to be altered slightly, so that, on the recommendation of the Tuition Committee at Balliol, Dixon received "£300 a year for his services to Trinity, Balliol and Exeter."[24] Trinity was to contribute £100 a year of the lecturer's salary and £25 a year for apparatus, assistance and other laboratory expenses. The Trust also made it possible to grant to Dixon £118 for apparatus in the year 1883–84,[25] and for Balliol to make up the greater part of the £50 deficit which occurred when Exeter withdrew from the arrangement with Balliol and Trinity.[26]

At the beginning of 1885, Dixon decided to start a cumulative record of the sort of work that was done in the laboratory. 'The Laboratory Day Book' is a large black volume, now rather damaged, in which those working in the laboratory, whether undergraduates or demonstrators, recorded details of their experimental work. Some of the entries are concerned with standard procedures, for example, the 'Determination of the Vapour Density of Methyl Alcohol by Victor Meyer's Method', written up by R.T. Bodey; while some appear to be more in the nature of minor research projects. Examples of the latter sort are the 'Explosion of Carbonic Oxide with Oxygen', and the 'Explosion of Gunpowder', both written up by H.B. Baker. J.E. Marsh attempted to determine whether hydrogen and oxygen combine below the temperature of ignition. He left mixtures of the two gases for periods of up to a couple of months and subjected them to some heating. He concluded that a certain contraction in volume did result.

These last three examples reflect the research interests of Dixon himself. After taking his degree, on the suggestion of Vernon Harcourt, his tutor at Christ Church, he started work on the explosion of gases. He continued this line of research at Balliol working in the cellar on Staircase XVI which had been the first laboratory. During the years 1876–81 his researches proved that Berthollet's 'law of mass action', enunciated in 1805, was applicable to gaseous explosions, contrary to what Bunsen had said in 1853. The latter held that continuous change in the composition of a gaseous medium led to a discontinuous change in the course and products of its explosion. Horstmann in Heidelberg disproved this simultaneously with Dixon, and the foundation was laid for much subsequent work on gas equilibria. A lot of his research in the 1880's was concerned with the velocity of gaseous explosions. He at first subscribed to the 'sound-wave' theory of Berthelot and Vieille, which held that explosions were governed by much the same laws as the propagation of sound. When this was proved by experiment to be inadequate, he modified his views to those expressed first by Hugoniot in 1887–88, who saw detonation as a 'shock-wave' propagated through a medium which is discontinuous at the wave front, i.e. the combustion causes there to be an abrupt change in pressure and density at the wave front. This modification of his views occurred some time after he left Balliol. While there, his most important piece of work was the paper on 'Conditions of Chemical Change in Gases: Hydrogen, Carbonic Oxide and Oxygen' published in *Philosophical Transactions* in 1884.[27] This was the product of several years' work, performed both at Christ Church and at Balliol. He dealt with explosive mixtures of carbonic oxide (CO) and hydrogen burning in oxygen and the dependancy of the final equilibrium position on moisture, pressure, temperature and the shape of the combustion vessel. A picture of the gas analyser he used is reproduced in Plate 3. He also touched briefly in this paper on the "rapidity of explosion of carbonic oxide and oxygen with varying quantities of aqueous vapour." For this part of the paper, most of the work was done neither at Christ Church nor at Balliol, but at Magdalen, in the Daubeny Laboratory. Dixon described the circumstances himself:[28]

> I think it was in 1881 that my friend, C.J.F. Yule, Fellow of Magdalen, showed me round the Magdalen Laboratory, and explained the electric chronograph with which he had been doing physiological experiments. This instrument seemed to be adaptable to my wants, so as he was no longer using it, I asked him to let me try it on my gases. This he allowed me to do, and I soon found it would accurately record the very rapid movements of the explosions. Accordingly I got leave from the College to work in the Laboratory and I worked there for about two years. In 1883 or 1884 I bought the chronograph from Magdalen, and removed it to Balliol.
> During 1881 and 1883 I used to go to the Magdalen Laboratory in the afternoons, and sometimes in the evenings.

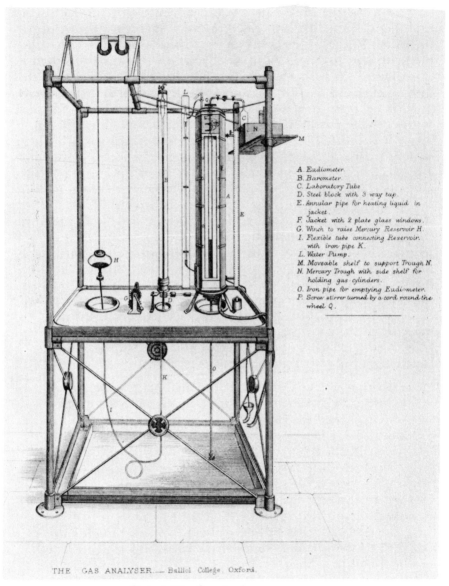

A. Eudiometer.
B. Barometer.
C. Laboratory Tube.
D. Steel block with 3 way tap.
E. Annular pipe for heating liquid in
     jacket.
F. Jacket with 2 plate glass windows.
G. Winch to raise Mercury Reservoir H.
I. Flexible tube connecting Reservoir.
     with iron pipe K.
L. Water Pump.
M. Moveable shelf to support Trough N.
N. Mercury Trough with side shelf for
     holding gas cylinders.
O. Iron pipe for emptying Eudiometer.
P. Screw stirrer turned by a cord round the
     wheel Q.

THE GAS ANALYSER.— Balliol College, Oxford.

Plate 3. The Gas Analyser.

I used the chronograph to determine the initial rate of explosion of mixtures of carbonic acid and oxygen with different quantities of moisture, and also for measuring the rates of the 'explosion-wave' in gases under different conditions.

In 1886 not only was Dixon elected F.R.S. and a Fellow of Balliol,[29] but he was also appointed to succeed Sir Henry Roscoe in the Chair of Chemistry at Owens College, Manchester. This was an important appointment, for under Roscoe and his assistant, Carl Schorlemmer, the Manchester School of Chemistry had become justly famous throughout the country. Indeed, many felt that it would suffer for the worse under a comparatively young and untried Oxford don. This was not to be the case, and under Dixon the School continued to flourish and expand.

He stayed on at Balliol until the end of the academic year 1886–87, but supervision of the laboratory was handed over at the start of 1887 to his successor in the Bedford and Millard Lectureships, Sir John Conroy, who had been at Christ Church, where he was a pupil of Vernon Harcourt's, first in the University laboratory and then in the Christ Church laboratory. Being a man of considerable private means, he was able to continue his scientific researches independently while living with his mother, to whom he was devoted. When she died in 1880, he was offered a lectureship at Keble by Edward Talbot, who had been a Christ Church contemporary, and was then Warden of Keble. Conroy remained at Keble, becoming a tutor after a few years, until his appointment at Balliol.

The last assistant that Dixon had in the laboratory was a young man named David Henry Nagel, who had obtained a First at Trinity in 1886. He continued to demonstrate under Conroy, and in the University Calendar of 1888 he is named as holding an official lectureship in Physics and Chemistry at Trinity.

On his appointment, Conroy's salary was £250, three-fifths coming from Balliol and two-fifths from Trinity. Nagel received a salary of £75 p.a., from the two Colleges. But Conroy chose to keep only £60 of his salary and give the remainder to Nagel. Conroy was both a wealthy and a generous man. Moreover, he spent several months of each year abroad for health reasons, and so was probably unwilling to accept any more than £60 p.a. He administered the annual grant of £150 for laboratory expenses.

On the teaching side it was agreed that Conroy should have general control of the laboratory and pupils, and would lecture in the Michaelmas term on electricity and in the Summer term, on heat and light. Nagel was to lecture on sound during the Hilary term, to take essays and papers, and to conduct the laboratory work alone in Hilary, and under Conroy's general supervision in the other two terms.[30] This highlights the point that during the latter part of Dixon's time and during Conroy's time the lectures given at Balliol were predominantly on aspects of physics. The majority of Balliol and Trinity scientists continued to take chemistry, however.

Students from other Colleges and Halls could attend lectures and use the laboratory, although there was not very much room to spare. The fees were £1 a term for lectures and £3 a term for the laboratory.

In 1893 Percy Elford, a Fellow at St. John's and formerly a Demonstrator at Balliol wrote to Conroy:

> I really enjoy working in the Lab. and if I could afford it I should ask to help without remuneration so that the real obligation lies on my side. I wonder if (when St. John's has a strong science side!) it would be possible for an arrangement to be made, by which I could act as an assistant without remuneration in exchange for the opportunity of St. John's men working in the lab. without having to pay Laboratory Fees.[31]

During the mid-'nineties Conroy came increasingly to feel that the laboratory's facilities were inadequate. The first move he made to rectify this was in the Trinity Term of 1895, when he wrote to Sir William Markby, the Senior Bursar at Balliol, requesting an increased grant to enable there to be assistants in the laboratory every working day rather than just for three days.[32]

It was also in that term that Conroy first made suggestions that an extension to the laboratory should be built on Trinity ground. He offered to pay for the fittings of the new part, and in a letter of 14 June 1895 he is thanked for this offer by H.G. Woods, President of Trinity. No firm commitment was given, however, as to whether the extension would be undertaken or not.[33] Nothing was said or done for eighteen months until Conroy wrote to Woods on 6 December 1896.[34] He explained that the laboratory was overcrowded: there were only thirteen working places, and at that time thirteen honours chemists in the two Colleges. This meant that others wishing to use the laboratory had to take a chance on there being a space available when they went along. Additional space was definitely needed. There was no room at Balliol, and so he requested permission for a new laboratory to be built on Trinity ground, east of the existing one, with the dividing wall between the two Colleges as one of the sides (see Appendix, Plan). He urged that it would not cost a lot, and he would pay for the fittings himself. It would be possible nearly to double existing accommodation and would be a great help to himself, Nagel and the two demonstrators. He stressed that it would have gas and water supplies separate from the other laboratory, so that it would be independent if the agreement between Balliol and Trinity ever broke down.

Conroy was successful in convincing Woods of the potential benefit of the scheme, and early in 1897 Trinity started to draw up plans. Conroy acted as intermediary for the two Colleges. He reported that Balliol had no objection to a breach being made in the wall,[35] and permission for this was formally granted on 24 March 1897.[36] The very next day Woods wrote to Conroy[37] to say that Trinity were ready to go ahead with the building. He made it clear that Conroy's offer to pay for the fittings, while much appreciated, would not be accepted. Trinity felt it was only fair that they should foot the bill themselves, especially "as some of the fittings are of the nature of fixtures."[38]

Good progress was made, despite the discovery that part of the foundations were being built over an old cesspool. This new laboratory, measuring about forty-five feet by twelve, cost Trinity just under £450. It was first used during Michaelmas 1897. At the end of that term Nagel reported to Conroy, who had taken both winter terms abroad, that: "The new building has worked very well; the only difficulty is to get it dry: the concrete remains obstinately damp in some places. The ventilation is satisfactory."[39] This building is today the only recognizable part of the Balliol-Trinity laboratories. It is used as a workshop, and in one place the cupboards and benches installed in 1897 remain untouched. It is also possible to see where the guttering along the centre of the floor and the stair well for access to the

Balliol teaching laboratory have been filled in. (See Plate 4, the Trinity teaching laboratory.)

The opportunities for research students in the Balliol-Trinity laboratory were limited, especially as research degrees only made a hesitant start in 1895 with the introduction of the B.Sc.. The problem was compounded by the fact that neither Conroy nor Nagel set an enthusiastic example as a research worker. Nagel did hardly any original practical work and published no papers. Conroy's field was optics. During his thirteen years at Balliol he published five papers. But as he spent more and more time abroad the amount of work he did decreased.[40] Therefore during the 'nineties it was not uncommon for students to go to study for a year or more in Germany, where many more opportunities were available.

A certain amount of informal research was carried on by students who had taken their degrees, as may be deduced from the letters of John Trengove Nance, who took a Second in 1898. Nance was immensely fond of Conroy and wrote him long letters while he was abroad in the winter of 1899. One of his letters contains a revealing insight into a man who was later to become Oxford's first Nobel Prize winner: "Soddy does seem to have a most unfortunate way of treading on people's corns . . . It is such a pity, for he's really such a nice fellow — but so obstinate (with a very big O)."[41] Soddy was at that time doing some work on the synthesis of camphoric acid in the cellar on Staircase XVI, or the Brodie Laboratory, as he called it.[42] His brief stay in Balliol came between his degree, from Merton, and his departure for Canada to work with Rutherford at McGill.

Three weeks later Nance wrote again to Conroy. A passage in this letter is a unique contemporary account of life in the laboratory:

> We are getting on, speaking from my point of view, very well down in the Lab., & a spirit of harmony prevails which could hardly be surpassed. Things go on much as usual — the usual amount of chaff over a pet idea & new piece of apparatus — the usual loss of hair in defence of the same — the usual ultimate triumph of one or the other tempered with sympathy, or with modesty as the case may be. The usual number of thermometers are smashed by being thrust into too narrow holes — the usual number of stirring rods put through the innocent hypocrisy of beaker sides & bottoms, the usual number of drying U-tubes crushed into twin

Plate 4. The Trinity teaching laboratory in the 1930's, looking North.

I's by excess of zeal; there is also the usual scarcity of india-
rubber tubing & of clamps — also the usual rumours of an
assault on the Domain of No. VI. These are inseparable
adjuncts of the history of the Balliol Lab. Everyone is, I
think, flourishing.[43]

Conroy's physical condition deteriorated towards the turn of the
century. He died while wintering abroad and was buried in Rome on
15 December 1900. At the start of the next term Balliol asked Nagel
to continue the work he had been doing for Conroy on the same conditions as he had done during Conroy's previous absences. It was agreed
"to pay him the sum formerly paid to Sir John Conroy for laboratory
expenses, together with the increase at the rate of £20 a year voted
last Term; this arrangement to last till the end of the Summer Term."[44]

There is evidence that, after Conroy's death, consideration was
given to the possibility of the joint science teaching of the two Colleges
being expanded to include physiology.[45] This was, after chemistry,
the second most popular of the options within the Natural Science
School. In the end the idea was dropped, for on 28 February 1901 it
was resolved "that an election be made to a Fellowship in Chemistry
and Physics"[46] and that "the stipend of the Fellow shall be £400 from
all sources inclusive of the Bedford Lectureship."[47]

Harold Brewer Hartley, who had come up to Balliol as a Brackenbury Scholar in 1896, was elected to the fellowship.[48] Hartley was
twenty-three and had taken Finals less than a year before. Balliol, in
order not to overburden him, resolved that

subject to the control of the Master and Fellows of Balliol
College, Mr. Nagel be asked to undertake for three years
the general management of the laboratory on behalf of the
College.[49]

Just before Hartley's first term as a Fellow, a new set of arrangements with Trinity was agreed upon.[50] The main points were:

1. That each College maintained its own part of the laboratory.
2. Fixtures belonged to the College on which they were sited, and
the College in question would pay for and own any additional fixtures.
3. All other instruments, materials and apparatus belonged to Balliol.

4. Balliol paid for all laboratory expenses, including wages and new furniture, apparatus and materials.
5. Trinity made a contribution of £90 p.a. to expenses.
6. That Nagel should keep the accounts and render them to Balliol.

The agreement was initially for three years but was subsequently renewed.[51]

In 1904 a scheme of cooperation between the various College laboratories was agreed. The Daubeny laboratories at Magdalen taught quantitative analysis, the Christ Church laboratory provided instruction in inorganic chemistry, the Balliol-Trinity laboratories provided a course in physical chemistry, and Queen's, whose small laboratory had been opened in 1900, supplemented the organic chemistry course then taught at the Museum.

For Balliol-Trinity this represented a progression from a physical tradition that had grown up under Dixon and Conroy. At the inception of the scheme the title of Hartley's post was changed from "Bedford Lecturer in Physics" to "Bedford Lecturer in Physical Chemistry."[52] In addition, preliminary physics was no longer taught at Balliol and for the first time women students were allowed to work in the laboratory.[53]

A brown canvas covered notebook labelled "Results" remains in the Balliol Library. It is not dated but the names mentioned appear roughly to correspond with the period 1898–1910. It gives a good idea of what experiments comprised the course during the period before World War I. Although actual entries of results are relatively few, the experiments listed are:

Spectroscopy; the Pulfrich Refractometer; Polarisation of Light; Optical Rotation; Freezing Point-Beckmann; Boiling Point-Beckmann; Boiling Point-Landsberger; Calorimetry; Viscosity; Density of a Solid; Density of a Liquid; Molecular Volumes; Coefficient of Expansion of Gases; Hydrolysis of an Ester; Electrolytic Separation of Metals; Vapour Density-Dumas; Vapour Density-Bleier; Vapour Density-Victor Meyer; Transport Numbers; Electrolysis of H_2SO_4; Cadmium Cell; Clark Cell; Conductivity of Electrolytes; EMF by Potentiometer; Solubilities by Meyerhoffer Pipette; Transition Temperatures; Surface Tension.

In 1908 Hartley and Nagel started to keep attendance records for the laboratory.[54] The names of individual students were recorded, and each week a different experiment was done and the fact noted in the book. The student attended the laboratory either on Monday, Tuesday and Wednesday or on Thursday, Friday and Saturday. In 1908 Jesus College opened a laboratory which, as part of the scheme of cooperation, provided instruction in general and physical chemistry. Thus students from a few Colleges did not work in the Balliol-Trinity laboratories, but since Jesus catered principally for the preliminary examination, most people would spend at least some time in the Balliol-Trinity laboratories. During the period up to 1914 about thirty people attended the laboratory every term, although in Michaelmas Term 1912 fifty-three names are entered in the attendance records. On working days the demonstrators were present from 11.00 a.m. to 1.00 p.m. and from 5.00 p.m. to 7.00 p.m., although in practice they were often present all afternoon and undergraduates could work then if they wished to. There was no distinction between the Balliol teaching laboratory and the Trinity teaching laboratory, and there was completely free circulation between the two.

Hartley's earliest scientific interest was with minerals. For a while he worked on the analysis of minerals, but found this too time-consuming for satisfaction.[55] Having come across the problem of spontaneous growth of very small crystals in a textbook of Ostwald's he decided to look into it. He chose triphenylmethane as his working material because it has a large number of derivatives. He conducted a phase-rule investigation of its solubility in several solvents, and over the next few years carried out a number of similar investigations. His work on the physical properties of a pyridine-water mixture cleared up some earlier misunderstanding on the supposed existence of a number of hydrates. A more important part of this research was a study of the electrical conductivity of lithium nitrate in pyridine-water mixtures. This was a first indication of his subsequent interest in the electrochemistry of non-aqueous solutions. All but a couple of the papers which Hartley published before World War I were written conjointly. He was himself an active researcher, and gave great encouragement to all his students to engage in original investigation themselves.

During World War I Hartley was absent on war service and Nagel was left in charge of the laboratory and the teaching for the two Colleges.[56] This was not a very onerous task as the only students in College at that time were those exempted from service for various reasons or those too young to serve. During the years 1915–1919 inclusive, only one man from Balliol sat chemistry Finals, and no-one from Trinity did. Numbers in the laboratory were never more than a few, and were often none at all.[57] In Hilary Term 1919, however, things began to return to normal when over forty people enrolled for the laboratory course.[58]

Following the death of Nagel on 27 September 1920, Cyril Norman Hinshelwood was elected a Fellow of Balliol. Hinshelwood had been unable to take up his Brackenbury scholarship at Balliol because of the war. In 1919 he returned to the special shortened course for War Service Candidates, gaining his degree with a distinction in the summer of 1920. The College had already appointed him a Lecturer, but Nagel's death prompted his election to a fellowship. The following academic year the teaching responsibility was again split between the two Colleges when he removed to the fellowship at Trinity which Nagel had held.

In 1923 the organisation of the teaching of chemistry at the University was reviewed. At a special meeting of the Sub-Faculty of Chemistry at the end of the year a so-called "ad interim" policy was agreed upon.[60] Under this policy the Department of Organic Chemistry consisted of the University's new Dyson Perrins laboratory and the Queen's College laboratory; the Department of Inorganic Chemistry of the Old Chemical Department and the Christ Church laboratory, and the Department of Physical Chemistry of the Balliol-Trinity laboratory and the Jesus College laboratory. If the intention regarding the "interim" nature of this policy was that it should be for a short period, it never quite worked out as such.[61] This arrangement was the foundation for the eighteen years during which the Balliol-Trinity laboratories remained active.

The laboratories' principal sources of income remained unchanged throughout this period.[62] The largest single source was fees from other Colleges, which produced between £600 and £800 a year. The laboratories also received, via the University Chest, about £600 a year as a grant from the Government.[63] Throughout the period Balliol and Trinity themselves paid £225 a year to the laboratories. Trinity's contribution was still the £90 p.a. which was agreed on in 1901. There was one other major source of income during these years. It was first received in 1923 when Brunner-Mond, the chemical manufacturers, made a grant of £100 towards research in the laboratories.[64] A year later, Brunner-Mond "having received a report of the use made last year of their grant of £100 to the College laboratory . . . expressed their willingness to make a grant of £200 for this year."[65] This generosity continued when the company became a division of Imperial Chemical Industries in 1927, and over the years 1925–41 an average of nearly £300 a year was granted to the Balliol-Trinity laboratories.

The principal costs were: fees to other laboratories, mainly the Old Chemical Department, the Dyson Perrins Laboratory and the Queen's laboratory, which came to £300–£400 a year; the salaries of demonstrators and the wages of assistants, which together came to about £600 a year; and the provision of funds for research, which accounted for £300–£500 a year. On top of this, about £300 was spent annually on apparatus and chemicals, roughly in the proportion two to one.

Teaching arrangements remained much as they had been before the war. Students worked either on Monday, Tuesday and Wednesday or on Thursday, Friday and Saturday. An average of seventy-five names was enrolled for the laboratory course each term,[66] considerably more than in the pre-war period. The attendance records cease in 1927, but numbers during the 'thirties must have been very much the same, since intake to the chemistry school remained at about sixty or seventy a year throughout the inter-war years. Laboratory hours were still officially 11.00 a.m. to 1.00 p.m., and 5.00 p.m. to 7.00 p.m., but were in practice much more flexible than that. A good student would spend about twenty to twenty-five hours a week in the laboratory during the rather busier winter terms.[67]

Among experiments which comprised the course were:

> The Variation of some Physical Properties of Aqueous Acetic Acid with the Dilution; Determination of Viscosity; Refractive Index; The Vapour Density of Acetic Acid at Various Temperatures; Molecular Weight of Chloroform by V. Meyer's Method; Molecular Weight of Camphor by Beckman's Method; Transport Numbers for Silver Nitrate; Depression of the Freezing Point of Aqueous Solutions by Richard's Method; Hydrolysis of Methyl Acetate; Melting

Point Curves; Thermal Analysis of Alloys; Determination of the Order of a Reaction; Decomposition of Acetone Bisulphite.[68]

It was the research side of the laboratories which really flourished, as it had not done before, in the inter-war years. Research was carried out at the various outposts of the laboratories shown in the appended plan.

Throughout the inter-war years Hinshelwood was the most dynamic of the research workers, always attracting around him a large number of research students. He was a skilled experimentalist, capable of using simple equipment to solve complex problems. His important work on homogeneous gas phase reactions led him to do much detailed work on the subject of chain reactions. It was principally for this work that he was awarded the Nobel Prize, jointly with N.N. Semenov, in 1956. His work was not confined to gas-phase reactions. He also investigated the kinetics of many reactions in various non-aqueous solvents and in liquids.[69] Throughout his life his work on kinetics was distinguished and very much in the vanguard of international thought.

Hartley continued his work on the electrochemistry of non-aqueous solutions.[70] He organised a Faraday Society discussion in Balliol in 1927, (See Plate 5, group photograph), on the theory of strong electrolytes. Among those who attended and made contributions were the distinguished physical chemists P. Debye, J.N. Brönsted, L. Onsager, and E. Hückel.

Others during the 'twenties and 'thirties produced distinguished work from the laboratories of Balliol and Trinity. E.J. Bowen was a Brackenbury Scholar at Balliol and from 1922 a Fellow of University College. His work on photochemistry formed the basis for a book, *The Chemical Aspects of Light* (Oxford 1942).

J.H. Wolfenden took a First at Balliol in 1923, spent a year at Princeton and then returned as a demonstrator to Balliol. In 1928 he was elected to a fellowship at Exeter College. His research interests reflected those of his tutor, Hartley, being concerned with the physical chemistry of non-aqueous solutions.

In 1930 Hartley left academic life to take up a post as Vice-President of the London, Midland and Scottish Railway. He was elected a Senior Research Fellow at Balliol, giving the College his assurance that he

Plate 5. The Faraday Society in Balliol College, 1927.

From left to right, Wolfenden, Onsager, Murray-Rust, Hückel, Hartley, Remy, Raikes, Brönsted, Scatchard, Ulick.

would complete the publication of his research work,[71] which he did by 1935.

Hartley's successor was Oliver Gatty, who was elected a tutorial Fellow in 1931[72] after one year as a Lecturer. After a short period of work on the thermochemistry of electrolytes he became interested in electrocapillarity. This in turn led him into biophysics, in which field he worked after his departure from Balliol in 1933.

In 1932 R.P. Bell returned from Copenhagen, where Hartley's influence had helped secure him a research post under Brönsted, to take up the Bedford Lectureship. On Gatty's resignation he was elected to a tutorial fellowship.[73] His early research interest was in aspects of solution chemistry, particulary exchange reactions. From here he moved into the field of acid-base catalysis, both in solution and in the gas phase, and was concerned with the role of the proton in reaction kinetics.

When Hinshelwood was elected to the Dr. Lee's Professorship in 1937, he became responsible for both the physical chemistry department (i.e. Balliol-Trinity and Jesus) and the teaching of inorganic chemistry. He continued to work in Trinity, but he was compelled to take up a professorial fellowship at Exeter College. To replace him, Trinity elected J.D. Lambert, who had demonstrated in the laboratory since 1934, to a tutorial fellowship in 1938.

At the very height of activity in the Balliol-Trinity laboratories, the question of the allocation of a site for a new Department of Physical Chemistry came up at a meeting of the Chemistry Sub-Faculty.[74] Shortly afterwards the site to the east of the Dyson Perrins Laboratory was approved.[75] The University was able to go ahead with the building only thanks to the generosity of Lord Nuffield. The building was sufficiently advanced for firewatching to begin at the end of 1940, and the first moves were made in March 1941 as the rooms became ready.[76]

When the laboratories closed down Balliol and Trinity agreed that the balance of accounts, amounting to £360 10s., should be invested and the interest used to augment the pension of James Warrell.[77] Warrell had been the laboratory assistant for fifty-one years, starting under Sir John Conroy. He always kept the laboratory running smoothly and was universally liked and respected.[78] It was also agreed that the £850 paid by the University for apparatus should be split, three-fifths going to Balliol and two-fifths to Trinity, this being the proportion in which each contributed to expenses.[79]

After the war the Trinity teaching laboratory became a workshop, which still stands today. The Balliol teaching laboratory became a joint science library, administered by the two Colleges until the summer of 1975. After that the books were dispersed, and the connecting door was permanently locked. It is now a music and exhibition room.

The contribution of the Balliol-Trinity laboratories to Oxford Chemistry was an important one. But during the laboratories' existence, Oxford Chemistry was not always healthy. The Report of the Royal Commission of 1922 on Oxford and Cambridge summed up the position as follows:

> There was a considerable period, during the most critical time in the history of modern Science at Oxford, in which the Departments of Chemistry and Physics, the most fundamental of the new developments at the Museum, did not avail themselves of their opportunities for vigorous, progress, and this probably caused a serious delay in the growth of the Science Schools.[80]

In the last twenty years of the nineteenth century the teaching provided by the University amounted to no more than a few lecture courses, and laboratory instruction which was available at the Museum. The number of lectures available to students did slowly increase towards the end of the century, but was never more than a dozen, covering both preliminary and honours work.[81] The College laboratories at this time (at Christ Church, Magdalen and Balliol) acted as a supplement to this rather inadequate teaching, but not on any kind of formal or systematic basis. Integration of the College laboratories became much more efficient, however, after 1904, when the scheme of cooperation already mentioned was adopted.

Oxford was fortunate in securing the services of W.H. Perkin Jr. as Professor of Chemistry in 1912. The son of the man who synthesized the first aniline dye, he had for a number of years been assistant to Professor Dixon at Manchester University. His most important contribution to the teaching of chemistry at Oxford was to have a new laboratory built. Mr. Dyson Perrins, the Worcestershire sauce manufacturer, gave generous financial assistance, and Perkin was able to move into the laboratory named after its benefactor in 1916.

In 1919 a second Professor of Chemistry was appointed in Oxford, Frederick Soddy. Soddy inherited the Old Chemistry Department at the Museum, where he was in charge of general and inorganic chemistry. He remodelled the rather dated laboratory on much more efficient lines, making good use of what space was available.

Despite these improvements in University facilities, the College laboratories still had an important part to play, with the number of chemistry students having increased after World War I. The 1922 Commissioners thought otherwise, though:

> There can be no doubt that the Teaching of Chemistry in a number of small College Laboratories is less economical and in some respects less effective than centralised teaching in the larger Laboratories of the University. At Cambridge it has been found advisable gradually to abolish the College laboratories altogether, and to concentrate the practical instruction entirely in the University Laboratories . . . it appears to us that all the practical instruction in Chemistry and Physics should, as in other subjects, be supplied in large and well-organised Laboratories belonging to the University.[82]

The Commissioners also pointed out that "The Board of the Faculty of Natural Science is strongly in favour of abandoning practical work in College Laboratories."[83] Accordingly, the Sub-Faculty defined its "ad interim" policy as described above. But the College laboratories continued to be teaching centres, despite the Commissioners' Report, and the views of the Faculty.

By 1935 the only active College laboratories were at Balliol-Trinity and Jesus, but as these were, between them, providing the entire physical chemistry course, they were indispensable for the time being.

Chemical research at Oxford in the nineteenth century was in an even poorer condition than chemical teaching. Benjamin Brodie, who held the Chair from 1855 to 1872, was a keen researcher, but the numbers of students at the time were insufficient for him to generate a research school of any kind. His successor, William Odling was notorious for his lack of interest in research. He considered it beneath the dignity of a Professor to appear in the laboratory.[84] Odling did no research himself, nor did he encourage his students or colleagues to undertake any. The result was that the University Chemistry Department produced practically no published work for forty years.

The College laboratories were the only research centres active in the nineteenth century. Mention has already been made of the work done at Balliol by Dixon and Conroy. The Curator of the Daubeny Laboratory at Magdalen, J.J. Manley, was also doing original chemical research at this time. The most important work to come from Oxford in the nineteenth century was that of A.G. Vernon Harcourt, which was done at Christ Church. His pioneer work on reaction rates represented something of a new direction in chemical thinking, chemists having previously been concerned more with the result rather than the progress of chemical action.

After the turn of the century it was still the College laboratories which gave impetus to research, through the work of Hartley, H.B. Baker at Christ Church, N.V. Sidgwick at the Daubeny Laboratory and D.L. Chapman at the Jesus laboratory. Research at Oxford received fresh impetus with the arrival of Perkin. He set a fine personal example by working for six or seven hours a day in his laboratory. More importantly, he was responsible for introducing the additional year of research to the degree course in 1918. He was also instrumental in the introduction of the D.Phil. in 1917. These changes did much to increase steadily the quantity and quality of chemical research at Oxford during the inter-war years.

Chemistry at Oxford was slow to develop, and for many years compared poorly both with other subjects at Oxford and with chemistry at other Universities. It was not until the 1920's that the school achieved any kind of eminence. By then the Balliol-Trinity laboratories had become a centre of excellence, and were so until their closure in 1941.

APPENDIX

PLAN OF THE BALLIOL-TRINITY LABORATORIES

Many of the rooms shown either do not now exist or are unrecogniz-
able owing to alteration. The plan cannot therefore claim to be wholly
accurate.

Key   ———— Boundary wall between Balliol and Trinity.

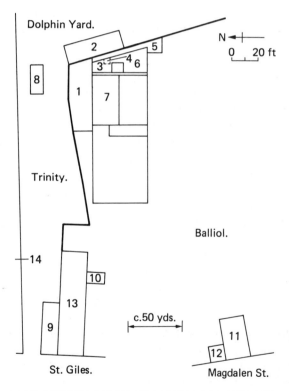

PLAN OF THE BALLIOL-TRINITY LABORATORIES

1. At basement level, the principal teaching laboratory, built in 1879. There was a central working bench down the middle, and a "box-office" for demonstrations at the western end. It is now used as a music and exhibition room.

2. At ground level, the Trinity teaching laboratory, built in 1897. A short staircase connected this with 1. There was also a door into Dolphin Yard. The balance room was at the southern end. This structure remains today and is used as a workshop. The original fittings are still visible in one place.

3. At ground level, the "library", connected to 1 by a short staircase. It was also possible to enter from the garden quadrangle. Books and periodicals were kept here, and experimental apparatus for conductivity and E.M.F. measurements. It was also known as the "physics" room, because it was here that preliminary physics was taught in the days of Dixon and Conroy. It has now been absorbed into the SCR.

4. At basement level, connected to 1 by a passage and to the ground level of Staircase XXIII by a flight of stairs from the passage. A small, dark room where experiments on refractive index and polarimetry were carried out. It no longer exists.

5. At basement level, at the end of the passage connecting 1, 4 and this room. The "thermostat room", initially used as part of the teaching laboratories, it was used more and more after World War I for research purposes. It no longer exists.

6. At basement level, a storeroom, probably belonging at some time to the laboratories.

7. At ground level, College lecture room, later fitted out as a teaching laboratory with benches, gas and water. Access from the passage running past the Senior Common Room.

8. At ground level, converted lavatories used by Hinshelwood and his pupils for research. It was demolished c.1930 to make way for new lavatories and baths in the vicinity. Hinshelwood then moved into 9.

9. At ground level, the Millard Laboratory, built in 1886 and used for nearly thirty years as a mechanical laboratory. It was converted to bathrooms by the War Office in 1914 and remained as such until 1930, when it became Hinshelwood's laboratory. E.J. Bowen and his pupils also worked there, at the eastern end. It no longer remains.

10. At basement level, a small cellar on Staircase XXII. It was used principally by J.H. Wolfenden, who set up a calorimeter there. It no longer remains.

11–12 At basement level on Staircase XVI. These form the original chemical cellar built in 1853. They fell into disuse after Brodie's departure, but after about 1880 were used continuously for research purposes, latterly principally by H.B. Hartley and R.P. Bell They are now part of the JCR beer cellar.

13. Solicitors' offices.

14. Southern extremity of St. John's College.

NOTES

Abbreviations

C.P.   Conroy Papers, Balliol College.
M.H.S.   Museum of the History of Science, Broad Street, Oxford.
P.R.S.   Proceedings of the Royal Society of London.
Phil. Trans.   Philosophical Transactions of the Royal Society of London.

1. College MS Register 1794–1875, 10 July 1851.
2. *Ibid.*, 8 Nov. 1853.
3. *Ibid.*, 2 Dec. 1853.
4. Bodleian Library, MS. Eng. Lett. d434, f.1.
5. *Report and Evidence upon the Recommendations of Her Majesty's Commissioners for inquiring into the State of the University of Oxford Presented to the Board of Heads of Houses and Proctors December 1, 1853* (Oxford 1853), *Report* p. 45.
6. *Ibid.*, p. 53.
7. Oxford University Commission (1852), *Report*, p. 191.
8. A.G. Vernon Harcourt 'The Oxford Museum and its Founders' *Cornhill Magazine*, 28 (1910), p. 359.
9. Balliol College Library, Scott letter books, 12 Dec. 1855.
10. M.H.S., MS Museum 71. Miscellaneous scientific papers of Brodie.
11. *Phil. Trans.*, 149 (1859), p. 249.
12. *P.R.S.* 9 (1859), p. 361.
13. *P.R.S.* 12 (1863), p. 655.
14. *Reports Commissioners* (1872) XII, 'Scientific Instruction and Advancement of Science', Minutes of Evidence, p. 305, q. 4820. This Commission was chaired by the Duke of Devonshire, is popularly known as the Devonshire Commission, and is cited hereafter as such.
15. *Ibid.*, q. 4836.
16. *Reports Commissioners* (1873) XI, Devonshire Commission, Third Report.
17. College MS Register 1794–1875, 21 March 1874.
18. College MS Register 1875–1908, 19 June 1879.
19. The details were negotiated with the President of Trinity by the Master and Professor Smith. Smith, although Keeper of the Museum and a Fellow of Corpus, was clearly still attached to and involved with Balliol.
20. College MS Register 1875–1908, 10 Oct. 1879.
21. *Ibid.*, 8 Feb. 1882.
22. Balliol College Archives D.18.8, Bedford Trust Deed.
23. *Idem.*
24. College MS Register 1875–1908, 13 Oct. 1882.
25. *Ibid.*, 12 Dec. 1883.
26. *Ibid.*, 17 Oct. 1885.
27. *Phil. Trans.* 175 (1884), p. 617.

28. R.T. Gunther *A History of the Daubeny Laboratory, Magdalen College, Oxford* (Oxford 1904), p. 24.
29. College MS Register 1875–1908, 16 Oct. 1886.
30. *Ibid.*, 12 Oct. 1888, entry headed "Laboratory and Bedford Lectureship".
31. C.P., Box 1A, Scientific Papers 1890–1900 (approx.), Bundle Four, "Laboratory 1893".
32. C.P., Box 4B, Letter Books 1893–1900, 9 vols., V. f.4. These letter books were a means by which an imprint of any letter could be taken. It appears that Conroy made such a copy of all his letters in the period 1893–1900.
33. C.P., Box 1B. Various letters, Balliol and Oxford 1889–1900, Bundle Eighteen "1895".
34. C.P., Box 4B. Letter Books 1893–1900, 9 vols., VI f.298.
35. *Ibid.*, VI f.479.
36. College MS Register 1875–1908, 24 March 1897.
37. C.P., Box 1B, Various Letters, Balliol and Oxford 1889–1900, Bundle Twenty-one "1897 Miscellaneous College."
38. *Idem.*
39. *Ibid.*, Nagel to Conroy, 24 Dec. 1897.
40. For a more detailed description of Conroy's scientific work, see *P.R.S.* 75 (1905), 247. An account, in Conroy's obituary notice, by Dr. A.E. Tutton.
41. C.P., Box 1A, Scientific Papers 1890–1900, Bundle Seven "Laboratory 1899", Nance to Conroy, 17 Feb. 1899.
42. H.B. Hartley, 'The Contribution of the College Laboratories', *Chemistry in Britain*, Nov. 1965, p. 522.
43. C.P., Box 1A, Scientific Papers 1890–1900, Bundle Seven "Laboratory 1899", Nance to Conroy, 11 March 1899. No. VI refers to Balliol's original chemical cellar. Before the garden quadrangle of Balliol was completed in 1915, the Staircase now numbered XVI was no. VI. Space for research would have been scarce in the teaching laboratories, so possession of the 'Brodie Laboratory' would have been greatly coveted.
44. College MS Register 1875–1908, 18 Jan. 1901.
45. A large balance sheet marked "Confidential" considering two possible alternatives with regard to the election of a science Fellow, and the financial implications of each possibility, Balliol College Library.
46. College MS Register 1875–1908, 28 Feb. 1901.
47. *Idem.*
48. *Ibid.*, 23 May 1901.
49. *Idem.*
50. *Ibid.*, 11 Oct. 1901.
51. *Ibid.*, 20 May 1905.
52. *Ibid.*, 13 Oct. 1904.
53. *Idem.*
54. Seven large books adapted from cash books covering the period 1908–27, hereafter cited as Attendance Records.
55. *Biographical Memoirs of Fellows of the Royal Society* 19 (1973), p. 350.

56. College MS Register 1909–1924, 4 Nov. 1914.
57. Attendance Records.
58. *Idem.*
59. College MS Register 1909–1924, 7, Oct. 1920.
60. M.H.S., MS Museum 136 "Minutes of Meetings of Chemistry Lecturers". At some point in the early twenties, it is not precisely clear when, the Chemistry Lecturers' meetings became meetings of the Sub-Faculty of Chemistry.
61. College MS Register 1909–1924, 21 May 1924. The College formally accepts the University's proposal for provision of practical instruction in physical chemistry. College "would prefer that the arrangements hold for 5 years, but would agree to 3 years if the University wishes."
62. "Cash Book". This is a well kept, stout, red volume covering the period 1925–41.
63. M.H.S., MS Museum 189, a laboratory account book covering the period 1922–41. A large book, bound in black leather, but in poor condition owing to damp. It seems to duplicate exactly the Cash Book (Note 62) remaining in Balliol. However the Balliol book refers to income from the University Chest, while the Museum copy refers to what is clearly the same source of income as Government grants.
64. College MS Register 1909–1924, 19 Jan. 1923.
65. *Ibid.,* 13 Feb. 1924.
66. Attendance Records. A peak was reached in Hilary Term 1922 when 106 names are recorded.
67. From a conversation with the late Dr. E.J. Bowen, F.R.S..
68. M.H.S., MS Museum 195. The list is from the practical book for Hilary and Trinity Terms 1923 of C.H. Collie, a New College man.
69. *Biographical Memoirs of Fellows of the Royal Society* 19 (1973), p. 375. H.W. Thompson gives a thorough account of Hinshelwood's work.
70. *Biographical Memoirs of Fellows of the Royal Society* 19 (1973), p. 349. An assessment of Hartley's scientific work is given.
71. College MS Register 1930–1936, 12 Dec. 1934.
72. *Ibid.,* 8 Oct. 1931.
73. *Ibid.,* 5 Oct. 1933.
74. M.H.S., MS Museum 137. Minutes of Meetings of the Sub-Faculty of Chemistry, 1927–41, 12 Feb. 1935.
75. *Ibid.,* 5 March 1935.
76. From a conversation with Dr. C.J. Danby.
77. College MS Register 1936–1942, 6 Dec. 1941.
78. From a conversation with the late Dr. E.J. Bowen, F.R.S..
79. College MS Register 1936–1942, 6 Dec. 1941.
80. *Reports Commissioners* (1922) X, p. 27 Royal Commission on Oxford and Cambridge Universities. *Report,* p. 144.
81. *The Oxford University Gazette* prints lecture lists at the beginning of each term.
82. Royal Commission 1922, *Report,* p. 145.
83. *Ibid.,* p. 146.
84. *Journal of the Royal Institute of Chemistry* 79 (1955), p. 123. From an article by Sir H.B. Hartley on chemistry at Oxford.

BIBLIOGRAPHY

ABBOTT, E. and CAMPBELL, L. *Life and Letters of Benjamin Jowett* 2 vols. (1897).

ACLAND, H.W. and RUSKIN, J. *The Oxford Museum* (1893).

BOWEN, E.J. 'Chemistry in Oxford. I - The Development of the University Laboratories', in *Chemistry in Britain* 1 (1965), pp. 517–21.

—— 'The Balliol-Trinity Laboratories Oxford 1853–1940' in *Notes and Records of the Royal Society of London* 25 (1970), pp. 227–36.

BREWER, F.M. 'The Place of Chemistry - I At Oxford', in *Proceedings of the Chemical Society*, July 1957 pp. 185–93.

CARDWELL, D.S.L. *The Organisation of Science in England* revised edn. (1972).

DAVIS, H.W.C. *A History of Balliol College*, revised edn. (Oxford 1963).

ELLIOT, I. ed. *Balliol College Register 1833–1933* (Oxford 1934).

—— ed. *Balliol College Register 1900–1950* (Oxford 1953).

GOWING, M. 'Science, Technology and Education: England in 1870', in *Notes and Records of the Royal Society of London* 32 (1977), pp. 71–90.

GUNTHER, R.T. *Early Science in Oxford*, XIV vols. (Oxford 1923–1945): see especially XI, *Oxford Colleges and their Men of Science* (Oxford 1937).

—— *A History of the Daubeny Laboratory, Magdalen College Oxford* (Oxford 1904).

HARTLEY, H.B. 'Chemistry in Oxford. II - The Contribution of the College Laboratories', in *Chemistry in Britain*, 1 (1965), pp. 521–24.

—— 'Schools of Chemistry in Great Britain and Ireland. XVI - The University of Oxford', Part I, *Journal of the Royal Institute of Chemistry* 79 (1955), pp. 118–27. Part II, *Ibid.*, pp. 176–84.

LEMON, E. ed. *Balliol College Register 1916–1967* (Oxford 1969).

MALLETT, C.E. *A History of the University of Oxford* 3 vols. (1927).

Oxford University Calendar.

Oxford University Gazette.

PARTINGTON, J.R. *A History of Chemistry*, 4 vols. (1961–1964). IV (1964).

Royal Commissions of Inquiry on:
  University of Oxford, 1852; Scientific Instruction and the Advance-
  ment of Science, 1872; Technical Instruction, 1882; Universities
  of Oxford and Cambridge, 1922.
VERNON, H.M. and Vernon K.D. *A History of the Oxford Museum*
  (Oxford 1909).
WARD, W.R. *Victorian Oxford* (1965).